Information Systems Foundations
Theory, Representation and Reality

Information Systems Foundations
Theory, Representation and Reality

Dennis N. Hart and Shirley D. Gregor (Editors)

THE AUSTRALIAN NATIONAL UNIVERSITY

E PRESS

Workshop Chair

Shirley D. Gregor *ANU*

Program Chairs

Dennis N. Hart *ANU*
Shirley D. Gregor *ANU*

Program Committee

Bob Colomb *University of Queensland*
Walter Fernandez *ANU*
Steven Fraser *ANU*
Sigi Goode *ANU*
Peter Green *University of Queensland*
Robert Johnston *University of Melbourne*
Sumit Lodhia *ANU*
Mike Metcalfe *University of South Australia*
Graham Pervan *Curtin University of Technology*
Michael Rosemann *Queensland University of Technology*
Graeme Shanks *University of Melbourne*
Tim Turner *Australian Defence Force Academy*
Leoni Warne *Defence Science and Technology Organisation*
David Wilson *University of Technology, Sydney*

E PRESS

Published by ANU E Press
The Australian National University
Canberra ACT 0200, Australia
Email: anuepress@anu.edu.au
This title is also available online at: http://epress.anu.edu.au/info_systems02_citation.html

---

National Library of Australia
Cataloguing-in-Publication entry

Information systems foundations : theory,
representation and reality

Bibliography.
ISBN 9781921313134 (pbk.)
ISBN 9781921313141 (online)

1. Management information systems–Congresses. 2. Information
resources management–Congresses.

658.4038

Cover design by Brendon McKinley with logo by Michael Gregor
Authors' photographs on back cover: ANU Photography

Table of Contents

Preface

This volume contains the papers presented at the Information Systems Foundations Workshop, 27-28 September, 2006. The workshop was the fourth in a series, begun in 1999 by Kit Dampney at Macquarie University and continued biennially from 2002 at The Australian National University (ANU), focusing on the theoretical foundations of the discipline of information systems. The workshop immediately followed the annual Australian Council of Professors and Heads of Information Systems (ACPHIS) workshop also held at the ANU.

The theme of the 2006 Workshop was 'Theory, Representation and Reality' and it once again allowed researchers and practitioners in the field of information systems to come together to discuss some of the fundamental issues relating to our discipline.

Information systems is still a quite young field of study that, perhaps uniquely, is a peculiar juxtaposition of the technological, in the form of computing and communication technology artifacts, and the non-technological, in the form of the humans and organisations that design, implement and use systems built with that technology. This has and still does present a problem for information systems theorists because typically theories in technologically oriented disciplines differ significantly from the more human oriented disciplines in their view of the world as well as how best to investigate it and intervene in it. Theory development and testing in information systems therefore presents a significant and continuing challenge since it must reconcile and integrate these differences at both the philosophical and practical levels in order to provide a secure foundation for the discipline. Moreover, it may and has been argued that what theoretical foundations exist in information systems are still weak, diffuse, poorly integrated and consist largely of imports from other fields of study with little that the field can really call its own. Accordingly, the primary aim of the Information Systems Foundations workshops is to provide those with an interest in the foundation of their discipline with an opportunity to discuss, debate and hopefully improve those foundations.

Typically the workshop gives authors an opportunity to present papers and get feedback on ideas that might be regarded as too new or risky for publication in conventional outlets. There have been some good outcomes from this approach, with revised papers going on to find a wider audience in mainstream journals. As the workshop is relatively small, and there is only one stream of papers, all paper presentations are typically attended by all participants, which leads to ongoing and vigorous discussion. We had some discussion at the 2006 workshop as to whether a small specialised workshop such as this should continue. The general consensus was positive, as participants felt that it was filling a niche not met by other conferences.

The papers presented here were accepted after a double-blind review process and we thank our program committee and reviewers for their assistance.

We also acknowledge and thank the sponsors of the workshop: The National Centre for Information Systems Research (NCISR) and the School of Accounting and Business Information Systems at the ANU.

Dr Lee Boldeman of the Australian Department of Communication, Information Technology and the Arts also provided, as the keynote speaker on the second day of the workshop, a thought provoking overview of the contribution made by Information Technology to productivity and his own views on related economic theory. All in all, therefore, the Workshop provided a stimulating and productive as well as an enjoyable couple of days for both the authors and attendees, and we hope that the papers that form this volume will provide similar stimulation, provoke similar productive outcomes, and perhaps provide some enjoyable reading as well, for a wider audience than those who were able to attend the Workshop itself.

Dennis Hart
Shirley Gregor

The Papers

The papers in this book are organised into three sections entitled 'Theory', 'Representation' and 'Reality', reflecting the sub-title of the 2006 Workshop. While convenient, it has to be said that this division is somewhat misleading, since no such hard categorial division can really be made: most if not all of the papers address more than one of these aspects at once. Nevertheless, in most cases an overriding interest in one or other of the three areas can be identified and this has formed the basis for the categorisation we have adopted in this volume.[1] For instance, the lead paper by Gregor and Iivari is primarily theoretical in focus, considering the nature of the information system artifact and even introducing a new term (semizoic artifact) to describe such artifacts. But the purpose of the theoretical discussion as well as the introduction of the new term is not only theoretically motivated but also has a distinctly practical ultimate aim: to help those who grapple with the messy reality of designing and developing information systems to better understand the nature of and achieve better results from their efforts. In a similar way, the papers of Vessey and Davern focus on the theoretical concept of 'fit' in an information systems context. Again, however, the aim of that focus is to identify and clarify ways in which it might be possible to improve the problem solving abilities and performance of both information system developers and users in the real world in which they work. The final paper in the 'Theory' section by Lederman and Johnston is essentially concerned with how the concept 'information system' is to be defined. This may appear to be a distinctly and exclusively theoretical issue, but even here there is crossover into the other categories: the intent of the authors is to contrast our usual understanding of 'information systems' with what they call 'routine manual systems' in order to glean ideas, lessons and implications about how we build information systems from looking at and considering how routine manual systems do their work in the world.

The papers in the 'Representation' section, like those in the 'Theory' section, also exhibit a multi-faceted nature in their concern for both theory and reality in addition to their primary focus. The paper by Recker and colleagues, for example, overtly deals with representational languages and their analysis, but is also concerned with how to integrate notionally different theories within information systems (IS) such as representation theory and the technology acceptance model, thereby providing an exemplar for how such theory integration efforts might be approached in similar domains. Likewise, though the paper by Lamp and Milton is targeted at the very practical problem of representing, through an appropriate categorisation scheme, published research

---

[1] See the paper 'Indexing Research: An Approach to Grounding Ingarden's Ontological Framework' by John Lamp and Simon Milton, in this volume, which is focused on exactly this issue.

in information systems, the approach is distinctly theoretical, based on the ontological framework of Roman Ingarden as well as grounded theory. In their paper on requirements engineering, Nguyen and Shanks also deal with a representational issue: the 'elicitation, modelling and specification of user requirements'. However, their concern is also theoretical, namely, how to best investigate the process of requirements elicitation (they propose protocol anaysis in the paper) so that its effectiveness in the reality of system development can be significantly improved. The final paper in this section by Hart and Warne deals with the vexed issue of IS success and failure, arguing that the representation of a system as one or the other is not as simple as is perhaps usually assumed. It proposes the new theoretical concept of stakeholder 'defining characteristics' that not only drives the distinction between the two but also carries implications for how user requirements gathering in particular is carried out in practice.

The final 'Reality' section of the book contains papers that are concerned with subjects such as: a new, action-based and radical approach to systems analysis and design (Waller et al); how 'conversational technologies' such as Wikis are impacting organisational work (Hasan and Pfaff); project management and its underlying theory viewed from a practice-driven perspective (Reynolds and Yetton); a case study in which grounded theory was applied, unusually if not uniquely in IS, using both quantitative and qualitative data gathering techniques (Fernandez et al); and the current state of the methodological and theoretical underpinnings of decision support systems research (Arnott and Pervan). Like the other papers in the book, most of these papers have distinct links to theory and/or representation. Waller and colleagues, for example, promote a unique representation and way of thinking about systems analysis and design; Hasan and Pfaff wonder about the theoretical implications (notably the 'democratisation' of organisational information) of systems such as those they consider; Reynolds and Yetton aim to show how to find the 'theory in the gap' from the 'gap in practice' of project management; Fernandez and colleagues illustrate, from a practical case, a more powerful and comprehensive way in which an increasingly popular research method in IS can be applied; and Arnott and Pervan, through analysis of the current reality of DSS reseach, throw out a challenge to the IS discipline to broaden and make more relevant the research that is done, the way it is done, and the theory that is developed.

Dennis Hart
Shirley Gregor

Theory

Designing for Mutability in Information Systems Artifacts

Shirley Gregor
School of Accounting and Business Information Systems,
The Australian National University
email: shirley.gregor@anu.edu.au

Juhani Iivari
Department of information Processing Science, University of Oulu
email: juhani.iivari@oulu.fi

Abstract

This paper aims to extend understanding of the nature of information systems and technology (IS/IT) artifacts and the manner in which information systems design theories address the mutable nature of these artifacts. The term 'semizoa' is introduced to refer to IS/IT artifacts as mutable systems that exhibit some of the characteristics of living creatures and that are only in part designable. It is shown that the mutability of semizoa can be both constrained and enabled in IS design theories, using concepts of homeostasis, situated action, autopoiesis, learning, evolution, emergence and redesign. Consideration of the range and nature of these characteristics provides a source of ideas for systems designers in designing for specific IS meta-requirements. In addition, we show that IS design theories should include a reflective structural component dealing with the mutability of not only the system state but also its structure (schema). The paper contributes by addressing the lack of attention to the distinctive characteristics of IS/IT artifacts and by extending current ideas of design theories and theorising.

Introduction

Information systems (IS) is increasingly represented as a discipline that is concerned with the design, construction and use of artifacts based on information technology (IT) (see Weber, 1987; March and Smith, 1995; Dahlbom, 1996; Orlikowski and Iacono, 2001; Benbasat and Zmud, 2003; Hevner et al., 2004). The term 'artifact', however, tends to be used in a rather unreflective and undifferentiated manner and the distinctive characteristics of this class of artifact are not discussed. There is little critical examination of the assumptions that underlie different treatments of artifacts. One assumption we believe should be questioned is the view that an IS/IT artifact is a relatively immutable result of a design process — an 'end state' that is arrived at as a result of a search process (see March and Smith, 1995; Hevner at al., 2004). A fixed end state is more characteristic of the inorganic artifacts that result from other design disciplines such as engineering (for example, a bridge, railway or painting).

Our argument is that IS/IT artifacts differ in fundamental ways from these other products of human design activity and that we need to talk about them and theorise about them in different ways. IS/IT artifacts are inherently *dynamic systems*. It was recognised early on that they evolve and change and that their real use may differ from their intended use (see Keen and Scott Morton, 1978). Dynamic systems are studied in many contexts and under many labels, including cybernetics, general systems theory, system dynamics, the systems approach and complex adaptive systems. Parallel lines of thought can be detected in structuration theory. Yet there is little if any attention paid in these fields to how such systems are *designed* — most effort is devoted into studying their behaviour as existing objects, following the natural science paradigm. The time is ripe to take ideas from the study of complex systems and see how they can be melded with ideas from the design science paradigm to give a much richer picture of design theorising in IS/IT. To date the borrowing from theories of complex systems has tended to be piecemeal and outside an encompassing framework.

The aim of this paper is to extend our meta-theoretical understanding of the nature of IS/IT artifacts as growing, changing and dynamic systems and the manner in which information systems design theories (ISDTs) can address the mutable nature of these artifacts. We provide a high-level framework for thinking about design theories that provide for the mutability in IS/IT artifacts in different ways. The need to explicitly include a component dealing with the mutability of designed artifacts in ISDTs is argued for in Gregor and Jones (2004, 2006).

We claim that a new way of thinking is required to capture design conceptualisations of IS/IT artifacts as complex phenomena that change and adapt in varying ways and to varying degrees. The term we introduce here to capture a more encompassing view of organic-type artifacts in IS and IT is *semizoa* a word derived from the Greek for living creatures (*zoa*). We define semizoa as IS or IT artifacts that exhibit the characteristic of mutability to some degree, that is, they grow, change (or are changed), and exhibit adaptive behaviour. Further, semizoa have the potential to modify, transform or constrain their surrounding environment.

Our work has theoretical significance because of the lack of prior attention to artifact mutability in the formal specification of design theories (as in Walls, et al., 1992, 2004). The paper also potentially has considerable practical significance.

We agree with van Aken (2004), who argues eloquently that one needs prescription-driven research that provides solutions for management problems in addition to description-driven research that enables us to understand the nature of problems, but leaves undone the task of developing interventions. Differing from van Aken, however, our focus lies in complex artifacts that require considerable design and development activity. A sounder and fuller basis for developing design theory for artifacts of this type offers opportunities for developing better theory to underpin design and development activities in practice.

Note that our investigation is meta-theoretical: it is not a specific theory but is a higher level analysis of a particular category of theorising — 'design theorising'.

The composition of the paper is as follows. The following section reviews perspectives in IS on the IS/IT artifact and proposes a continuum between designed and natural artifacts and argues there is a need to recognise IS/IT artifacts as semizoa. We then proceed by considering a number of the ways in which designing for mutability occurs with semizoic artifacts. Our discussion leads to a number of suggestions as to how design theories and design theorising could benefit from our arguments. We conclude with some suggestions for further work.

The nature of IS artifacts

IS and IT artifacts

While it is currently quite common in the IS literature to talk about IT or IS artifacts, there is not a great deal of discussion of exactly what is meant by these terms and some divergence in views can be detected. Dahlbom suggested in 1996 that our focus should be on IT rather than IS artifacts because the latter do not easily cover, for instance, personal computing, communication, electronic publishing, air traffic control and intelligent houses. Subsequently, Orlikowski and Iacono (2001) popularised the phrase 'IT artifact' within the IS research community. These authors distinguished 13 different views of IT artifacts in the 188 articles published in the journal *IS Research* in the decade beginning in 1990 and ending in 1999. Most of these conceptualisations viewed IT artifacts as black boxes without looking inside the artifact. The articles reviewed focused on the building of IT artifacts with particular capabilities (the computational view of technology), their intended uses (the tool view of technology), technology as a variable (the proxy view of technology), and the interaction between people and technology (the ensemble view of technology). All IT artifacts were treated as a homogenous set in this review. As a whole, the discussions of IS/IT artifacts are characterised by somewhat convoluted definitions (see Orlikowski and Iacono (2001)) and Benbasat and Zmud (2003)) and some lack of recognition of IS as artifacts in themselves.

In this paper we will consider the range of artifacts that includes both IT and IS artifacts, the major focus lying in IT application artifacts. In the terms of Walls et al. (1992), March and Smith (1995) and Lee (1999), an information system is an instantiation of more general information technology. Information systems form a subset of IT artifacts, which obviously include various computer hardware and software artifacts. The word 'artifact' is used in the sense that it is an object designed, manufactured, used or modified by human activity.

Both IS and IT artifacts are also *systems*, where a system is:

> Any portion of the material universe which we chose to separate in thought from the rest of the universe for the purpose of considering and discussing the various changes which may occur within it under various conditions (Gibbs, cited in the Principia Cybernetica Web, 2004).

Both an IS and an IT artifact qualify as a system because they have somewhere within their boundary a computer system that allows the artifact to change and exhibit mutability — the essential nature of a computer system being that it can be self-modifying. Information systems also exhibit mutability because they encompass the human users of technology, a further source of change. These basic definitional matters are important because we need to recognise that we have the interesting situation where the objects of interest for IS and IT are both artifacts *and* complex dynamic systems with the capability of self-modification.

From artifacts to semi-artifacts to semizoa

Simon (1969/1996) makes a distinction between artificial or man-made things and natural things. He associates artifacts with design, in that they are designed (synthesised) by human beings, even though not necessarily with full forethought. We feel that the dichotomy between designed artifacts and natural objects is too simple. Many 'artifacts' are only partly the work of a designer.

Interestingly, Dahlbom (1996) adopts a very broad interpretation of the concept of artifact, claiming that 'People and their lives are themselves artifacts, constructed, and the major material in that construction is technology'. Referring more to IT, he continues:

> When we say we study artifacts, it is not computers or computer systems we mean, but information technology use, conceived as a complex and changing combine of people and technology. To think of this combine as an artifact means to approach it with a design attitude, asking questions like: This could be different? What is wrong with it? How could it be improved?

The concept of artifact in this view implies that an artifact is at most partially man-made and designed. Perhaps it is more appropriate to say that they are cultivated rather than designed (Dahlbom, 2005).

Figure 1 gives an example of this continuum of 'artifacts' starting from completely designable artifacts such as mathematical theories and ending with natural objects in our environment that nevertheless are partly man-made because of factors such as cultivation, breeding, genetic engineering, and training.

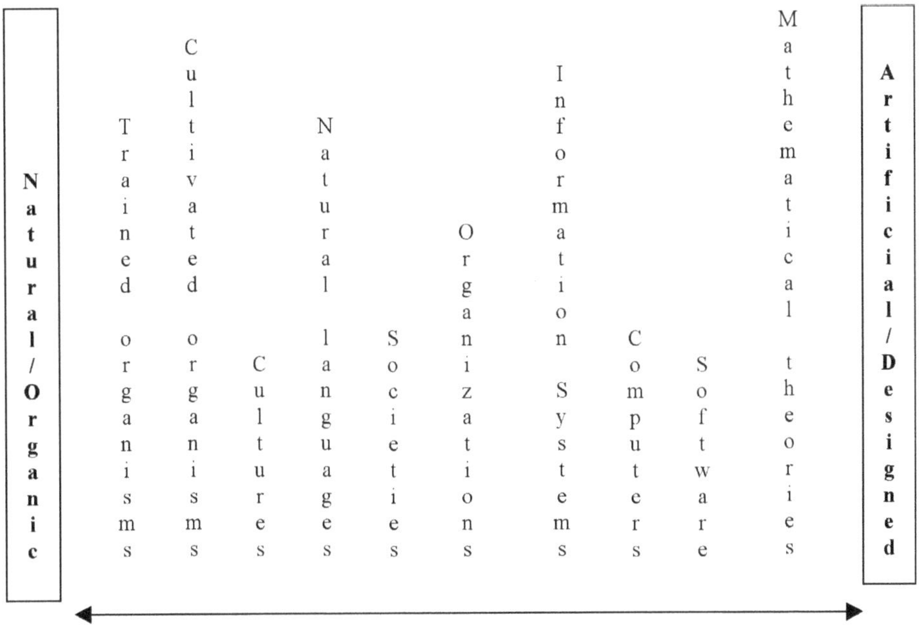

Natural/Organics — Trained organisms — Cultivated organisms — Cultures — Natural languages — Societies — Organizations — Information Systems — Computers — Softwares — Mathematical theories — Artificial/Designed

Figure 1: A natural-artificial continuum.

The positions of the different phenomena on the continuum of Figure 1 are only indicative. Software, in Figure 1, is interpreted as a system of algorithms, close to mathematical theories. Computers have a physical implementation that gives them a natural element. In addition to software and computers, IS comprise an information base that is only partially designable and makes IS additionally organic or emergent. On the opposite side, trained organisms (such as human beings and some animals) are considered less 'designed' because the influence of training is only ontogenetic with cultivated organisms, and the influence of cultivation and breeding is phylogenic.[1] One should also observe that there may be internal variation within each phenomenon. For example, some natural languages such as Finnish may be more designed than others such as English. Similarly, some societies may be more designed than others and organisations can also differ in the degree to which they are designed.

Our purpose here is to illustrate that the traditional dichotomy between artificial and natural is a simplification. It is also obvious that the term 'artifact' emphasises

---

[1] Ontogenetic: Of, relating to, or characteristic of ontogenesis; relating to the development of the individual organism. Phylogenic or phylogenetic: Relating to the race history of an organism or organisms (Oxford English Dictionary, Online version, 2004)

the artificial, designed end of the continuum but, unfortunately, we were unable to find a better existing term than 'artifact' that avoids this implication. 'Technology', when interpreted as 'a design for instrumental action that reduces the uncertainty in the cause-effect relationship involved in achieving a desired outcome' (Rogers, 1995), might be an alternative, but it has too technical a connotation. Järvinen (2004) prefers to speak about 'innovations' rather than 'artifacts', but the concept of an 'innovation' may lose the connotation of artificiality in contrast to natural or behavioural science theories. Recognising the bias in the concept of an artifact towards a static, designed object, we looked for an adjective to counterbalance this bias, ending with the adjective '*semizoic*'. The term we use for the class of IS/IT artifacts as a whole is *semizoa*, a term created from the Greek '*zoa*' for living creatures and '*semi*' for 'almost'. The singular is '*semizoan*' and the adjectival form is '*semizoic*'. We believe that this, perhaps paradoxical, phrase '*semizoic artifact*' better captures the richness of IS/IT artifacts.[2]

Figure 1 also suggests that information systems differ in their degree of artificiality from other IT artifacts such as software and computers. Many IT artifacts are only partly the work of a single designer. Systems are increasingly outcomes of distributed design where numerous designers engage in designing without being directly aware of each other. Many Web-based systems are examples of this. A resulting system may exhibit emergent features as an outcome of numerous local actions (for example, use, interpretation, negotiation and redesign), but these emergent features cannot be anticipated by reference to any *a priori* design. At a more theoretical level, the literature on the social construction of technology (Bijker et al., 1989; Bijker and Law, 1992; Orlikowski and Gash, 1994) discusses this emergent aspect of many artifacts. The provocative article of Truex et al. (1999) suggests that emergent organisations need continuous redevelopment of their systems but, in spite of the 'Growing systems in emergent organisations' title of their paper, the authors fail to recognise emergent information systems that grow without any continuous redevelopment. More recently, Markus et al. (2002) have analysed the provision of IT support for emergent knowledge processes (EKPs), which they define as organisational activity patterns characterised by:

- an emergent process of deliberations with no best structure or sequence;
- an actor set that is unpredictable in terms of job roles or prior knowledge; and
- knowledge requirements for general and specific distributed expertise.

---

[2] It is with some hesitation that we introduce this new term to a field with a proliferation of invented terms. Language, however, is influential. Our way of talking about things and the words we use can circumscribe thought. Particular words have particular connotations. It is preferable to recognise the special nature of IS/IT artifacts as 'semizoic artifacts' by finding a new word for them.

To summarise the discussion to this point, we see IS/IT artifacts as complex systems that exhibit mutability. They are in part designable and in part they exhibit characteristics typical of organic life in that they change in ways that could not be completely anticipated. This special class of artifact we have given the label semizoa. In the next section we describe theories that inform the design of semizoic artifacts and some of the design mechanisms for achieving mutability.

Towards design theory for semizoic artifacts

Kernel theories

Our conceptualisation of IS/IT artifacts as complex systems means there is a wide array of reference disciplines to draw upon as ideas for design. Three reference disciplines are particularly promising sources of underlying kernel theories for the design of semizoic artifacts: biology, computer science and especially Artificial Intelligence (AI), and systems theory. The interactions among these fields is traced by Richardson (1991) who shows how a number of disciplines, including biology, engineering, mathematics and the social sciences came together in the Macy Cybernetics Conferences, with cybernetics subsequently leading to further streams of thought including control theory, information theory, digital computing, system dynamics and systems theory.

We have depicted semizoa as only in part designable and also as exhibiting growth and change in ways that parallel the mutability of organic life forms. Thus, it is not surprising biology forms a significant source of kernel theories for semizoa. Biology has provided a number of ideas and metaphors for computing. De Castro and Von Zuben (2004) suggest that 'natural computing' encompass these three types of approaches:

- biologically-inspired computing;
- artificial life and fractal geometry of nature; and
- computing with natural means.

Similar ideas are expressed by Christopher Langton (1989), the 'father' of artificial life (Alife), who describes the concept as 'the study of man-made systems that exhibit behaviours characteristic of natural living systems'.

Computer scientists, especially in the field of AI, have adopted ideas and metaphors for computing from biology to develop computational systems and algorithms capable of solving complex problems; for example, with artifical neural networks and evolutionary algorithms. More fundamentally, the increased distribution of computing has led computer scientists to develop new paradigms for computing based on interaction rather than algorithms (Wegner, 1997; Wegner and Eberbach, 2004). The interaction paradigm, in which one sees computation as a distributed ongoing interaction of interaction machines, provides a theoretical model of computation that is more consistent with the idea of mutability, change and evolution than the algorithm paradigm based on the Turing machine.

Even though biologically inspired computing, artificial life and artificial intelligence provide a bundle of technologies, many of them reflect the algorithmic paradigm of search, problem solving and optimisation, rather than an interaction paradigm. To analyse and understand the mutability and change of semizoic artifacts, systems theory provides a third perspective (von von Bertalanffy, 1973; Ashby 1956). IT artifacts are systems and, as digital systems, very complex ones (Parnas, 1985). Systems theory has paid considerable attention to the analysis of complex and dynamic systems (see Aulin, 1989; Bar-Yam, 1997).

These potential sources of kernel theories for ISDT provide for many concepts that can be recognised in existing designs for semizoic artifacts. Characteristics of these artifacts include homeostatic mechanisms, situated action, autopoiesis, learning, evolution and emergence; although not necessarily all of them together, but at least one of them. These requirements constrain or enable mutability in the semi-designed artifact, as explained further in the following section.

Designing for mutability in semizoic artifacts

In this section we examine a number of the ways in which mutability can be enabled or constrained in semizoic IS/IT artifacts. These different categories of mutability have been identified by studying the theories discussed above and the different ways in which the mutability of semizoic artifacts are dealt with in existing design theories. We do not claim that our list is exhaustive, although we believe that it captures the most salient aspects of providing for mutability. Nor do we claim that the different categories we present are mutually exclusive; some IS/IT artifacts will have several types of mutability allowed for. In keeping with our previous ideas about designed and semi-designed artifacts, some types of mutability can be more 'designed-in' than others. With some types the designer can set up some initial pre-conditions that allow for change, but it is unlikely to be possible to anticipate completely the direction change will take.

Nilpotence

A nilpotent system is a memory-less system (without any persistent information base) that gives the same response to the same stimulus and returns to its initial rest-state after a finite number of units of time (Aulin 1989; Järvinen 2004). Many real-time computer systems are nilpotent systems. They are designed to react to different external events, to give the same response to the same type of event, and to return to the idle state after processing the external event. We are including nilpotent systems to demonstrate a dimension of minimum mutability in a designed artifact.

Homeostatic mechanisms

Biologists use the term homeostasis for the state where an organism is relatively insensitive to its environment. That is, it has mechanisms that allow it to function despite wide variability in external conditions. Homeostasis normally refers to the maintenance of the internal environment of the body within narrow and rigidly controlled limits (for example, a body temperature of around 37°C in human beings).

Computers are, of course widely used as control systems where the goal is to maintain the homeostatic state of the controlled process, such as keeping the temperature of a process within specified limits. Information systems can be designed to exhibit homeostatic behaviour. For example, the aim might be to control the response time of a distributed database. If the response time approaches an allowed upper limit, the system may automatically reorganise its database. In this way mutability is restricted.

Autopoiesis

Living beings are characterised by their autopoietic organisation. The term autopoiesis was coined in cybernetics by Humberto Maturana to refer to a special case of homeostasis in which the critical variable of the system that is held constant is that system's own organisation (Maturana and Varela, 1980). Maturana recognised that the autonomous quality of the living cell or organism was captured by the term self-creation, self-making, or self-producing. The organism is capable of maintaining its own organisation as a unity, in terms of its components and the relationships between them, without outside interference. That is, the basic structure of the organism remains the same. In simple terms, all the cells in a living creature might change, but it appears to have much the same appearance to an observer. An important aspect of autopoietic theory is that there is a boundary around the system. It can obtain matter and energy from its environment while at the same time being operationally closed. Closed, that is, to instruction or control. Further explanation of this concept and its relevance to IS and IT can be found in Mingers (1989, 1994) and Winograd and Flores (1986).

Application of the concept to IS design is not straightforward. In terms of the theory of Maturana and Varela, the focus should be on the internal dynamics of the system, and not on an ascription of outwardly-focused behaviour such as recognition and reaction to external events. An example with living organisms is the immune system's distinction between self and non-self. An analogy with a database system would be the principles of self-organisation that it is given to maintain database integrity. For example, it might have a consistency rule that says a department has only one manager. The system should then never contain data that violates this consistency rule.

Situated action

The idea of 'situated action' has been discussed in a number of contexts — in biological systems, but also in robotics, human-computer interaction design and with parallels in structuration theory and actor-network theory (see Johnston, 2001). We will mainly base our discussion on the work of Lucy Suchman (1987), who introduced the idea in the context of design theory for human-computer interaction. This design theory sees people's behaviour as contextualised; that is, the situation in part determines what they will do. In situated action individuals continuously monitor their flow of action and the context in which the action takes place.

To what extent can IS/IT artifacts exhibit situated action in the sense of Suchman (1987)? Lieberman and Selker (2000) discuss context-aware systems that adapt to and learn from context.[3] Erickson (2002) expresses serious concerns about context-aware artificial systems, about their capability to sense their rich context in a way comparable to human beings, and about their capability to intelligently select an action appropriate in the context. And when one takes into account that situated action as introduced by Suchman (1987) comprises artful improvisation (Orlikowski and Hofman, 1997) as an essential aspect, the possibilities of artificial situated action become still slimmer.

Despite these difficulties, some researchers have applied the concepts of situated action to the design of information systems, showing how, in an environment such as a manufacturing plant, the need for high-level planning of interrelated complex processes can be reduced by allowing some of the actors in the system to respond in a situated way to their environment (Johnston, 1995, 2001; Johnston and Milton, 2002). One of the authors, in the course of writing this paper, realised that a situated action perspective could help in another project involving designing 'zero intelligence' trading agents and decision aids in a complex trading environment.

Learning

A further characteristic that distinguishes intelligent life is the capacity to learn and acquire knowledge. The attempt to model this characteristic is one that occupies designers who develop theories of machine learning and build 'systems that learn' (see Jain et al., 1999). Machine learning has, of course, a long tradition in AI (Langley and Simon, 1995) but it is beyond the scope of the present paper to review this research tradition.

All information systems that have a memory (information base) have a potential for learning in the simple sense that they can accumulate more information into their information base. A more advanced form of learning implies changes in

---

[3] In our view context-awareness does not necessarily include learning even though it often does.

the structure and functionality of the system at the IS schema level. For example, the interconnections of system components and the behaviour of components may be changed because of learning (as in, for example, neural computing).

An example of an IS incorporating learning is provided by Hall et al (2003) who propose a theory for the design of learning-oriented knowledge management systems.

Evolution

The term 'evolution' is used with a number of meanings in information systems and software engineering, often without any connection to biological evolution (for examples, see Hawgood, 1982; Lehman and Belady, 1985). Generally, 'evolution' refers to a trial-and-error process of variation and natural selection of systems at all levels of complexity. In the Darwinian theory of biological evolution, 'natural selection' is distinguished from 'artificial' selection where, for example, the breeding of animals is controlled so that certain traits are retained or eliminated.

Swanson (1982) discusses to what extent biological concepts such as genotypes and phenotypes and natural selection apply as analogies to information systems. He parallels design with genotype, implementation with phenotype, and utilisation with natural selection.[4] In the case of design (genotype) he points out that, contrary to biological organisms, which have a fixed genotype, information systems may be redesigned during their implementation, and concludes that effective IS design must provide for its own conceptual adaptation. In the context of implementation (phenotypes) he mainly discusses modifications during implementation, arguing that, instead of a 'faithful' implementation, 'a strong case can be made for a "faithless" implementation which corrects in action that which has been misconceived in thought'. Finally, in the context of utilisation Swanson (1982) notes that over time utilisation tends to decline, not necessarily because of any observable failings in system implementation, but because the user may be better served by a new IS design (genotype).[5] Helylighen (1997a, 1997b) provides a further interpretation of evolution in which there is no need for competition between simultaneously present configurations.

Evolutionary concepts underlie the design architectures of some computer systems. Evolutionary and genetic algorithms (Chaudry et al., 2000) model the

---

[4] Genotype: The genetic constitution of an individual, esp. as distinguished from its phenotype; the sum-total of the genes in an individual or group. Phenotype: A type of organism distinguishable from others by observable features; the sum total of the observable features of an individual, regarded as the consequence of the interaction of its genotype with its environment (Oxford English Dictionary, 2004)

[5] Swanson's discussion is weakened by the fact that he does not make a difference between the IS model (schema) and the IS state. Applying this distinction, one can interpret a genotype as an IS model, even though an information system may experience a number of redesigns during its life, and a phenotype as an IS state.

evolution of a population of individuals and provide methods for solving optimisation problems. Evolutionary concepts have also been utilised in the context of software architectures, to model how software systems can evolve (e.g. Paderewski-Rodríguez et al., 2004) and Scharl (2000) describes evolutionary methods for Web development.

Emergence

The terms 'emergence' and 'emergent' are finding increasing use in the field of information systems, although the labels are on occasion applied rather loosely. In systems theory the concepts encapsulated are those of the 'whole being more than the sum of its parts' or the 'generation of complex systems from simple ones' (see Bar-Yam, 1997, for a more detailed analysis).

John Holland (1996, 1999), the originator of genetic algorithms, proposed that the study of emergence was relevant to the development of complex systems in the arts, business, the evolution of society and the generation of new ideas. Problems studied include the evolution of organisations — how a collection of initially independent but interacting agents can come to organise themselves so as to form a coordinated system that can tackle problems too complex for the individual agents themselves (Heylighen 1997b).

One can identify emergence at different levels — at the structural level or in the changes of state that arise. Knowledge Management Support Systems such as *Answer Garden* (Ackerman, 1998) provide good examples of emergent information systems in which the support provided by the information system is much more dependent on the growth of the system than on its design. A system like *Answer Garden* is a learning system in the sense that it can accumulate more knowledge into its knowledge base but it may also exhibit emergence. To illustrate, existing knowledge in the knowledge base may be like a puzzle where pieces of knowledge are interrelated, but do not quite fit together. However, a new piece of knowledge may be the critical missing piece in the puzzle that allows the integration of the existing pieces of knowledge and their interpretation in a new light. This case shows emergence at the level of the IS state.

Information systems in which the design is distributed over a number of decisions illustrate emergence at the IS structural level. Imagine a hypertext or multimedia information system on certain topics to which several people can provide content. Their design decisions to insert hyperlinks form an emergent structure that cannot be predicted in advance. The World-Wide Web, with its distributed hypermedia architecture, is an example of an emergent system on a large scale.

In IS/IT systems, emergence cannot be totally planned or designed in. Yet, conditions can be set up that allow emergence to develop (like the plan for a garden). Examples are the standards for interfaces that allow new systems to join to existing systems, and open systems.

Redesign as a response to externally initiated change

Unlike the previous examples of change in an artifact, and reflecting their 'designed' rather than 'natural' creation, some changes to IS/IT artifacts do not have strong parallels with those that occur in living creatures.

After its original design and implementation, an IS/IT artifact will generally be subjected to further change and modification to meet changing requirements, to correct errors and to allow re-design by new designers. The ability to change in this respect is mostly a desirable aspect of computer software and systems. That is, they should be easy to modify and maintain, and often substantial modification is required. Examples of similar occurrences with living systems are not common. Perhaps the closest is genetic manipulation, or an artificial limb, or a bionic ear.

A number of influential design theories for programming and systems construction were motivated by the need to make programs easy to maintain, modify and change. Many of these design theories make use of the idea that change can be more easily accomplished if it is limited to one section or module of a program. Thus, we have the ideas of modularisation and module de-coupling in structured program design, and encapsulation in object-oriented methods.

A further example is the database concept of 'data independence', which involves the idea that the internal schema of a database can be changed without any change implications for the conceptual schema. Also, Codd's provision of views in relational database design (Codd, 1970, 1982) means that the database can appear differently to different users at different times and those users can adapt the views from outside as they wish. Further, in the case of relational databases, the database schema can be changed while use is ongoing.[6]

Implications for IS design theorising

The review of the different mechanisms for providing for the mutability of semizoic artifacts leads us to some conclusions as to how design theories for ISDT should be specified. Walls et al. (1992) omitted Dubin's (1978) concept of 'system states' in their formulation of ISDT components. In Dubin's terms, one should specify in a theory what states of a system will be covered by a theory that is proposed (see Gregor and Jones, 2004, 2006, for further elaboration). Our discussion above demonstrates that such a component is valuable in ISDT because they deal with changing semizoic artifacts, which will almost certainly demonstrate some form of mutability over their life and thus changes in state. We argue that an ISDT will be improved if the proponents of a theory consciously

---

[6] Note, however, that even though it is easy to redesign the relational schema, it is not that easy to get the system state to correspond to the new schema. This requires that existing tuples be extended to include attribute values of the new attributes. Relational DBMSs manage this by inserting null values into the new attributes.

reflect on the degree of change they anticipate for their designed artifacts. Some degree of change may be provided for deliberately in the meta-requirements (as in being flexible in the face of future amendments). In addition, however, the theorist should document what changes in state the theory will cover.

A further interesting conclusion can be drawn by careful study of the nature of the changes that can occur in achieving the meta-requirements listed in the previous section. It is not only system states that can change but also the basic structure of the system itself. One way of conceptualising these broad directions in which information systems change is to think of an IS schema or model (structure and functions of the system) in addition to the IS states that the system can occupy at different times.[7] When thinking of the way in which an information system changes, we can think of changes both to:

- its model/schema (its basic form and functional capacities), and
- its state (i.e. the changes as it moves from one state to another over time).

A system's model/schema (its basic form) is related to its design and is the subject of design theory in IS, but it is also significant to recognise state changes. A system's capability to change its structure (IS schema) requires that the system has a reflective capability, including a self-representation (Maes, 1987). The system has a model of itself (schema) and it has the capacity to change itself by its computation (Maes, 1987).

Table I summarises our findings by showing the types of mutability discussed and their appearance at the levels of the IS schema and IS state. With some types of mutability the changes to the schema (structure) can be anticipated to some extent and facilitated (as with re-design), or the degree of change can be limited (as with nilpotent systems, homeostasis and autopoiesis). With other types of mutability the extent or nature of change cannot easily be anticipated, although the designer may set up conditions for change to take place (learning, evolution and emergence), meaning that the resultant system is only in part designed.

Concluding remarks

We have, in this paper, highlighted the varying degrees to which IS/IT artifacts can be 'designed' and how these artifacts can be viewed as occupying a space along a continuum that exists between artificial, completely designed artifacts, and more natural, organic entities, which may yet also be partly designable.

---

[7] More formally, the IS model can be conceived as the pair <Information base schema, Process schema>. The IS state s $\in$ R $\subseteq$ D (Information base schema) X D (Process schema). D (Information base schema) describes the potential lawful states of the information base and D (Process schema) the possible execution states of the software (programs) in the system.

Type of mutability	Nature of change	
	Changes in the IS structure/schema	Changes in the IS state
Nilpotent systems	No change.	Returns to the single rest (idle) state.
Homeostasis	No change.	Maintains the state within specified limits.
Autopoiesis	Limited change.	Maintains its own organisational state.
Situated action	Possible change in IS structure/schema (e.g. new learned response).	Changes state to correspond to the context (situation) and responds depending on the context.
Learning	Structural and functional change, with gaining of new knowledge.	New states by accumulating new knowledge in the knowledge base.
Evolution	Competitive selection among new designs.	Competition between potential successive states.
Emergence	Emergent structure and functionality because of parallel, interdependent design decisions that shape the IS schema without any *a priori* design.	Emergent states as new data, knowledge and/or activity occur.
Redesign	Structural and functional change in the IS model, as determined by the external designer.	Dependent on changes to the schema

Table 1: The mutability of IS/IT artifacts and the nature of change

We introduced the term semizoa to refer to these organic-type IS/IT artifacts, which exhibit the property of mutability to some degree; that is they grow, change or are changed, and exhibit adaptive behaviour to some degree. The properties of mutability that IS/IT artifacts possess are identified as being a consequence of the essence of their nature, which is that of computer systems and living beings. Varying types of mutability have been explored, drawing on work in a number of disparate areas, including systems theory, systems dynamics, complexity theory, sociology, and IS/IT design theories. The mechanisms for providing for mutability examined included nilpotence, homeostasis, situated action, autopoiesis, learning, evolution, emergence and re-design. Our exploration shows that many metaphors used in connection with IS/IT artifacts are borrowed from the study of living creatures. The dimensions of mutability are not mutually exclusive, and a single semizoic artifact could exhibit a number of these characteristics.

Implications of the paper

Our paper has significance in that, despite recent attention having been paid to the artifactual nature of IS and IT, the term 'artifact' has been used with little reflection and without differentiating among various types of artifacts. That is, there has been relatively little attention paid to the ontology of IS/IT artifacts. Our paper provides a unifying perspective on ideas that have originated in quite different paradigms, but can be recognised in different forms across many fields. The perspective that brings all these ideas together is the recognition that they all deal with different aspects of change, or mutability, which is a distinguishing characteristic of systems, living creatures and semizoic IS/IT artifacts, and all have parallels in ideas for design of IS/IT.

The paper has further significance in the implications for design theorising for semizoic artifacts. Our analysis suggests that:

- An IS artifact should not be regarded as a static goal that is the end product of a search process. Our many examples show the mutability of these artifacts. Designers should consider establishing the basis for a design trajectory, rather than aiming at a completely designed finished artifact. The partially-designed nature of some semizoa, for example those that exhibit emergence, means that the final form and behaviour of the artifact can not be specified in advance. The challenge is to find design principles that allow 'desirable' forms and behaviours to develop.
- Some of the characteristics of semizoa can be explicitly specified as design meta-requirements: for example, the ability to acquire new information (learning) or the requirement for systems to be easily modifiable, or extensible. The discussion in this paper shows some of the kernel theories that can inform designing for these requirements.
- Other characteristics of semizoa, while they may not be explicitly thought of as first-order, primary design goals, can help a semizoic artifact accomplish a first-order goal. For example, in the case of a trading agent in a stock market, the main goal is to maximise gains from trading. Considering how living organisms cope in situations of extreme complexity suggests that situated action concepts can help design an effective agent (AI researchers have been using these same concepts successfully in robotics).
- Designers should note that some of the dimensions of mutability may be mutually antagonistic. For example, the maintenance of self-stabilisation, or an autopoietic condition, is opposed to a condition where a semizoan is open to externally-originated modification or change, which could destroy or irrevocably alter its essential nature.
- IS designers and IS design theories should explicitly reflect on the dimensions of mutability that have been considered when they specify their theories, both for system structure and for system states. In this way what the theory encompasses is specified more fully, and stronger and more practical theory should ultimately result.
- The range in forms of mutability provides a fertile source of ideas, a 'menu', for new designs and new design theories.

Many of the ideas in this paper are not new. A number of existing approaches recognise that information systems are dynamic and can exhibit emergent behaviour (eg. Orlikowski and Gash, 1994). This prior work, however, tends to stop at the stage of analysing and describing some aspects of the behaviour of these systems: it does not go on to show how designers can explicitly confront and manage mutability through a variety of means, as we have tried to do here.

Further research: semizoa as actors

The above analysis is the first attempt to analyse information systems and information technology as semizoic artifacts. Obviously it can be deepened in many details. One aspect, not addressed in this paper is that semizoic IS/IT artifacts have the potential to modify, transform, or constrain their surrounding environment. They can also be thought of as actors that cause or bring about change, and their success may depend on the extent to which they are able to serve in this role. To illustrate, the success of a Knowledge Repository System for a certain domain (topic) may depend on to the extent to which the system is able to stimulate the domain experts to contribute to the knowledge repository. If an expert finds the existing knowledge in the domain and the debate related to its validity is stimulating and rewarding, he or she may be more motivated to contribute (as with scientific debate and progress). Relevant here is actor-network theory, which is a high-level meta-theory that views non-human entities as actors (Law, 1992). Another high-level meta-theory that deals with the interaction between actions, whether or not of human origin, and structure (environment) is structuration theory (Giddens, 1984).

Further, Heidegger (1993) was concerned that modern technology, as opposed to previous technologies, modifies and challenges the natural order. It controls and reorders the natural order rather than simply using it. Heidegger uses the comparison between a windmill, which harnesses the wind but doesn't change it, and a hydro-electric dam, which captures and changes the river. The objects within the natural order are modified to become a standing reserve for technology. The water of the river becomes the power source for hydro-electric power generation. The way in which these objects are perceived is framed with a different perspective provided by modern technology. Heidegger saw the 'enframing' (*ge-stell*) offered by modern technology and its capacity to overwhelm and restrict all other ways of revealing as the essence and danger of modern technology. Heidegger's concerns were expressed before computer technology was much in evidence but they could be expected to hold with even more force given the increasing pervasiveness of IS/IT artifacts. Heidegger offers some possibility of a counterbalance to the pessimistic outlook of enframing through *poiesis*. However, different meanings are given to this concept in Heidegger's own writing and it is almost impossible to represent it clearly, especially in a limited space as here. Nevertheless, a simplistic attempt to do so might run along the lines that humankind can perhaps escape from the technical order through thinking and poetry (*poiesis*), which provide a different manner of revealing from that of technology.

A further challenge is to consider how we design for emergence. The coupling of ideas between what can be observed with existing emergent systems such as the Web, and ideas from the field of complex and dynamic systems may be worthwhile.

To conclude, we present the idea that regarding IS/IT artifacts as semizoa and dealing with their forms of mutability provides real prospects for the development of 'grand theories' of information systems that we would like to achieve. Some existing design theories that consider aspects of mutability have been influential, including Codd's relational database design theory, structured systems analysis and design theories, concepts of situated action, and object-oriented approaches. However, unlike prior work we have brought together a range of different forms of mutability, showing how they differ and how they can all be used in design work. We believe that building design theories that explicitly deal with the mutability of designed semizoic artifacts provides a means of differentiating IS and allied fields from other design disciplines and can give our discipline a more readily identifiable theoretical base.

References

Ackerman, M. 1998, 'Augmenting organisational memory: A field study on Answer Garden', ACM Transactions on Information Systems, vol. 16, no. 3, pp. 203-24.

Ashby, W. R. 1956, *An Introduction to Cybernetics*, Chapman and Hall, London.

Aulin, A. 1989, *Foundations of mathematic system dynamics: The fundamental theory of causal recursion and its application to social science and economics*, Pergamon Press, Oxford.

Benbasat, I. and Zmud, R. W. 2003, 'The identity crisis within the discipline: Defining and communicating the discipline's core properties', MIS Quarterly, vol. 27, no. 2, pp. 183-94.

Bar-Yam, Y. 1997, *Dynamics of Complex Systems*, Addison-Wesley, Reading, MA.

Bijker, W. E., Hughes, T. P. and Pinch, T. J. (eds) 1989, *The Social Construction of Technological Systems, New Directions in the Sociology and History of Technology*, The MIT Press, Cambridge, MA.

Bijker, W. E. and Law, J. (eds) 1992, *Shaping Technology/Building Society*, The MIT Press, Cambridge, MA.

Chaudry, S. S., Varano, M. W. and Xu, L. 2000, 'Systems research, genetic algorithms and information systems', Systems Research and Behavioral Science, vol. 17, no. 2, pp. 149-62

Codd, E. F. 1970, 'A relational model of data for large shared data banks', Communications of the ACM, vol. 13, no. 6, pp. 377-87.

Codd, E. F. 1982, 'Relational database: A practical foundation for productivity. The 1981 Turing Award Lecture', Communications of the ACM, vol. 25, no. 2, pp. 109-17.

De Castro, L. N. and Von Zuben, F. J. 2004, 'From biologically inspired computing to natural computing', in De Castro, L. N. and Von Zuben, F. J. (eds), *Recent Developments in Biologically Inspired Computing*, Idea Group Publishing, Hershey, PA.

Dahlbom, B. 1996, 'The new informatics', Scandinavian Journal of Information Systems, vol. 8, no. 2, pp. 29-48.

Dahlbom, B. 2005, Personal communication, June 13.

Dubin, R. 1978, *Theory Building*, Revised ed., Free Press, London.

Erickson, T. 2002, 'Some problems with the notion of context-aware computing, ask not for whom the cell phone tolls', Communications of the ACM, vol. 45, no. 2, pp. 102-4

Giddens, A. 1984, *The Constitution of Society: Introduction of the Theory of Structuration*, University of California Press

Gregor S. and Jones, D. 2004, 'The formulation of design theories', in Linger, H., Fisher, J., Wojtkowski, W., Zupancic, J., Vigo, K. and Arold, J. (eds) *Constructing the infrastructure for the knowledge economy: Methods and tools, theory and practice*, New York, Kluwer Academic.

Gregor, S. and Jones, D. 2006, 'Improving the specification of Information Systems design theories', Working Paper, The Australian National University.

Hall, D., Paradice, D. and Courtney, J. 2003, 'Building a theoretical foundation for a learning-oriented management system', Journal of Information Technology Theory and Application, vol. 5, no. 2, pp. 63-85.

Hawgood, J. (ed.) 1982, *Evolutionary Information Systems*, North-Holland.

Heidegger, M. 1993, 'The question concerning technology', in *Basic Writings*, Harper, San Francisco, pp. 311-41, translated from Martin Heidegger 1954, *Vortrage and Aufsatze*, Gunther Neske Verlag, Pfullingen, pp 13-44.

Helylighen, F. 1997a, 'Basic concepts of the systems approach', in Heylighen, F., Joslyn, C. and Turchin, V. (eds), *Principia Cybernetica*, Brussels, viewed 1 November, 2004, <http://pespmc1.vub.ac.be/ SYSAPPR.html>.

Helylighen, F. 1997b, 'Evolutionary theory', in Heylighen, F., Joslyn, C. and Turchin, V. (eds), *Principia Cybernetica*, Brussels, viewed 1 November, 2004, <http://pespmc1.vub.ac.be/EVOLUT.html>.

Hevner, A., March, S., Park, J. and Ram, S. 2004, 'Design science in information systems research', MIS Quarterly, vol. 28, no. 1, pp. 75-105.

Holland, J. H. 1996, *How Adaptation Builds Complexity*, Addison-Wesley.

Holland, J. H. 1999, *Emergence: From Chaos to Order*, Addison-Wesley.

Jain, S., Osherson, D., Royer, J., and Sharma, A. 1999, *Systems That Learn* (2nd ed.), Bradford Books.

Järvinen, P. 2004, *On Research Methods*, Opinpajan kirja, Tampere, Finland.

Johnston, R. B. 1995, 'Making manufacturing practices tacit: A case study of computer aided production management and lean production', Journal of the Operational Research Society, vol. 46, no. 10, pp. 1174-83.

Johnston, R. B. 2001, 'Situated action, stucturation and actor-network theory: An integrative perspective', in *Proceedings of ECIS 2001 the 9th European Conference on Information Systems*, Bled, Slovenia.

Johnston, R. B. and Milton, S. K. 2002, 'The foundational role for theories of agency in understanding of information systems design', Australian Journal of Information Systems, vol. 9, Special Issue, pp. 40-9.

Keen. P. and Scott Morton, M. 1978, *Decision Support Systems: An Organisational Perspective, Reading*, Addison-Wesley.

Langley, P. and Simon, H. A. 1995, 'Applications of machine learning and rule induction', Communications of the ACM, vol. 38, no. 11, pp. 55-64.

Langton, C. G. 1989, 'Artificial Life', in Langton, C. G. (ed.), *Artificial Life*, Volume VI of SFI Studies in the Sciences of Complexity, Addison-Wesley, Redwood City.

Law, J. 1992, 'Notes on the theory of the actor-network ordering: Strategy and homongeneity', Systems Practice, vol. 5, no. 4, pp. 379-93.

Lee, A. S. 1999, 'Researching MIS', in Currie, W. L. and Galliers, R. (eds) *Rethinking Management Information Systems*, Oxford University Press.

Lehman, M. M. and Belady, L. A. 1985, *Program Evolution: Processes of Software Change*, Academic Press.

Lieberman, H. and Selker, T. 2000, 'Out of context: computer systems that adapt to, and learn from, context', IBM Systems Journal, vol. 39, nos. 3 and 4, pp. 617-32.

Maes, P. 1987, 'Concepts and experiments in computational reflection', OOPSLA'87 Proceedings, pp. 147-55.

March, S. T., and Smith, G. F. 1995, 'Design and natural science research on information technology', Decision Support Systems, vol. 15, pp. 251-66.

Markus, M., Majchrzak, L. A., and Gasser, L. 2002, 'A design theory for systems that support emergent knowledge processes', MIS Quarterly, vol. 26, pp. 179-212.

Maturana, H. R. and Varela, F. J. 1980, *Autopoiesis and Cognition*, D. Reidel, Dordrecht, Holland.

Mingers, J. 1989, 'An introduction to autopoiesis — implications and applications', Systems Practice, vol. 2, no. 2, pp. 159-80.

Mingers, J. 1994, *self-producing systems: implications and applications of autopoiesis*, Plenum Publishing, New York.

Orlikowski, W. J. and Gash, D. C. 1994, 'Technological frames: Making sense of information technology in organisations', ACM Transactions on Information Systems, vol. 12, no. 2, pp. 174-207.

Orlikowski, W. J. and Hofman, J. D. 1997, 'An improvisational model for change management: The case of groupware technologies', Sloan Management Review, vol. 38, no. 2, pp. 11-21.

Orlikowski, W. J. and Iacono, C. S. 2001, 'Research commentary: Desperately seeking the "IT" in IT research — A call to theorising the IT artifact', Information Systems Research, vol. 12, no. 2, pp. 121-34.

Paderewski-Rodríguez, P., Torres-Carbonell, J. J., Rodríguez-Fortiz, M. J., Medina-Medina, N. and Molina-Ortiz, F. 2004, 'A software system evolutionary and adaptive framework: application to agent-based systems', Journal of Systems Architecture, vol. 50, pp. 407-501.

Parnas, D. L. 1985, 'Software aspects of strategic defense systems', Communications of the ACM, vol. 28, no. 12, pp. 1326-35.

Principia Cybernetica Web 2004, viewed November, 2004 <http://pespmc1.vub.ac.be/DEFAULT.html>.

Richardson, G. P. 1991, *Feedback thought in social sciences and systems theory*, University of Pennsylvania Press, Philadelphia.

Rogers, E. M. 1995, *Diffusion of innovations*, (4th ed.), The Free Press, New York.

Scharl, A. 2000, *Evolutionary Web development*, Springer.

Simon, H. 1996, *The sciences of the artificial*. (3rd ed.), MIT Press, Cambridge, MA, (1st ed., 1969, 2nd ed., 1981).

Suchman, L. A. 1987, *Plans and situated actions: the problem of human-machine communication*, Cambridge: Cambridge Press.

Swanson, E. B. 1982, 'A view of information system evolution', in Hawgood, J. (ed.), *Evolutionary information systems*, North-Holland.

Truex, D., Baskeville, R., and Klein, H. 1999, 'Growing systems in emergent organisations', Communications of the ACM, vol. 42, no. 8, pp. 117-23.

Van Aken, J. 2004, 'Management research based on the paradigm of the design sciences: The quest for field-tested and grounded technological rules', Journal of Management Studies, vol. 41, no. 2, pp. 219-46.

von Bertalanffy, L. 1973, *General system theory* (revised ed.), George Braziller, New York.

Walls, J. G., Widmeyer, G. R., and El Sawy, O. A. 1992, 'Building an information system design theory for vigilant EIS', Information Systems Research, vol. 3, no. 1, pp. 36-59.

Walls, J. G., Widmeyer, G. R., and El Sawy, O. A. 2004, 'Assessing information system design theory in perspective: How useful was our 1992 rendition?', Journal of Information Technology Theory and Practice, vol. 6, no. 2, pp. 43-58.

Weber, R. 1987, 'Toward a theory of artifacts: a paradigmatic base for information systems research', Journal of Information Systems, vol. 1, pp. 3-19.

Wegner, P. 1997, 'Why interaction is more powerful than algorithms', Communications of the ACM, vol. 40, no. 5, pp. 80-91.

Wegner, P. and Eberbach, E. 2004, 'New models of computing', The Computer Journal vol. 47, no. 1, pp. 4-9.

Winograd, T. and Flores, F. 1986, *Understanding computers and cognition*, Addison-Wesley, Reading, MA.

The Effect of the Application Domain in IS Problem Solving: A Theoretical Analysis

Iris Vessey
UQ Business School, University of Queensland
email: i.vessey@business.uq.edu.au

Abstract

This study presents theory that formalises, and generalises to problems of different levels of structure, the role of the application domain in IS problem solving. It does so by developing a unifying theory to explain the diverse findings from two experiments that focused on the role of the application domain in IS problem solving. The theoretical framework that we use to form the structure for our theory is a dual-task problem-solving model based on the theory of cognitive fit. Cognitive fit applies to problem solving in each of the contributing domains (application and IS), as well as to the interaction between the two. The theory of cognitive fit allows us to distinguish different types of interactions between the tasks that must be conducted in the IS and application domains when the two types of tasks 'match' and when they do not. Those interactions may be supportive, neutral, or conflicting, depending on whether the problem under investigation is well- or ill-structured.

Introduction

Domain knowledge, which is fundamental to all disciplines (Alexander, 1992), is knowledge of the area to which a set of theoretical concepts is applied. Domain knowledge has long been acknowledged as an important avenue of inquiry in educational research (see, for example, Alexander, 1992; Alexander and Judy, 1988) with studies being conducted in such diverse areas as physics and economics, on the one hand, and history and reading, on the other. Such studies have found that thinking is dominated by content and skills that are domain-specific (McPeck, 1990), and that the lack of domain knowledge results in inelegant problem-solving strategies (Alexander and Judy, 1988).

In the information systems (IS) discipline, the term 'domain knowledge' has dual significance. First, *IS domain* knowledge provides representations, methods, techniques, and tools that form the basis for the development of application systems. Second, those application systems are developed to organise or structure solutions to real-world problems that exist in a given business area, or *application domain*. IS problem solving therefore applies theoretical concepts from the IS domain to the application domain of interest. Hence, knowledge of the IS and the application domains go hand-in-hand in solving IS problems.

A number of studies argue that application domain knowledge impacts IS problem-solving effectiveness (see, for example, Blum, 1989; Curtis et al., 1988; Glass and Vessey, 1992). Few studies have, however, addressed this relationship empirically. Exceptions are Burton-Jones and Weber (1999), Khatri et al (2006), Purao et al (2002), Shaft and Vessey (1995, 1998, 2006), and Vessey and Conger (1993). Most research has examined processing aspects, with far fewer studies addressing data aspects, such as conceptual modelling. Finally, no studies have presented theory that seeks to explain the role of application domain knowledge in IS problem solving.

Given the pervasiveness of the application domain in IS development, it is important to understand why and how application domain knowledge can aid IS problem solving. In this paper we present theory that explains the roles of both IS and application domain knowledge, and the interactions between the two. We use theory related to dual-task problem solving as the theoretical framework. We then introduce the theory of cognitive fit as the fundamental theory for identifying and explaining different types of interrelationships between IS and application domain knowledge. Finally, we use theory from cognitive psychology in suggesting that the types of interaction between IS and application domain knowledge differ depending on the nature of the problem under investigation. We illustrate our theory with two recently published studies, each addressing different types of problems (Khatri et al., 2006; Shaft and Vessey, 2006).

In the next section, we present the theoretical foundations on which our theory is based. The following two sections present our theory of cognitive fit in dual-task problem solving in well- and ill-structured problems and then we present the implications of our theory for both the IS and cognitive psychology communities. Lastly, we present our conclusions.

Theoretical foundations

In this section, we present three theoretical perspectives that serve as the basis for theory that explains the role of the application domain in IS problem solving. The theoretical framework for establishing roles for both IS and application domain knowledge is provided by research in cognitive psychology that examines problem solvers engaging in the simultaneous solution of two tasks. Formulating problem solving in IS as a dual-task model, that is, with tasks in each of the IS and application domains, allows us to consider situations in which a cognitive task in one domain has different types of influences on the performance of a cognitive task in the other domain. We present the theory of cognitive fit (Vessey, 1991) as the theoretical basis for determining what happens in such circumstances. Finally, we present theory on the structured nature of the problems under investigation, which we propose as a contingency factor in establishing cognitive fit between the dual tasks.

Theoretical framework of dual-task problem solving

Following an introduction to the cognitive psychology literature on the simultaneous solution of two tasks, we present a model of dual-task problem solving as a way of thinking about the interrelationship between the two tasks.

Introducing dual-task problem solving

Cognitive psychologists have long investigated what the community calls 'dual-task interference', a phenomenon that occurs when problem solvers perform two tasks in rapid succession. It is manifested in performance degradation on one or both of the tasks (see, for example, Durso et al.,1998; Koch and Prinz 2002; Navon and Gopher, 1979; Pashler, 1994; Van Selst and Jolicoeur, 1997; Wickens, 2002). When dual-task interference occurs, it is difficult for the individual to allocate attention effectively between tasks, resulting in reduced performance.

Much of the research in the area has focused on the resources needed to conduct the two tasks simultaneously, and therefore the allocation of resources between them (see, for example, Durso and Gronlund, 1999; Kahneman, 1973; Wickens, 2002) and the likelihood of a processing bottleneck (Pashler, 1994; Pashler and O'Brien, 1993; Van Selst and Joliceour, 1997). Although there is still substantial debate regarding the mechanisms that underlie the phenomenon, the effects have been observed consistently (see, among others, Koch and Prinz, 2002; Navon, 1990; Navon and Miller, 1987; Pashler, 1994; Pashler and O'Brien, 1993; Van Selst and Joliceour, 1997; Whitaker, 1979).

In this research, we apply the basic premises of research on dual-task interference to our specific context of IS problem solving in which interaction occurs between the IS and application domains and therefore between tasks in each of those domains. Under these circumstances, we propose that dual-task problem solving does not always lead to dual-task interference, and we address the circumstances in which the simultaneous solution of the two tasks does lead to dual-task interference and when it does not. We therefore use the term dual-task problem solving in our current analyses, rather than dual-task interference.

Model of dual-task problem solving in IS

As we have seen, IS problem solving consists of solving problems in a variety of application domains, and therefore knowledge in both the IS and application domains may play a role in problem solution. The basic premise of our theoretical model is, therefore, that tasks in each of those domains must be solved to reach a solution. We present a dual-task problem-solving model as the framework for examining the interrelationship between the two types of tasks.

Figure 1 presents the dual-task problem-solving model that describes the cognitive process involved in solving a problem in which two types of relevant knowledge interact. This model is based on three repetitions of the basic problem-solving model used to describe cognitive fit (Vessey, 1991), extended to include the notions of distributed cognition proposed in Zhang (1997) and Zhang and Norman (1994). One problem-solving model is used to describe each contributing cognitive task, shown in dashed boxes in Figure 1, with a further model for their interaction.

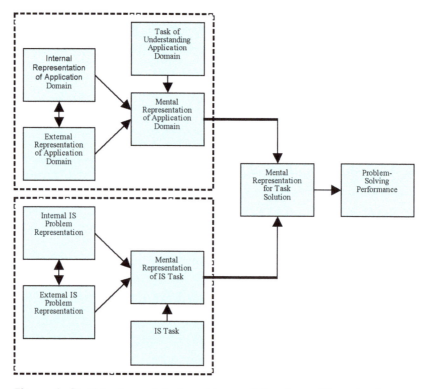

Figure 1: Dual-task model of problem solving in an IS context.

Problem solvers first form mental representations for each contributing task, that is, the cognitive tasks of understanding the application domain (developing a *mental representation of the application domain*) and the IS domain (developing a *mental representation of the IS task*). They must then integrate these two representations into a mental representation that facilitates task solution (the *mental representation for task solution*).[1] Each contributing task is supported by an *internal problem representation* (knowledge the problem solver has of the domain of interest: IS or application) and an *external problem representation* that presents explicit knowledge related to the solution of the task in the IS domain.

The theory of cognitive fit

Formulating IS problem solving as a dual-task model opens the way for us to consider situations in which one task might either facilitate or inhibit the other. The theory of cognitive fit that is used as the foundation for the dual-task problem solving model therefore serves as the basis for a theoretical analysis of the circumstances in which application domain knowledge facilitates problem solving, and those in which interaction between the IS and application sub-tasks results in dual-task interference, thereby inhibiting performance.

Here we present the basic notions of the theory of cognitive fit (Vessey, 1991). Although more complex forms of cognitive fit have now been identified (see Vessey, 2006), the theory of cognitive fit is most simply explained in terms of its original formulation as the performance effects resulting from matching the *external IS problem representation* to the *IS task* to be solved (Vessey, 1991). A match or cognitive fit occurs when the information emphasised in a particular *external IS problem representation* matches that required to complete the type of *IS task* under investigation. Decision making is facilitated because the problem-solving processes used to act on the problem representation are similar to those needed to solve the problem.

Using decision making using graphs and tables as our example (see Vessey, 1991) 'symbolic' tasks such as determining train departure and arrival times, which involve discrete data values, require the use of analytical processes and are therefore best supported with *external IS problem representations* that also require the use of analytical processes. In this case, such tasks are better supported using tables (symbolic formats) than by graphs. On the other hand, 'spatial' tasks such as determining the relationships among the performances of a number of sales regions, which involve making associations or perceiving relationships in the data, require the use of perceptual processes and are therefore best supported with *external IS problem representations* that also require the use of perceptual processes. In this case, such tasks are better supported using graphs (spatial formats) than by tables. Note that when problem-solving processes match, the decision maker is effectively guided in reaching a task solution.

Alternatively, when the type of information emphasised in the *external IS problem representation* does not match that emphasised in the *IS task*, there is nothing to guide the decision maker in working toward task solution, and they must

---

[1] Note that references to specific constructs in our model are shown in italics.

exert greater cognitive effort to transform the information into a form suitable for solving that particular type of problem (Vessey, 1994). This increased effort will result in decreased performance (that is, decreased decision accuracy, increased decision time, or both).

Theory on problem structure

We propose that the types of interactions between the tasks in the IS and application domains differ depending on the nature of the problem under consideration. The aspect of the problem that is key in these circumstances is whether it is well- or ill-structured. We distinguish different 'fit' situations based on whether the problem to be solved is well-structured or ill-structured in nature (see Reitman, 1964).

Well-structured problems are those that have a well-defined initial state, a clearly-defined goal state, a well-defined, constrained set of transformation functions to guide the solution process, well-defined evaluation processes, and a single optimal solution path (Greeno, 1978; Sinnott, 1989; Voss and Post, 1988). Further, the information needed to solve the problem is contained in the problem statement.

On the other hand, ill-structured problems are those for which the initial and goal states are vaguely defined or unclear (Voss and Post, 1988), and for which there are multiple solutions and solution paths, or no solution at all (Kitchner, 1983). Further, with such a problem the problem statement does not contain all of the information needed for its solution; hence it is not clear what actions are required to solve it (Chi and Glaser, 1985).

Dual-task problem solving in well-structured problems

We first present a theoretical analysis of the role of dual-task problem solving and cognitive fit in well-structured problem areas. We then apply the theory to a study of problem solving on the well-structured problem of understanding conceptual schemas (Khatri et al., 2006).

Implications of problem structure

When the problem is well-structured, both the *external IS problem representation* and the *IS task* itself are sufficiently well formalised for problem solution to occur directly; that is, with reference to the problem statement alone and the associated representations, and without reference to the application domain. In terms of the dual-task problem-solving model presented in Figure 1, problem solving can take place in terms of the cognitive fit model related to the IS task alone (presented at the lower left of the model). In this case, the second task, that of forming a mental representation of the application domain, is not essential to forming the *mental representation for task solution* and therefore plays only a minor role in solving such a problem.

Role of cognitive fit in dual-task problem solving of well-structured problems

We use the theory of cognitive fit to understand the interrelationship between knowledge of the IS and application domains and the role of each in well-structured problem domains.

Because only IS domain knowledge is required to solve well-structured problems, any effect of application domain knowledge will occur in addition to the effect of IS domain knowledge. There will therefore be no interaction between the two types of knowledge and each therefore has independent effects on performance. We state the following proposition.

- Proposition WS-1: In well-structured IS problem areas, the effects of IS and application domain knowledge are independent.

We can now explore the independent effects of both IS and application domain knowledge on performance. Because IS domain knowledge is essential to solving well-structured problems, we expect that it will influence performance on all types of well-structured problems. We state the following proposition.

- Proposition WS-2: IS domain knowledge influences performance on all tasks in well-structured IS problem areas.

From the viewpoint of the application domain, although application domain knowledge is not essential to the solution of well-structured problems, we expect that its effect will be contingent upon the nature of the task in the well-structured problem area under investigation. Two situations may arise. First, in addressing certain tasks, the knowledge required for task solution can be acquired directly from the *external IS problem representation*; that is, cognitive fit exists. The problem solving that takes place is therefore both accurate and timely (Vessey, 1991). Hence knowledge of the application domain does not influence performance. We state the following proposition.

- Proposition WS-3: When cognitive fit exists, problem solvers addressing tasks in well-structured IS problem areas are equally accurate irrespective of their knowledge of the application domain.

Second, while all of the information essential to solving well-structured problems is available in the *external IS problem representation*, it may not always be available directly. In this case, the knowledge required to address the task and that available for task solution do not match; that is, cognitive fit does not exist. Problem solvers must transform either knowledge emphasised in the *external IS problem representation* to match that emphasised in the *IS task,* or vice versa, in order to form a *mental representation of the IS task* and ultimately a mental representation that facilitates task solution (*mental representation for task solution*). The need to transform such knowledge to solve the task effectively increases the complexity of the task at hand. In this situation, the presence of application domain knowledge may play a role in problem solution, thereby effectively reducing the complexity of the task under consideration. In terms of the dual-task problem-solving model presented in Figure 1, the formulation of the *mental representation for task solution* may be aided by the presence of application domain knowledge. Hence the cognitive fit model to the upper left of Figure 1 may also play a role in such problem-solving situations. We state the following proposition.

- Proposition WS-4: When cognitive fit does not exist, problem solvers solving tasks in well-structured IS problem areas are more accurate when they have knowledge of the application domain.

Theoretical analysis of conceptual schema understanding

For our application of dual-task problem solving to well-structured problem areas, we draw on Khatri et al. (2006), who examined conceptual schema understanding in the context of high and low application domain knowledge. Note that, in what follows, we use the practical term 'schema' to denote the *external IS problem representation*.

We first address the well-structured nature of conceptual schema understanding, followed by theory on conceptual schema understanding tasks so that we can then examine the situations of fit and lack of fit that may arise.

The well-structured nature of conceptual schema understanding

A conceptual schema represents the structure and inter-relationships in a set of data. The structure of data has been subject to extensive formalisation over the past four decades (see, among others, Chen, 1976; Codd, 1970; Elmasri and Navathe, 1994). As a result, all of the information required to solve conceptual schema understanding tasks (*IS task*) can be gained from the schema itself, which, from the viewpoint of the model of dual-task problem solving, is represented by the *external IS problem representation*. There is, therefore, a clearly-defined initial state, a well-defined goal state, a formal set of transformation and evaluation paths, as well as a well-defined solution path. Conceptual schema understanding can therefore be addressed using IS domain knowledge alone and we can characterise conceptual schema understanding as a well-structured problem area.

Characterising conceptual schema understanding tasks

In keeping with the cognitive theories we use to explain the role of application domain knowledge in IS problem solving, we characterise conceptual schema understanding tasks based on the cognitive nature of the task.

Based on prior IS research we can identify two basic types of conceptual schema understanding tasks: comprehension tasks and problem-solving tasks. Comprehension tasks are supported by the education literature, which identifies two different types of knowledge, syntactic and semantic (Shneiderman and Mayer, 1979; Mayer, 1991).[2] We therefore refer to such tasks as *syntactic* and *semantic comprehension tasks*. Syntactic knowledge involves understanding the vocabulary specific to a modelling formalism, for example, the ER model. *Syntactic comprehension tasks* are therefore those that assess the understanding of just the syntax of the formalism (conceptual model) associated with a schema. For example, the syntax for an entity type is a rectangle. Semantic knowledge refers to a set of mappings from a representation language to agreed-upon concepts in the real world. Thus, *semantic comprehension tasks* are those that assess the understanding of the data semantics conveyed through constructs in the schema; for example, a rectangle, the symbol for an entity type, represents a collection of entity instances, that is, objects, things, events, or places (in the 'real world') (Elmasri and Navathe, 1994).

Problem-solving tasks require a deeper level of understanding than comprehension tasks (see Gemino, 1999). Khatri et al. (2006) refer to a problem-solving task that can be solved using knowledge represented *in* the schema as a *schema-based problem-solving task*. Such tasks resemble query tasks; respondents are requested to determine whether, and how, certain information is available from the schema (see also, Shanks et al., 2003). A further type of problem-solving task, which Khatri et al. (2006) refer to as an *inferential problem-solving task*, requires conceptual modellers to use information *beyond* what is provided in the schema (see, for example, Bodart et al., 2001; Burton-Jones and Weber, 1999; Gemino and Wand, 2003; Shanks et al., 2002; Shanks et al., 2003).

In this study, we examined syntactic and semantic comprehension tasks and schema-based problem-solving tasks (in order of increasing complexity) based on their relevance to practicing conceptual modellers.

Study findings

Khatri et al. (2006) investigated the effects of IS and application domain knowledge on conceptual schema understanding using problem solvers with high and low IS knowledge in both familiar and unfamiliar application domains.

The study findings were as follows. First, there was no interaction between IS and application domain knowledge supporting our theory, as presented in Proposition WS-1, that tasks in well-structured problem areas can be solved

---

[2] While their work was set in the context of programming languages, these concepts are also relevant to conceptual models.

using IS knowledge alone.[3] Second, as expected, IS domain knowledge influenced the solution of all types of conceptual schema understanding tasks, supporting Proposition WS-2. Third, application domain knowledge did not influence the solution of syntactic and semantic comprehension tasks because the information required for their solution is available directly from the *external IS problem representation*. Hence Proposition WS-3 is supported. The solution of schema-based problem-solving tasks is, however, influenced by the presence of application domain knowledge because the information represented in the schema requires transformation to support the formulation of a consistent *mental representation for task solution*. As we have seen, the presence of application domain knowledge aids in the transformation process, effectively reducing the complexity of these types of tasks. Hence Proposition WS-4 is supported.

Dual-task problem solving in ill-structured problems

In this section, we first present a theoretical analysis of the role of dual-task problem solving and cognitive fit in ill-structured problem areas. We then apply the theory to a study of problem solving on the ill-structured problem of software maintenance (Shaft and Vessey, 2006).

Implications of lack of problem structure

When the IS problem is ill-structured, the problem statement does not contain all of the information required to solve it, and the tasks of developing mental representations of the application and IS domains are both essential to solving the problem. When the knowledge required to solve each of the tasks is consistent (that is, 'fit' exists), then solution performance will be facilitated. When that knowledge is not consistent (that is, 'fit' does not exist), however, there will be a mismatch between the two types of knowledge required for problem solution. In this case, the mental representation of one of the sub-tasks must be transformed to match the other in order to facilitate problem solving. Hence the task is rendered much more complex than when cognitive fit exists.

Role of cognitive fit in dual-task problem solving of ill-structured problems

We again draw on the theory of cognitive fit (Vessey, 1991) to provide the theoretical basis for what happens when knowledge of two tasks is essential to problem solving.

Matching representations

When cognitive fit exists, the problem solver's *mental representation of the application domain* and their *mental representation of the IS task* emphasise similar

---

[3] Note that this hypothesis was not tested in the original study (Khatri et al., 2006) because conceptual schema understanding was not presented as an example of dual-task problem solving.

types of knowledge and therefore have similar processing requirements. Hence, no transformations are required to form the *mental representation for task solution,* effectively reducing the cognitive resources needed for problem solving (Vessey, 1991). The problem solver can therefore more readily allocate attention between tasks. A problem solver is able to shift attention relatively easily, therefore, between the tasks in the IS and application domains with efforts in the application domain being directed toward the information most relevant to solving the IS task. As a result, *problem-solving performance* is likely to be more accurate and quicker than would otherwise be the case.

We state the following proposition:

- Proposition IS-1: In ill-structured IS problem areas, when the *mental representation of the application domain* is consistent with (i.e., matches) the *mental representation of the IS task*, increased knowledge in the application domain is associated with higher levels of performance on the IS task (*problem-solving performance*).

Mismatching representations

When cognitive fit does not exist (that is, when knowledge in each of the two task areas does not mutually support problem solving), the problem solver's *mental representation of the application domain* and the *mental representation of the IS task* emphasise different types of knowledge. Without cognitive fit, there is nothing to guide the problem solver in working towards task solution (Vessey, 1991). As a result, activities in the application domain are likely to interfere with the problem solver's ability to complete the IS task, the problem solver may experience difficulty in allocating attention effectively between tasks in the IS and application domains that are not mutually supportive, and performance suffers.

In these circumstances, some kind of transformation must be brought about for problem solving to proceed: either the *mental representation of the application domain* must be transformed to emphasise the same type of knowledge as the *mental representation of the IS task*, or vice versa. The problem solver confronted with these challenges may take one of two approaches to resolve the situation: 1) focus further on the task in the application domain; or 2) focus further on the task in the IS domain.

In the first case, because the *mental representation of the application domain* tends to drive the solution process (Burkhardt et al., 2002), there is a tendency for the problem solver to heed information in the application domain that is consistent with the knowledge already emphasised in the *mental representation of the application domain*, rather than the knowledge consistent with their *mental representation of the IS task* (cf., Broadbent, 1971). Changing the *mental representation of the application domain* to reflect an increased understanding of knowledge that is consistent with their *mental representation of the IS task* does not, however, enhance the problem solver's ability to complete the *IS task*. Hence, both efficiency and effectiveness are likely to be affected and it is likely that improved knowledge of the application domain will be associated with lower levels of *problem-solving performance.*

In the second case, problem solvers who focus more on task solution perform more effectively than those who focus on the present state (Durso et al., 1998; Hogg et al., 1995; Vessey, 1991). Such an approach would require them to switch attention to their *mental representation of the application domain* only when necessary to resolve an issue directly related to solving the *IS task*. Focusing on the *IS task*, however, has its own difficulties. First, because a problem solver's *mental representation of the application domain* tends to be quite stable over time (Corritore and Wiedenbeck, 1999), problem solvers find it difficult to shift to a different *mental representation of the application domain* after they have invoked an inappropriate one (Taylor et al., 1997). Second, when a problem solver attempts to acquire knowledge consistent with that required to conduct the IS task they find difficulty in mapping that knowledge into their mismatched *mental representation of the application domain*. The process of building up the knowledge essential to conducting the IS task (that is, developing the *mental representation for task solution*) is therefore quite challenging. Hence, again, both efficiency and effectiveness are likely to be affected and it is likely that improved problem-solving performance will be associated with lower gains in application domain knowledge.

Based on these arguments, therefore, when there is a mismatch between the problem solver's *mental representation of the application domain* and their *mental representation of the IS task*, *problem-solving performance* will be inversely related to improvements in knowledge of the application domain that occur during problem solving. Note that the situation we are describing is that of dual-task interference. We state the following proposition.

- Proposition IS-2: In ill-structured problem areas, when the *mental representation of the application domain* is inconsistent with (i.e., does not match) the *mental representation of the IS task*, greater increases in knowledge of the application domain are associated with lower levels of performance on the IS task, and higher levels of performance on the IS task are associated with lesser increases in knowledge of the application domain.

In summary, then, when the *mental representation of the application domain* does not support the *mental representation of the IS task* to be conducted:

- paying increased attention to the application domain distracts the programmer from the primary IS task of completing the modification; and

- focusing on the *IS task* interferes with the problem solver's understanding of the application domain.

In both cases, the relationship between knowledge of the application domain and performance on the IS task is an inverse one and this is indicative of dual-task interference.

Theoretical analysis of software maintenance

For our application of dual-task problem solving to ill-structured problems, we draw on Shaft and Vessey (2006). In order to evaluate *problem-solving performance*, the authors used two different types of software maintenance tasks in both familiar and unfamiliar application domains to conduct a study in which the IS task (making a modification to software) and the application domain (represented by the software) were both matched and mismatched.

We first address the ill-structured nature of software maintenance, followed by the nature of both mental representations of the software (*mental representation of the application domain*) and modification tasks (*mental representation of the IS task*). Finally, we present details of the experiment and its findings.

The ill-structured nature of software maintenance

Software maintenance requires knowledge of both the application area that is being addressed and how to develop as well as maintain software, both of which represent application domain knowledge. Hence application domain knowledge is essential to the solution of ill-structured problems. Allocating attention between tasks in the IS and application domains is particularly relevant to software maintenance because maintainers must comprehend the existing software in order to be able to make relevant changes. Comprehending the software, alone, is a substantive task because maintainers must divide their attention among multiple elements within the software itself (e.g., different modules), as well as understand information other than that in the software (e.g., the external software documentation, etc). Modifying software is also a substantive task, as maintainers must both understand the modification to be conducted as well as make appropriate changes to the software.

Software maintenance is therefore a task for which the initial and goal states are vaguely defined and for which there are no well-defined solution paths. Further, because the problem statement does not contain all of the information needed for solution, it is not clear what actions are required to solve them. We therefore characterise software maintenance as an ill-structured problem area.

Roles of dual-task interference and cognitive fit in dual-task problem solving

We first examine the intrinsic characteristics of software. We then apply that knowledge to the mental representations that software maintainers form when they examine software (*mental representation of the application domain*), as well as to the types of modification tasks that they may be requested to accomplish (*mental representation of the IS task*).

Part of the essential difficulty of building and maintaining software comes from the need to represent the numerous types of information that are embedded in a piece of software (see Brooks, 1987). We address the characteristics of software and software tasks using these types of information (see, for example, Brooks, 1987; Curtis et al., 1988; Pennington, 1987a, 1987b). The most important types of information embedded in software are function, data flow, control flow, and state information (see, for example, Pennington 1987a, 1987b). Function information reflects the main goals of the program and the hierarchy of sub-goals. Data flow information reflects the series of transformations that data objects undergo. State information relates to the condition-action information embedded in a program; that is, the program actions that result when a set of conditions is true. Control flow information reflects execution sequence; that is, the order in which actions occur.

The mental representations of the software (application domain) formed from these types of information are typically characterised as domain, program, and situation models (von Mayrhauser and Vans, 1995).

First, a software maintainer's *domain model* is a high-level model that focuses on software functionality (Vans et al., 1999). It is more closely aligned to the problem (that is, what the software accomplishes) than how the software accomplishes it (Vans et al., 1999; von Mayrhauser and Vans, 1996) and therefore represents the maintainer's understanding of function information embedded in the software. Second, a software maintainer's *program model* emphasises how the software accomplishes tasks (von Mayrhauser and Vans, 1995) and is quite closely aligned with the programming domain (Pennington, 1987a). It therefore represents the maintainer's understanding of state and control flow information embedded in the software. Control flow reflects the sequencing of actions within software, while state information reflects connections between execution of an action and the state of the software when the action occurs (Pennington, 1987a). Third, a software maintainer's *situation model* allows a maintainer to avoid cognitive overload by reorganising the knowledge gained through detailed study of the software into higher level chunks and reflects the maintainer's understanding of data flow information in the software. It therefore serves as a bridge between the domain and program models (Vans at al., 1999). We can consider the domain and program models as being at the opposite ends of a continuum, with the situation model residing between them.

When engaging in software comprehension, a software maintainer invokes one of the possible mental representations of the software (domain, program, or situation model) (Vans at al., 1999), which then drives the comprehension process (Burkhardt et al., 2002). Because the domain model is linked to what the software accomplishes, software maintainers tend to invoke it when they are familiar with the application domain (von Mayrhauser and Vans, 1995). When maintainers lack application domain knowledge, they tend to invoke the program model thereby relying on their understanding of the programming language and standard programming constructs (von Mayrhauser and Vans, 1995). Because the situation model tends to develop after the program model, and only after extensive interaction with a piece of software, it is unlikely to be invoked at the outset of comprehension (von Mayrhauser et al., 1997).

Software modification tasks can be conceptualised as emphasising one of the types of information embedded within software. In this study, we investigated two types of tasks that have been examined in prior modification studies: a control flow modification task and a function modification task. A control flow modification task should be consistent with a program model because it emphasises the way in which software accomplishes tasks (von Mayrhauser and Vans, 1995), while a function modification task should be consistent with a domain model because it emphasises function information (Vans et al., 1999).

We conceptualise software maintainers as creating a *mental representation of the IS task* based on the requirements of the modification task, the way in which the modification task is presented (*external IS problem representation*), and their existing knowledge of software development (*internal representation of the application domain*). The external representation of the modification (*external IS problem representation*) is a specification of the software modification task such as a narrative or graphic. Essentially, then, the maintainer's *mental representation of the IS task* will emphasise the type of knowledge that is emphasised in the task requirements *(IS task)*. The maintainer's *mental representation of the* software *(application domain)* and *mental representation of the* modification task *(IS task)* may or may not match in that they may or may not emphasise the same type of information.

Operationalisation of the study and study findings

This study operationalised cognitive fit by crossing familiarity with the application domain with the type of modification task. A maintainer's domain model was invoked by using software from a familiar application domain (Vans et al., 1999) and their program model by using software from an unfamiliar application domain (von Mayrhauser and Vans, 1995). A maintainer's *mental representation of the IS task* was invoked using a modification task that emphasised function information or one that emphasised control flow information. Hence cognitive fit exists when maintainers conduct either a function task in a familiar application domain or a control flow task in an unfamiliar application domain. Such a match facilitates *problem-solving performance*. Correspondingly, cognitive fit does not exist when a control flow task is conducted in a familiar application domain and a function task in an unfamiliar application domain. This mismatch results in dual-task interference, which results in lower *problem-solving performance*.

The theory presented suggests that the fit conditions established would moderate the effectiveness of the comprehension that occurs during problem solving, which is reflected in changes to the *mental representation of the* software (*application domain*). Hence the dependent variable in the study was change in the level of comprehension observed during the modification task. The data analysis therefore evaluated the three-way relationship between application domain familiarity, type of modification task, and changes in comprehension.

The propositions presented earlier were supported in this study; that is, the three-way interaction between application domain familiarity, type of modification task, and changes in comprehension was significant. As shown in Figure 2, when cognitive fit exists (familiar application domain/function modification and unfamiliar application domain/control flow modification), the relationships between percent change in comprehension and modification performance are positive; that is, increases in comprehension of the software are associated with higher levels of performance on the modification tasks, and Proposition IS-1 is supported. In contrast, as shown in Figure 3, when cognitive fit does not exist (familiar application domain/control flow modification and unfamiliar application domain/function modification) the relationships are negative, demonstrating dual-task interference; that is, increases in comprehension are associated with lower levels of modification performance. Proposition IS-2 is supported.

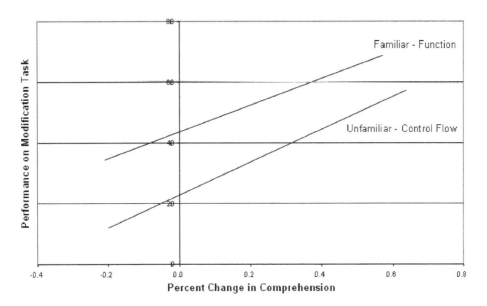

Figure 2: Relationship between percent change in comprehension and performance on modification task in conditions of cognitive fit.

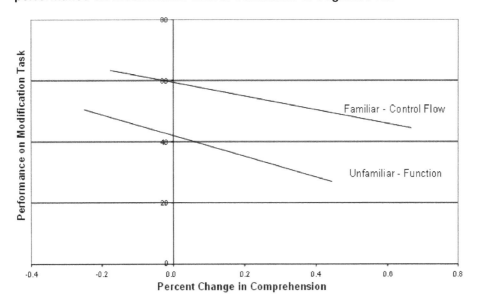

Figure 3: Relationship between percentage change in comprehension and performance on modification task in conditions where cognitive fit does not exist.

Discussion and implications

Although the application domain has long been acknowledged as playing a significant role in IS problem solving, very little research has been conducted into the effect that it has on performance on IS tasks, and even less theory has been developed. In this paper, we present theory that explains the role of application domain knowledge that is contingent upon the structured nature of the IS task under consideration. We then illustrate the theory on the well-structured problem area of conceptual schema understanding, and on the ill-structured problem area of software maintenance.

Discussion of the findings

This research develops a unifying theory of the role of the application domain in IS problem solving that explains the findings from two experiments that focused on the role of the application domain in IS problem solving and that produced different results.

The theoretical framework that we use to form the structure for our theory is a dual-task problem-solving model based on the theory of cognitive fit. Cognitive fit applies not only to problem solving in each of the contributing domains (application and IS), but also to the interaction between the two. The theory of cognitive fit allows us to distinguish different types of interactions between the tasks in the IS and application domains, when the two types of tasks match and when they do not. Those interactions may be supportive, neutral, or conflicting, depending on the structured nature of the problem area under investigation.

In solving tasks in well-structured problem areas, all of the information needed for problem solution is available in the *external problem representation* and problem solving can take place with reference to IS domain knowledge alone. In this case, knowledge of the application domain plays a role only in solving problems in which cognitive fit does not exist. Analysis of the well-structured problem-solving area of conceptual schema understanding (Khatri et al., 2006) revealed that knowledge of the application domain aided problem solving only in schema-based problem-solving tasks (fit does not exist), and not in syntactic and semantic comprehension tasks (fit exists). When cognitive fit does not exist, the information required for task solution is not available directly in the conceptual schema and transformations are required.

In solving tasks in ill-structured problem areas, on the other hand, the information needed for problem solution is not available in the *external problem representation* and application domain knowledge is essential to problem solution. When knowledge of the application domain matches the knowledge required to solve the problem, cognitive fit exists and problem solving is facilitated. However, when knowledge of the application domain does not match that required to solve the problem, dual-task interference, which is manifested in an inverse relationship between knowledge of the software gained during problem solving and performance on the IS task, occurs. Analysis of software maintenance tasks (Shaft and Vessey, 2006) revealed that when knowledge of the application domain matched that required to solve the maintenance task, improved knowledge of the application domain during conduct of the modification task was linked to better problem-solving performance. However, when the two types of knowledge did not match, an inverse relationship between knowledge of the application domain and problem-solving performance resulted.

Implications and future research directions

Our theory has implications for research in both IS and cognitive psychology. From the viewpoint of research in IS, there are two major implications. First, the dual-task problem-solving model presents a new way of viewing IS problem-solving. Its foundation in theory in cognitive psychology provides the opportunity for IS researchers to investigate the role of what is acknowledged to be an important and under-researched area of IS problem solving: the role of the application domain. The dual-task problem-solving model and its theoretical underpinnings therefore open the way for the development of a stream of research on the role of the application domain. It should always be remembered, however, that the research needs to be conducted in the context of the degree of structure in the problem area under investigation.

Second, this research adds to the strength of a growing body of literature that further testifies to the pervasiveness of cognitive fit in problem solving (see Vessey, 2006). There are a number of possible avenues for further investigation. For example, the distributed model of problem-solving suggests other factors in the fit models, such as the nature of the internal and mental representations in each of the domains, may either facilitate or inhibit problem solving in a given set of circumstances, and could be the subject of future research.

From the viewpoint of research in cognitive psychology, the community has focused on 'people's ability (or inability) to perform two or more activities concurrently' (Pashler, 1994). The findings of dual-task interference have been pervasive, and research does not appear to have been undertaken to examine other possible types of interactions (and their underlying mechanisms), although a number of authors have observed that problem solvers have a greater ability to perform two tasks that are compatible, as opposed to incompatible, at the same time, thus reducing the impact of dual-task interference (see, for example, Koch and Prinz, 2002; Whitaker, 1979).

What is specific to the types of tasks we investigated is that they either interact with each other, or have the potential to interact. Therefore, instead of focusing on the mechanisms by which dual-task interference occurs, we focused on the circumstances in which knowledge in each of the contributing domains interacts, and the type of interaction that results. Our contribution to the theory of dual-task problem solving in general, therefore, lies in introducing theory to determine when dual-task problem solving results in synergies between the two types of interacting tasks, when it results in interference, and when there are no effects. The cognitive psychology community could extend the focus of its research to determine the mechanisms by which certain tasks that are conducted simultaneously facilitate, while others inhibit, problem solving.

Conclusion

This research presents theory that formalises, and generalises to tasks in well-structured and ill-structured problem areas the role of the application domain in IS problem solving, thus opening the way to furthering knowledge on this important aspect of IS problem solving. The dual-task problem-solving model that forms the overarching framework for the theory was inspired by research on dual-task interference in cognitive psychology. The true contribution of this model lies in the use of the theory of cognitive fit to determine the different types of interactions that may arise.

References

Alexander, P. A. 1992, 'Domain knowledge: evolving themes and emerging concerns', Educational Psychologist, vol. 27, no. 1, pp. 33-51.

Alexander, P. A. and Judy, J. E. 1988, 'The interaction of domain-specific and strategic knowledge in academic performance', Review of Educational Research, vol. 58, no. 4, pp. 375-404.

Blum, B. A. 1989, 'A paradigm for the 1990s validated in the 1980s', Proceedings of the AIAA Conference, pp. 502-11.

Bodart, F., Patel, A., Sim, M. and Weber, R. 2001, 'Should optional properties be used in conceptual modelling? a theory and three empirical tests', Information Systems Research, vol. 12, no. 4, pp. 384-405.

Broadbent, D. E. 1971, Decision and Stress, London: Academic Press.

Brooks, F. P. 1987, 'No silver bullet: essence and accidents of software engineering', IEEE Computer, vol. 20, no. 4, pp. 10-9.

Burkhardt, J., De tienne, F. and Wiedenbeck, S. 2002, 'Object-oriented program comprehension: effect of expertise, task and phase', Empirical Software Engineering, vol. 7, no. 2, pp. 115-56.

Burton-Jones, A. and Weber, R. 1999, 'Understanding relationships with attributes in entity-relationship diagrams', Proceedings of the Twentieth International Conference on Information Systems, pp. 214-28.

Chen, P. P. 1976, 'The Entity-Relationship Model — Toward a unified view of data', ACM Transactions of Database Systems, vol. 1, no. 4, pp. 9-36.

Chi, M. T. H. and Glaser, R. 1985, 'Problem solving ability', in Sternberg R. J. (ed.), *Human Abilities: An Information Processing Approach*, NY: W. H. Freeman and Company.

Codd, E. F. 1970, 'A relational model of data for large shared data banks', Communications of the ACM, vol. 13, no. 6, pp. 377-87.

Corritore, C. L. and Wiedenbeck, S.1999, 'Mental representations of expert procedural and object-oriented programmers in a software maintenance task', International Journal of Human-Computer Studies, vol. 50, pp. 61-83.

Curtis, B., Krasner, H. and Iscoe, N. 1988, 'A field study of the software design process for large scale systems', Communications of the ACM, vol. 31, no. 11, pp. 1268-87.

Durso, F. T., Hackworth, C., Truitt, T. R., Crutchfield, J., Nikolic, D. and Manning, C. A. 1998, 'Situation awareness as a predictor of performance in en route air traffic controllers', Air Traffic Control Quarterly, vol. 6, no. 1.

Durso, F. T. and Gronlund, S. D. 1999, 'Situation awareness', in Durso, F. T., Nickerson, R. S., Schvaneveldt, R. W., Dumais, S. T., Lindsay, D. S. and Chi, M. T. (eds), *Handbook of Applied Cognition,* John Wiley and Sons.

Elmasri, R. and Navathe, S. B. 1994, *Fundamentals of Database Systems*, (2nd ed.) Benjamin/ Cummings Publishing Co., Redwood City, CA.

Gemino, A. 1999, 'Empirical methods for comparing system analysis modelling techniques', Unpublished PhD thesis, University of British Columbia, Vancouver, B.C., Canada.

Gemino, A. and Wand, Y. 2003, 'Evaluating modelling techniques based on models of learning', Communications of the ACM, vol. 46, no. 10, pp. 79-84.

Glass, R. L. and Vessey, I. 1992, 'Toward a taxonomy of application domains: history', Journal of Systems and Software, vol. 17, no. 2, pp. 189-99.

Greeno, J. 1978, 'Natures of problem-solving abilities', in Estes W. (ed.) *Handbook of Learning and Cognitive Processes*, vol. 5, Hillsdale, NJ: Lawrence Erlbaum Associates.

Hogg, D. N., Folleso, K., Strand-Volden, F. and Torralba, B. 1995, 'Development of a situation awareness measure to evaluate advanced alarm systems in nuclear power plant control rooms', Ergonomics, vol. 11, pp. 394-413.

Kahneman, D. 1973, *Attention and Effort*, Englewood Cliffs, NJ: Prentice-Hall.

Khatri, V., Vessey, I., Ramesh, V., Clay, P. and Park, S-J. 2006, 'Comprehension of conceptual schemas: Exploring the role of application and IS domain knowledge', Information Systems Research, vol. 17, no. 1, pp. 81-99.

Kitchner, K. S., 1983, 'Cognition, metacognition, and epistemic cognition: A three-level model of cognitive processing', Human Development, vol. 26, pp. 222-32.

Koch, I. and Prinz, W. 2002, 'Process interference and code overlap in dual-task performance', Journal of Experimental Psychology: Human Perception and Performance, vol. 28, no. 1, pp. 192-201.

Mayer, R. E. 1991, *Thinking, Problem Solving, Cognition*, W. H. Freeman and Company, New York, NY.

McPeck, H. 1990, 'Critical thinking and subject specificity: a reply to Ennis', Educational Researcher, vol. 19, no. 4, pp. 10-2.

Navon, D. 1990, 'Exploring two methods for estimating performance tradeoff', Bulletin of the Psychonomic Society, vol. 28, no. 2, pp. 155-7.

Navon, D. and Gopher, D. 1979, 'On the economy of the human processing systems', Psychological Review, vol. 86, pp. 254-5.

Navon, D. and Miller, J. 1987, 'Role of outcome conflict in dual-task interference', Journal of Experimental Psychology: Human Perception and Performance, vol. 13, no. 3, pp. 435-48.

Pashler, H. 1994, 'Dual-task interference in simple tasks: Data and theory', Psychological Bulletin, vol. 116, no. 2, pp. 220-44.

Pashler, H. and O'Brien, S. 1993, 'Dual-task interference and the cerebral hemispheres', Journal of Experimental Psychology-Human Perception and Performance, vol. 19, no. 2, pp. 315-30.

Pennington, N. 1987a, 'Stimulus structures and mental representations in expert comprehension of computer programs', Cognitive Psychology, vol. 19, pp. 295-341.

Pennington, N. 1987b, 'Comprehension strategies in programming', in Olson G. M., Sheppard S., and Soloway, E. (eds), *Empirical Studies of Programmers: First Workshop*, Ablex Publishing, Norwood, NJ.

Purao, S., Rossi, M. and Bush, A. 2002, 'Toward an understanding of the use of problem and design spaces during object-oriented system development', Information and Organisation, vol. 12, pp. 249-81.

Reitman, W. R. 1964, 'Heuristic decision procedures, open constraints, and the structure of ill-defined problems', in Shelly, M. W. and Bryan, G. L. (eds), *Human Judgements and Optimality*, New York: John Wiley and Sons.

Shaft, T. M. and Vessey, I. 1995, 'The relevance of application domain knowledge: The case of computer program comprehension', Information Systems Research, vol. 6, no. 3, pp. 286-99.

Shaft, T. M. and Vessey, I. 1998, 'The relevance of application domain knowledge: Characterising the computer program comprehension process', The Journal of Management Information Systems, vol. 15, no. 1, pp. 51-78.

Shaft, T. M. and Vessey, I. 2006, 'The role of cognitive fit in the relationship between software comprehension and modification', MIS Quarterly, vol. 30, no. 1, pp. 29-55.

Shanks, G., Tansley, E., Nuredini, J., Tobin, D, Moody, D. and Weber, R. 2002, 'Representing part-whole relationships in conceptual modelling: An empirical evaluation', Proceedings of the Twenty-Third International Conference on Information Systems, pp. 89-100.

Shanks, G., Nuredini, J., Tobin, D, Moody, D. and Weber, R. 2003, 'Representing things and properties in conceptual modelling: An empirical investigation', European Conference on Information Systems.

Shneiderman, B. and Mayer, R. E. 1979, 'Syntactic/semantic interactions in programmer behavior: A model and experimental results', International Journal of Computer and Information Science, vol. 8, pp. 219-38.

Sinnott, J. D., 1989, 'A model for solution of ill-structured problems: Implications for everyday and abstract problem solving', in Sinnott, J. D. (ed.), Everyday problem solving: Theory and application, Praeger, New York.

Taylor, R. M., Finnie, S. and Hoy, C. 1997, 'Cognitive rigidity: The effects of mission planning and automation on cognitive control in dynamic situations', 9th International Symposium on Aviation Psychology, Columbus, OH.

Vans, A. M., von Mayrhauser, A. and Somlo, G. 1999, 'Program understanding behavior during corrective maintenance of large-scale software', International Journal of Human-Computer Studies, vol. 51, pp. 31-70.

Van Selst, M. and Jolicoeur, P. 1997, 'Decision and response in dual-task interference', Cognitive Psychology, vol. 33, no. 3, pp. 266-307.

Vessey, I. 1991, 'Cognitive fit: A theory-based analysis of the graph versus tables literature', Decision Sciences, vol. 22, no. 2, pp. 219-40.

Vessey, I. 1994, 'The effect of information presentation on decision making: An analysis using cost-benefit theory', Information and Management, vol. 27, pp. 103-19.

Vessey, I. 2006, 'The theory of cognitive fit: One aspect of a general theory of problem solving?', in Zhang, P. and Galletta, D. (eds), Human-computer *interaction and management information systems: Foundations*, Advances in Management Information Systems Series, Armonk, NY: M.E. Sharpe.

Vessey, I. and Conger, S. 1993, 'Learning to specify information requirements: The relationship between application and methodology', Journal of Management Information Systems, vol. 10, no. 2, pp. 177-201.

von Mayrhauser, A. and Vans, A. M. 1995, 'Industrial experience with an integrated code comprehension model', Software Engineering Journal, vol. 22, no. 6, pp. 171-82.

Von Mayrhauser, A. and Vans, A. M. 1996, 'Identification of dynamic comprehension processes during large scale maintenance', IEEE Transactions on Software Engineering, vol. 22, no. 6, pp. 424-37.

von Mayrhauser, A., Vans, A. M. and Howe, A. E. 1997, 'Program understanding behavior during enhancement of large-scale software', Software Maintenance: Research and Practice, vol. 9, pp. 299-327.

Voss, J. F. and Post, T. A., 1988, 'On the solving of ill-structured problems', in Chi M. H., Glaser, R. and Farr M. J. (eds), *The Nature of Expertise*, Hillsdale, NJ: Lawrence Erlbaum Associates.

Whitaker, L. A. 1979, 'Dual-task interference as a function of cognitive processing load', Acta Psychologica, vol. 43, no. 1, pp. 71-84.

Wickens, C. D. 2002, 'Multiple resources and performance prediction', Theoretical Issues in Ergonomic Science, vol. 3, no. 2, pp. 159-77.

Zhang, J. 1997, 'The nature of external representations in problem solving', Cognitive Science, vol. 21, no. 2, pp. 179-217.

Zhang, J. and Norman, D. A. 1994, 'Representations in distributed cognitive tasks', Cognitive Science, vol. 57, pp. 87-122.

Towards a Unified Theory of Fit: Task, Technology and Individual

Michael J. Davern
Department of Accounting and Business Information Systems,
University of Melbourne
email: m.davern@unimelb.edu.au

Abstract

Fit between task requirements, user abilities and system characteristics has both intuitive appeal and empirical support as a driver of performance with information technology. Yet despite the volume of research on the construct, there is no unified theory that encompasses the key elements of the different fit constructs. Different studies employ different definitions of fit, both conceptually and operationally. Furthermore, while greater insight is obtained by considering the dynamics of fit and performance over time, prior work has largely focused on fit as a static point-in-time construct. In this paper a unified theory of fit is developed and a comprehensive fit taxonomy is derived. Finally, the theory and definition are shown to extend to a more dynamic conceptualisation of fit.

Introduction

Predicting and explaining how information technology (IT) affects human and organisational performance is a key task for information systems (IS) researchers (e.g. Seddon, 1997; Hitt and Brynjolfsson, 1996; Delone and McLean, 1992). Such research can improve understanding of the business value impacts of information technology (e.g. Davern and Kauffman, 1998), and can yield managerial interventions and design prescriptions for more effective use of IS.

The focus in this study is how IT affects individual task performance. IT value creation becomes concrete and most controllable at the level of the individual user, within a specific task and business process context (Davern and Kauffman, 2000). At this level problems with aggregated economic measures are eliminated; and established theory bases in psychology and the cognitive sciences can be used to predict and explain human behaviour.

Fit between task requirements, user abilities and system characteristics has been shown to be a key predictor of individual performance with information systems. Notable examples include Goodhue's task-technology fit (TTF) construct

(Goodhue and Thompson, 1995) and Vessey's (1991) cognitive fit construct. Intuitively, a better fit yields a better performance. Beyond this intuitive argument however there seems substantial divergence in the literature as to what actually constitutes 'fit'. For example, Zigurs and Buckland (1998) present 'a theory of task/technology fit' built on Venkatraman's (1989) work on fit in the strategic management literature. Surprisingly, Zigurs and Buckland do not even cite any of the work related to Goodhue's TTF construct, or Vessey's cognitive fit construct.

What is clearly required is a comprehensive theory of fit, from which it is possible to derive a taxonomy of the different types of fit that may drive individual performance with information technology. Without such a theory it is difficult to relate fit to other constructs in the literature. Moreover, without a comprehensive theory of fit the definition of the construct itself is confused. The intuitive appeal of the concept is both a key to its popularity, but also hides the lack of any comprehensive theory and definition.

To date, empirical investigations of fit have largely been static. Little is known of how fit changes over time — how users learn and systems evolve. In part, this is an artifact of the field's experience with the construct. Research logically starts with a static view because it is simpler. Understanding weaknesses of the static view can enrich subsequent efforts to develop a dynamic theory. Prior fit research has recognised the issue of dynamics, but left it unexplored. For example, Goodhue and Thompson's (1995) technology-to-performance chain model includes feedback, and Vessey and Galletta (1991) state that cognitive fit is 'an emergent property' of their model, although these dynamic aspects receive virtually no empirical attention. A dynamic theory of fit holds the prospect of identifying new interventions for improving user performance with information technologies (e.g. it could provide a basis for determining the sorts of training interventions that may be useful). It is also consistent with trends in the behavioural sciences more broadly, which have begun to focus on the explanation of behaviour as an emergent outcome of individual-environment interactions (e.g. McClamrock, 1995; Port and van Gelder, 1995; Thelen and Smith, 1994; Anderson, 1990).

The purpose of this paper is to present a comprehensive theory of fit that is explicitly able to consider the dynamic aspects of fit. The structure of the paper is as follows. Firstly, a theory and definition of fit is presented. Then, a taxonomy of the different types of fit, followed by an exploration of the dynamics of fit that draws on theory from ecological psychology, is presented. Finally, the conclusions and implications for research and practice are presented.

Fit: theory and definition

The need for a theory of fit

Vessey and Galletta (1991) define cognitive fit as the match between task, problem representation (e.g. mode of presentation of data) and individual problem solving skills. Goodhue (1995) defines TTF as the 'extent that technology functionality matches task requirements and individual abilities'. Three components appear consistent across these two definitions: task, technology (which in Vessey and Galletta's work is what provides the problem representation) and individual abilities.

Operationally, these two widely used fit constructs are quite different. For example, the survey instrument for measuring TTF identifies 12 components (see, for example, Goodhue, 1998), whereas cognitive fit is not measured per se, but rather manipulated in experimental studies that employ the construct. While it is possible to make some mappings between the two constructs, such mappings are not the same as an integrated theory of fit. For example, one of the 12 dimensions of TTF is 'presentation', which is operationalised with items like 'data is presented in a readable and useful format' (Goodhue, 1998). This dimension may loosely capture the relationship between problem presentation and task that is at the crux of the graphs versus tables debate that cognitive fit has attempted to resolve (Vessey and Galletta, 1991). While the mapping is possible, it is still unclear theoretically what precisely constitutes a comprehensive definition of fit.

Examining fit relative to other behavioural constructs in information systems requires mapping again from scratch. There is no unifying theoretical framework to provide guidance. Consider the well-known constructs of perceived usefulness and ease of use (e.g. Davis, 1989). From a fit perspective, perceived usefulness could map into how well the technology supports the task requirements, and ease of use could correspond to the 'fit' between user abilities and the technology. While these mappings seem intuitive, there is no clear theory of fit to justify them and empirical investigation of the relationships has not been forthcoming.

Components of a theory and definition of fit

At the outset, fit has three key components — task, technology, and individual characteristics. A unified theory of fit must therefore address these components. For expositional ease, the components are described separately below, although they are inextricably linked in practice.

Technology

Following Wand and Weber (1990), a two-part view of information systems is employed here: technology-as-tool and technology-as-representation. Technology-as-tool provides the physical interface for manipulating the technology as representation. 'Representation' implies a model of the real world task (e.g. a mathematical model embedded in a decision support system, or a graphical representation of a document) as opposed to a designer's system metaphor or a mental model inside the head of the user. In decision support systems terms, it is the Representation part of the ROMC (Representations, Operations, Memory Aids and Controls) design approach (Sprague and Carlson, 1982).

Distinguishing between technology as tool and as representation is useful. It can help organise various literatures addressing behaviour with information technology. For example, research on the psychology of decision models (e.g. Cooksey, 1996; Hoch and Schkade, 1996; Melone et. al., 1995; Blattberg and Hoch, 1990; Kleinmuntz, 1985; Einhorn, 1972) bears on technology as representation, whereas work in human-computer interaction (e.g. Davern, 1997; Gerlach and Kuo, 1991; Norman, 1986; Card et. al., 1983) bears on understanding technology as tool.

When considering fit with technology, the question thus arises as to whether it is fit with the tool, the representation, or indeed the fit between the tool and the representation. The tool versus representation dichotomy thus provides at least one basis for conceptualising different types of fit to populate a taxonomy. Any definition of fit must be able to capture both roles of technology: tool and representation.

More broadly, the value of this tool-representation dichotomy is evident in considering other behavioural constructs in the information systems literature. Consider the well-known constructs of ease-of-use and perceived usefulness from the technology acceptance model (Davis, 1989). Does the ease-of-use pertain to the technology as tool or as representation? Likewise for the usefulness construct. By capturing the dichotomy explicitly in a theory and taxonomy for the fit construct there is no such confusion.

Task

Following Wood (1986), task is defined here as comprising three components: products, required acts, and information cues. Products are ends, required acts and information cues are means for achieving the ends or goals. Specification of products or goals should detail the level of performance (in other words, the quality of the product, such as the accuracy of a sales forecast). Behavioural requirements (acts to be carried out and information cues to be used) will vary with the level of performance required in the task product. In practice there may often be substantial choice amongst sets of required acts (more than one way to achieve the goals of the task), even given a specific target level of performance.

The decomposition of task into goals and acts can be carried even further. User interactions with computer-based systems have often been described in terms of a hierarchy of tasks (Gerlach and Kuo, 1991; Card et. al., 1983). Rasmussen (1988) identified three levels of abstraction for computer supported work tasks: functional purpose, generalised, and physical (for an application of this framework in information systems, see Davern, et. al., 2000). In a similar vein, Silver (1990) distinguished between mechanical and conceptual tasks in decision support system usage.

To illustrate the task hierarchy consider the example of producing a sales forecast. There is the *substantive task* for which the product is the sales forecast. The required acts and information cues for making the forecast could involve collating and modelling a sizable time series of past sales. The size of the time series (the information cues) and the collation and modelling efforts (required acts) are contingent on the level of performance at which the product (sales forecast) is defined (i.e. the desired accuracy). Typically, the task leads the human forecaster to use some computer-based aid. Using technology support to produce a forecast involves running the time series data against some forecasting model. Thus there is the task that has as its product a computer model of sales (a sub-task of the substantive task), which involves the technology as representation. Subordinate to this task are the series of sub-tasks the products of which are specifications of some part of the model inside the computer or refinements to it (e.g. adding variables, etc). There is also a series of subtasks, the product of which is the time series data in a form suitable for running against the model. These more operational tasks involve the use of technology as a tool rather than as a representation, and are a primary concern of human-computer interaction research.

The type of fit and relevant measures of performance vary with the level at which a task is defined. At a minimum, it is necessary to distinguish among three key levels in the task hierarchy. There is the level of the super-ordinate or *substantive task* that motivates the whole exercise (e.g. producing a sales forecast). There is also the level of the *computer modelling task* [1] which involves the technology as representation (e.g. conceptual development and manipulation of a sales forecasting model inside the computer). Finally, there is the level of the more *operational tasks* in the hierarchy that involve the use of technology as a tool (e.g. data entry and other more physical operations). It is also evident that different users will work on different and multiple tasks and sub-tasks at different stages of interaction with an information system. By way of example, Figure 1 depicts a sample task hierarchy for a production mix optimisation problem using the spreadsheet package Excel.

---

[1] The term modelling is used here in its broadest sense. Even when using a word processor there is a 'model' being developed that corresponds, ultimately, to the paper document that gets printed.

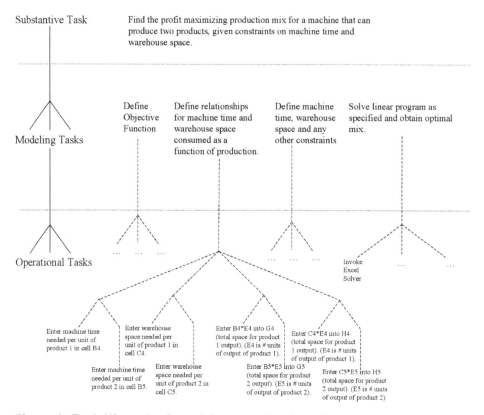

Figure 1: Task Hierarchy for solving a production mix problem using Excel.

Individual user

Newell (1982) provides a framework by which it is possible to understand individual behaviour in terms of knowledge and goals — the principle of rationality — which states:

> If an agent has knowledge that one of its actions will lead to one of its goals, then the agent will select that action (Newell 1982, p. 102).

In simple terms, if an individual's goals are known then from observing their behaviour his knowledge can be inferred. Alternatively, if the goals and knowledge of an individual are known his behaviour can be predicted.[2] Newell's framework complements the definition of task in terms of products, required acts and information cues presented above. Products are goals. Information cues and required acts define the structure of the task to which the individual user

---

[2] While this may appear to be a circularity, Anderson (1990) demonstrates this not to be the case as he notes: 'if we know a person's goals and observe his behaviour, we can infer his knowledge. Now that we have determined his knowledge, if we manipulate his goals, we should be able to predict his new behaviour ... [we] infer knowledge from one situation and make potentially disconfirmable predictions in a new situation. The appearance of circularity is only illusory.'

must apply their knowledge and abilities. Thus, such questions arise as: Does the user have the knowledge to carry out the required acts? Does he or she have the requisite knowledge to effectively utilise relevant information cues? Does the user's knowledge and abilities about how to achieve the task goal/product correspond to the set of acts and information cues supported by the technology?

To understand behaviour (and ultimately performance) with information technology thus requires understanding both the goals and the knowledge of the user. Importantly, this does not require absolute definition of how an individual will achieve a goal. The Principle of Equifinality (McClamrock, 1995) suggests that there are multiple ways to achieve a given goal or product. Colloquially, this is often rendered as 'there is more than one way to skin a cat'. Equifinality and the task hierarchy suggest that multiple actions may achieve a goal and there may be multiple goals implying different actions. Thus, the principle of rationality simply constrains actions, rather than dictates them. This degree of flexibility and equifinality evident in the application of the principle of rationality will prove important in understanding fit as a dynamic emergent property of user-technology interactions, as discussed in section four below.

Fit defined

Any definition of fit must consider task (goals/products, required acts, and information cues), technology (tool and representation, both of which support finite sets of goals, acts and relevant information cues), and user (goals, knowledge of how to carry out relevant acts and knowledge of how to make use of relevant information cues). It must also be consistent with the principle of equifinality. In its most general form fit is defined here as:

An agent's potential to achieve a given performance level at a given task.

Notably, the definition is silent on the mechanics of how potential becomes performance, which is consistent with the principle of equifinality. The distinction between fit and performance is somewhat analogous to the distinction in physics between the potential energy of a ball about to be dropped and the kinetic energy of the ball in motion, having just been dropped. More formally, it draws on Chomsky's (1965) classic distinction between competence and performance theories of behaviour that is the foundation of much of modern linguistics. Competence, as used by Chomsky, defines the capability for idealised performance. Performance is the realisation of this capability, which in practice may not quite achieve the full potential.

The general definition above is purposely couched in terms of an 'agent'. Changing the agent in question provides a basis for generating different types of fit. For example, the agent may be the individual user, the technology-as-tool or the technology-as-representation. The roots of this definition are in the broader cognitive science literature, where Johnson et al. (1992) provide a powerful definition of the fit a cognitive agent has with their task environment:

> Fit, then, characterises the degree to which an agent's expertise (a) reflects the requirements for success in … performing tasks and (b) is in accordance with the structure of available task information. (p. 307)

Adapting Johnson et al's definition to the present context, fit is formally defined here as:

Fit: The degree of functional correspondence between an agent's knowledge and the structure and features of the environment that specify supported actions and available information, relative to a specific task.

With its roots in psychology (e.g. Gibson, 1979; Kochevar, 1994) this definition lends itself to a theory of dynamics as discussed below. Importantly, it can also be readily mapped on to the different components of fit described earlier.

A fit taxonomy: the ATT-Fit framework

Fit, then, is a mapping amongst the required acts and information cues of a task, an agent's knowledge of relevant acts of which they are capable and information they can interpret and use, and finally the acts supported and information provided by the environment. The term 'environment' here refers conceptually to the location in which the task is carried out. Given the three levels of the task hierarchy, it logically follows that there are three 'task-environments'. The environment for the substantive task is reality — the real world context of the task. Similarly, the environment for the modelling task is the technology as representation. Finally, the environment for the operational task is the technology as tool. Table 1 summarises the taxonomy of different fits that arise in considering the different agents and task-environment combinations. Figure 2 summarises this visually in the ATT-Fit framework: A framework of Agent-Task-Technology Fit. The figure succinctly demonstrates that the taxonomy is exhaustive (all possible combinations are included).

Agent	Task-Environment	Type of Fit
User	Substantive-Reality	User-Reality Fit
	Modelling-Representation	User-Representation Fit
	Operational-Tool	User-Tool Fit Fit
Technology (Representation)	Substantive-Reality	Representation-Reality Fit
Technology (Tool)	Modelling-Representation	Tool-Representation Fit
	Substantive-Reality	Tool-Reality Fit

Table 1: A fit taxonomy

Interestingly, technology can play a role as both agent and environment. This role is twofold again because it can play agent or environment either as tool or as representation. In theory, therefore, the technology can be both agent and environment. In practice, this can be simplified by recognising that tools may act on representations, but not the other way around. Consequently, the only task-environment for technology as representation is reality — at the substantive task level.

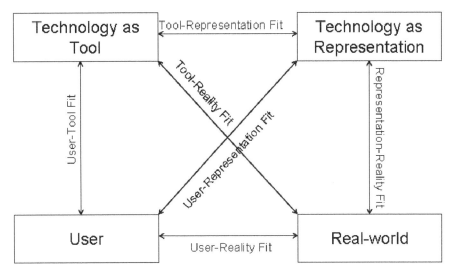

Figure 2: Visualising the fit taxonomy: the ATT-Fit framework.

Defining the different types of fit

User-Reality fit is the functional correspondence between the user's knowledge of the relevant set of acts and information cues that could achieve the task goals (e.g. a sales forecast) and the actions supported and information available in the organisational and business process context of the user's work (the substantive-task/real-world task environment). It is the user's potential for substantive task performance, unaided by technology.

User-Representation fit pertains to the user's potential performance in the modelling task (e.g. producing a sales forecast from a computer-based model). It is the degree of functional correspondence between the user's knowledge of the set of acts (e.g. model manipulation and analysis) and information cues (variables) that could achieve the desired goal (e.g. a computer based sales forecast and associated model). The task-environment here is the modelling task/technology-as-representation (e.g. the variables in the model and the analysis methods supported by the model's formulation).

User-Tool fit pertains to the user's potential performance in the operational task. It is a measure of the functional knowledge the user has of the acts and information cues supported by the technology-as-tool in carrying out operational tasks (i.e. a correspondence between what is known by the user and what is supported by the tool). Such knowledge, for example, could include the commands to execute data and model manipulation tasks in the sales forecasting scenario).

Representation-Reality fit is the degree of functional correspondence between the technology as representation's knowledge of relevant acts and information cues relative to the required acts and information cues of the substantive task (e.g. sales forecasting), in reality. It is the system's potential for performance, assuming it is effectively used. For example, in a decision support system, representation-reality fit is a measure of how well the model embedded in the decision support system functionally approximates the real world decision environment.

Tool-Representation fit is the tool's potential performance in manipulating the representation (i.e. the modelling-representation task-environment). It is the degree of functional correspondence between the representation manipulation and processing acts supported by the tool, and the acts required in manipulating the representation to achieve the modelling task goal (e.g. an appropriately specified sales forecasting model and suitably organised time series data).

Tool-Reality fit recognises that the demands of the modelling task are somewhat determined by the demands of the substantive task. Consequently, it is the tool's potential for manipulating appropriate representations of reality. *Tool-Reality fit* is the degree of functional correspondence between the technology as tool's knowledge of (support for) procedures of data and model manipulation that are implied by the substantive task, and consistent with the actions and information supported in real-world context (i.e. the substantive-reality task-environment).

Performance and the ATT-Fit framework

When considering the fit to performance relationship it is necessary to identify the specific task-environment of interest — the goals of the task and its place in the hierarchy of operational tasks, modelling tasks, substantive tasks. Indeed, location in the task hierarchy determines the relevant set of performance measures. In practice, performance is a multi-attribute construct; it can rarely be defined in terms of a single all encompassing measure (in part because good measures are often hard to come by, and in part because users have multiple goals to satisfy).

In its most general form, performance can be measured in terms of effectiveness and efficiency. Effectiveness relates to the output quality of the task (the task as product). Efficiency relates to the costs of inputs (information cues, required acts) for a given level of output (product). At higher levels in the task hierarchy, effectiveness measures dominate user attention. For example, in the substantive task of producing a sales forecast, forecasting accuracy is the key performance measure. Of course, the forecast must be completed in reasonable time (i.e. the required acts cannot be too onerous) and the relevant data must be readily available at a reasonable price (i.e. the information cues employed must be accessible economically), but these are matters of efficiency. At the higher hierarchical levels these efficiency performance measures act more as minimum requirements that, once satisfied, become relatively inconsequential. For example, the time it takes (a function of the required acts) to produce the sales forecast will not be of consequence unless it delays the production of the forecast past the point when management can act on the information. This is not to say that the manager will not prefer tools that take less time (e.g. require fewer keystrokes to manipulate data or models). Rather, it suggests that in the context of the super-ordinate task of producing a good forecast, enhanced modelling and data manipulation capabilities are likely to be more important than interface improvements (within some 'reasonable' limits).

In contrast, at lower levels in the task hierarchy efficiency issues take on greater importance (e.g. operations such as downloading files, printing documents, or booting up a machine always seem to take too long). Thus, at lower levels in the task hierarchy efficiency measures become more important, largely because effectiveness (product or output) performance tends to be binary (e.g. either the document printed out correctly or it did not, the data were sorted appropriately or not).

For each of the three key tasks in the task hierarchy, performance can be more formally defined as a function of the different fits, in principle, as follows:

Substantive Performance = f (All Six Fits)

Modelling Performance = f (User-Tool Fit, Tool-Representation Fit, User-Representation Fit)

Operational Performance = f (User-Tool Fit)

More completely, any fit based predictions and explanations of performance must recognise the dynamic nature of fit. Fit is subject to change over time as users learn and systems are refined. Pragmatically, it is also important to recognise that perceptions of fit may often differ greatly from what is actually the case (Davern, 1996; 1999).

A dynamic view of fit

Under a dynamic view, fit is an emergent property of an interaction between adaptive knowledge agents and the properties of the task environment that specify relevant information cues and required behavioural acts. Fit changes over time as the agent learns and the task environment changes. To understand fit as an emergent property requires analysis of the feedback system from which it emerges. Such an analysis considers the effects of both user learning and system evolution on performance — two critical factors that are not readily accommodated by simply considering the state of fit at a given point in time.

Although prior IS research on fit has recognised in theory that feedback is important (e.g. Goodhue and Thompson, 1995), feedback has not been the main focus of study either theoretically or empirically (e.g Goodhue, 1998; Vessey and Galletta, 1991; Umanath and Vessey, 1994; Goodhue, 1995).

Prior research on behaviour with information technology evidences the value of understanding the dynamics of technology usage. For example, DeSanctis and Poole's (1994) Adaptive Structuration Theory (AST) takes a dynamic process view of technology usage. AST suggests that the way in which a technology may be used is not deterministic but rather adaptive. AST views behaviours in using technology as emerging from interactions between users and technology features. Thus, a technology may be used in a variety of ways, not necessarily consistent with the intentions of the system designers, which may constitute what DeSanctis and Poole (1994) call unfaithful appropriations of the technology. Importantly, DeSanctis and Poole also note that 'unfaithful appropriations are not "bad" or "improper" but simply out of line with the spirit of the technology' (DeSanctis and Poole, 1994). Unfaithful appropriations suggest that achieving a good fit is not simply a matter of engineering; rather it emerges from user interactions with the system. Other research has shown the value of conceptualising technology usage as adaptive and exploratory behaviour (e.g. Davern and Wilkin, forthcoming; Bagozzi et al.,1992; Seely Brown, 1986). A dynamic theory of fit could thus provide improved explanations of the behaviour and performance outcomes in technology usage that involve user learning and adaptive usage — for both faithful and unfaithful appropriations.

Dynamic fit: an ecological psychology theory

As a scientific concept, fit has its origins in the biological sciences where the emphasis is on understanding the process of fitting in order to understand the fit that emerges. Evolutionary selection is viewed as a process of survival of the fittest. In this evolutionary context, the explanatory power of fit is not so much in the outcome of the process of fitting (i.e. selection of some biological feature of a species) as in the process itself; that is, in how the biological feature came to be selected in the evolutionary process (see, for example, Dawkins, 1982). In a human behavioural context, as opposed to a purely biological context, ecological psychology has explored the dynamic and emergent nature of fit (e.g. Kochevar, 1994). The definition of fit presented earlier can be shown to be entirely consistent with the concept of dynamic fit in ecological psychology.

In ecological psychology behaviour is the product of the interaction between an individual and the environment. Gibson (1979) coined the term *affordance* to refer to the possible actions that may result from this interaction between an individual's knowledge and the properties of the environment. A situation can afford a particular action for an individual with appropriate knowledge and abilities, and an individual can have the knowledge and abilities to carry out a particular action in an environment that affords such actions (Greeno et al., 1993). As Kochevar (1994) puts it: 'Environments provide information structured to support specific behaviours, and adapted individuals are sensitive to such information patterns'. Thus, the concept of an affordance is concerned with the complementarities between an agent's knowledge and abilities and the features of the environment (i.e. the information it provides and actions it supports). This notion of complementarities is essentially one of fit, but 'fitness' for what purpose? A given environment may afford many different actions for agents of even limited abilities. Affordances do not determine action; they merely define the set of possible actions available to a given agent in a particular environment. Newell's Principle of Rationality, discussed earlier, provides the 'filter' for action selection: an agent will select the action (realise the affordance) that appears to best attain his or her task goals. Indeed, Heft (1989) states that the affordances an individual perceives in a given environment are determined by his or her intentions or goals. Notably, the other aspects of task, information cues and required acts, relate to the affordances themselves — what information the environment provides and what actions it supports.

Ecologically, what a situation affords an individual at a given point in time depends on the fit amongst the individual's knowledge and abilities, the actions supported by the environment and the information it provides, in the context of the task goals that are present. Thus, the earlier definition of fit as the degree of the correspondence between an individual's knowledge and the structure and features of the environment that specify supported actions and information, in the context of a specific task goal, is entirely consistent with ecological psychology principles. The complementarities between the environment (information cues provided and actions supported) and an individual's knowledge define the set of all possible actions the individual may take in that environment — the affordances. The task at hand (goals, required acts and information cues) determines what affordances an agent perceives in that environment at a given point in time. More specifically, the task goals serve as a filter in the selection of the appropriate action to take. At least implicitly, this filtering reflects the degree of fit amongst the environment (information provided and acts supported), the agent's knowledge (ability to use information and carry out acts), and the demands of the task (goals, required acts, and information cues — of which goals is the most determinative element since equifinality implies substitutions may be possible with respect to acts and cues).

This filtering is not a cognitively complex task. Rather, ecological psychology argues the somewhat extreme position that individuals 'directly perceive' the task relevant affordances in an environment. As Gibson (1979) notes:

> Perceiving is an achievement of the individual, not an appearance in the theater of his consciousness. It is a keeping-in-touch with the world, an

experiencing of things rather than a having of experiences. It involves awareness-of instead of just awareness.

Ecologically speaking individuals engage in a continuous perception-action cycle as they seek to maintain the fit between their knowledge and the environment in their attempts to satisfy specific task goals — fit is dynamic and task specific. Maintaining fit is a process of becoming sensitised to the affordances in a given environment and task context, and of fine-tuning this sensitivity. Problem solving behaviour can be characterised as 'gap closing' (Lave, 1988); attempting to improve the fit between the individual's knowledge and the environment in the task context. Gap closing involves taking the processes used in the past to handle similar classes of problems or tasks and iteratively manipulating them until the present task or problem can be accomplished or resolved.

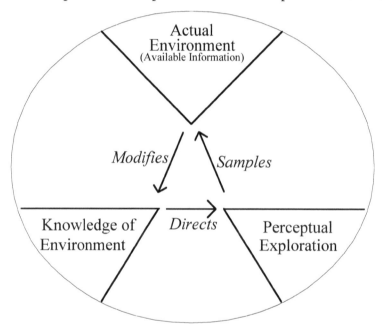

Figure 3: Neisser's perceptual cycle (adapted from Neisser, 1976).

Neisser's (1976) Perceptual Cycle characterises this gap closing process (see Figure 3). The individual has some knowledge of the environment based on past experiences. This knowledge drives exploratory action in the actual environment; for example, behaviour driven by a crude notion such as 'my experience suggests that this [action] usually fixes problems like this' (Orr, 1990). Feedback about the success of the action relative to the goals results in modifications to the individual's knowledge (their sensitivity to the affordances of the environment is fine-tuned) that then drives further action. This process iterates until the individual is satisfied that his or her knowledge of the environment and the actions that derive from it adequately address the problem (i.e. the task can be completed). Satisfactory fit is achieved. Importantly, this conception of fit allows for new and unique combinations of actions to emerge (Kochevar, 1994). In AST terms, it allows for novel, unique and unexpected or 'unfaithful' appropriations of a technology environment.

Judgments of fit: implications for learning and systems change

Neisser's perceptual cycle is essentially a model of learning. Learning is thus an integral component of a dynamic, ecological view of fit. As an individual learns more about the environment, his or her fit with it changes and the affordances (possible actions) available change. Old ways of doing things are supplanted by new and better ways. However, in technology supported work environments, there are multiple types of fit, as there are multiple knowledge agents (user, technology-as-tool, technology-as-representation as per Table 1). While an individual may be able to 'directly' perceive affordances and consequently their fit with an environment for a given task, the assessment of fit for an agent other than themselves (e.g. as in representation-reality fit) is clearly a more cognitively complex task.

From a cognition perspective, two information processes influence an individual's judgments of fit: inference from past performance, and prospective analysis of available affordances in light of one's goals. Both of these processes can introduce errors into fit judgments. For example, performance feedback is often delayed in real world environments. Moreover, it is also difficult for an individual to causally separate performance variations due to actions taken from those due to natural variation in a stochastic world. Indeed, prior research has shown that human decision makers do not cope well with dynamic feedback systems, particularly when there are delays (Diehl and Sterman, 1995; Sterman, 1989a; 1989b).

Inferring fit from a goal-based consideration of available affordances as a form of prospective thinking — evaluating the desirability of realising an available affordance without actually taking the action — is also subject to error and bias as it is likely to be carried out heuristically (e.g. Tversky and Kahneman, 1974). The problem is exacerbated when a user is inferring fit when the technology is the knowledge agent. For example, assessing representation-context fit requires that the user have knowledge of what the environment affords the representation. Consequently, this implies that the accuracy of subjective judgments of representation-reality fit by a user is influenced by the degree of user-representation fit.[3]

---

[3] There is already support for this notion in the literature. Melone et al. (1995), following Sharda et al. (1988), attribute the conflicting performance outcomes in experimental DSS studies to the influences of differences in user knowledge of the system model (representation) on users' abilities to appropriately calibrate their use of a DSS.

Judgments of fit, whether directly perceived or otherwise, drive individual learning and motivate efforts in task or systems refinement and development. Learning in this dynamic view of fit can be proactive, reactive, or passive. Proactive learning aims at improving fit by making available to the individual new affordances. It is driven *a priori* on an assessment of how well the current affordances correspond to the individual's goals. Reactive learning occurs in response to dissatisfaction with the performance evaluation of actions taken. Learning can also occur passively as an individual acquires knowledge in a non-purposeful manner while interacting with the environment. In the information systems context, proactive learning could occur when a user works through an interactive tutorial before attempting a task with a new piece of software. Reactive learning could occur through resorting to the tutorial after having difficulties carrying out a task with a new piece of software. Passive learning could occur when a user discovers new ways of using a software application through casual observation or interaction with another user — it is merely an incidental outcome rather than a deliberate goal of the user.

Judgments that fit is unsatisfactory can also lead to efforts to change the environment to improve fit; through system refinement and development, for example. Such efforts could be as radical as a major hardware or software upgrade, or as simple as a change to the toolbars displayed in a word processor. Importantly, these changes may also occur exogenously if they are imposed on users rather than instigated by them.

Since users' inferences about the different types of fit can become biased, their subjective judgments of fit may differ substantially from more objective measures of fit. In the IS context this is problematic both for the user who seeks to maximise job performance through IT and for the researcher or practitioner trying to evaluate a system. More specifically, misjudgements that fit is good, when it is not, reduce the motivation for learning (as per the perceptual cycle) or to refine a system to improve fit. In a similar vein misjudgements that fit is bad when it is actually good (such as may occur in highly stochastic environments) could lead to unwarranted efforts at system refinement or task learning.

Implications and conclusions

Theoretical contributions

A unified theory of fit has been developed and a comprehensive definition has been derived from the theory. The definition recognises the key aspects of technology, individual, and task that are present in prior research. It also provides the basis for an explicit description of a taxonomy of the different types of fit in technology supported work and the interrelationships amongst them.

Furthermore, it has demonstrated theoretically that performance and fit are distinct but related constructs.

The theory and definition of fit developed in the paper is shown to be consistent with a move to a dynamic understanding of fit. The development of theories of the feedback processes and dynamics of fit and performance over time is itself a promising and under-researched area, but a direction consistent with trends in the broader behavioural sciences literature to consider the dynamics by which behaviour emerges over time (e.g. Port and Van Gelder, 1995; Sterman, 1989a; 1989b). It also highlights the potential for user misjudgements of fit (Davern, 1996; 1999).

Practical implications

One of the difficulties facing both researchers and practitioners in using the various behavioural of constructs in information systems is understanding precisely what is being measured. The taxonomy of fits in the ATT-Fit framework serves as a useful foundation in this regard. It clearly articulates a basis for distinguishing between different types of fit. For example, it highlights some of the distinctions (e.g. between technology as representation and as tool) that are glossed over by existing measures of fit, and indeed a number of other widely used IS constructs.

More specifically, the explication of the task hierarchy calls practitioners and researchers alike to specifically identify the task for which they anticipate the technology will provide performance gains. Alternatively, it serves as a diagnostic tool for identifying where a technology solution may be failing. Again, it provides a clear and theoretically grounded foundation for understanding the different aspects of fit in information technology contexts.

Finally, the richer understanding of behaviour with technology provided by the dynamic conceptualisation of fit may lead to new and more successful methods and interventions in systems and training that are cognisant of these dynamics.

References

Anderson, J. R. 1990, *The Adaptive Character of Thought*, Hillsdale, NJ, L. Erlbaum Associates.

Bagozzi, R. P., Davis, F. D. and Warshaw, P. R. 1992, 'Development and test of a theory of technological learning and usage', Human Relations, vol. 45, no. 7, pp. 659-86.

Blattberg, R. C. and Hoch, S. J. 1990, 'Database models and managerial intuition: 50% model + 50% manager', Management Science, vol. 36, no. 8, pp. 887-99.

Card, S., Moran, T. and Newell, A. 1983, *The Psychology Of Human-Computer Interaction*, Hillsdale, NJ: Lawrence Erlbaum and associates.

Chomsky, N. 1965, *Aspects Of The Theory Of Syntax*, M.I.T. Press, Cambridge.

Cooksey, R. W. 1996, *Judgment Analysis: Theory, Methods, And Applications*, San Diego, CA, Academic Press.

Davern, M. J. 1996, 'When good fit is bad: The dynamics of perceived fit', Proceedings of the Seventeenth International Conference on Information Systems, Cleveland, OH.

Davern, M. J. 1997, 'Human-Computer Interaction', in Davis, G. B. (ed.), *Blackwell's Encyclopaedic Dictionary of Management Information Systems*, Blackwell, Oxford, UK, pp. 98-99.

Davern, M. J. 1999, 'Performance with information technology: Individual fit and reliance on decision support systems', unpublished doctoral dissertation, University of Minnesota.

Davern, M. J. and Kauffman, R. J. 2000, 'Discovering Value and Realising Potential from IT Investments', Journal of Management Information Systems, vol. 16, no. 4, pp. 121-44.

Davern, M. J., Te'eni, D. and Moon, J. 2000, 'Content versus structure in information environments: A Longitudinal analysis of website preferences', Twenty-First International Conference on Information Systems, Brisbane, Australia.

Davern, M. J. and Wilkin, C. L. Forthcoming, 'Evolving Innovations Through Design and Use', Communications of the ACM.

Davis, F. D. 1989, 'Perceived usefulness, perceived ease of use, and user acceptance of information technology', MIS Quarterly, vol. 13, no. 3, pp. 319-40.

Dawkins, R. 1982, *The Extended Phenotype*. San Francisco, CA, W. H. Freeman.

Delone, W. H. and McLean, E.R. 1992, 'Information systems success: The quest for the dependent variable', Information Systems Research, vol. 3, no. 1, pp. 60-95.

DeSanctis, G. and Poole, M. S. 1994, 'Capturing the complexity in advanced technology use: Adaptive structuration theory', Organisation Science, vol. 5, no. 2, pp. 121-47.

Diehl, E. and Sterman, J. D. 1995, 'Effects of feedback complexity on dynamic decision making', Organisational Behavior and Human Decision Processes, vol. 62, no. 2, pp. 198-215.

Einhorn, H. J. 1972, 'Expert measurement and mechanical combination', Organisational Behavior and Human Performance, vol. 7, no. 1, pp. 86-106.

Gerlach, J. H. and Kuo, F-Y., 1991, 'Understanding human-computer interaction for information systems design', MIS Quarterly, vol. 15, no. 4, pp. 527-49.

Gibson, J. J. 1979, *An Ecological Approach to Visual Perception*. Boston, MA: Houghton Mifflin.

Goodhue, D. L. 1995, 'Understanding user evaluations of information systems', Management Science, vol. 41, no. 12, pp. 1827-44.

Goodhue, D. L. 1998, 'Development and measurement validity of a task-technology fit instrument for user evaluations of information systems', Decision Sciences, vol. 29, no. 1, pp. 105-38.

Goodhue, D. L. and Thompson, R. L. 1995, 'Task-technology fit and individual performance', MIS Quarterly, vol. 19, no. 2, pp. 213-36.

Greeno, J. G., Moore, J. L. and Smith, D. R. 1993, 'Transfer of situated learning', in Detterman, D. K. and Sternberg, R. J. (eds), *Transfer on Trial: Intelligence, Cognition and Instruction*, Norwood, NJ, Ablex Publishing Co.

Heft, H. 1989, 'Affordances and the body: An intentional analysis of Gibson's ecological approach to visual perception', Journal for the Theory of Social Behaviour, vol. 19, no. 1, pp. 1-30.

Hitt, L. M. and Brynjolfsson, E. 1996, 'Productivity, business profitability, and consumer surplus: three different measures of information technology value', MIS Quarterly, vol. 20, no. 2, pp. 121-42.

Hoch, S. J. and Schkade, D. A. 1996, 'A psychological approach to decision support systems', Management Science, vol. 42, no. 1, pp. 51-64.

Johnson, P. E., Kochevar, L. K. and Zaulkernan, I. 1992, 'Expertise and fit: Aspects of cognition', in Pick, Jr., H. L., Van den Broek, P. and Knill, D. C. (eds) *Cognition: Conceptual And Methodological Issues*, pp. 305-331. Washington, DC: American Psychological Association.

Kleinmuntz, D. N. 1985, 'Cognitive heuristics and feedback in a dynamic decision environment', Management Science, vol. 31, no. 6, pp. 680-702.

Kochevar, L. K. 1994, 'Generativity of Expertise', unpublished doctoral dissertation, University of Minnesota.

Lave, J. 1988, *Cognition in Practice: Mind, Mathematics and Culture in Everyday Life*, New York, NY, Cambridge University Press.

McClamrock, R. A. 1995, *Existential Cognition: Computational Minds in the World*, Chicago, IL: Chicago University Press.

Melone, N. P., McGuire, T. W., Chanand, L. W. and Gerwing, T. A. 1995, 'Effects of DSS, modelling, and exogenous factors on decision quality and confidence', Proceedings of the Twenty-Eighth Hawaii International Conference on System Sciences, Wailea, HI, pp. 152-9.

Neisser, U. 1976, *Cognition and Reality: Principles and Implications of Cognitive Psychology*, San Francisco, CA, W. H. Freeman.

Newell, A. 1982, 'The knowledge level', Artificial Intelligence. vol. 18, no. 1, pp. 87-127.

Norman, D. A. 1986, 'Cognitive engineering', in Norman, D. A. and Draper, S. W., (eds) *User Centered System Design: New Perspectives on Human-Computer Interaction*, pp. 31-61. Hillsdale, NJ: Lawrence Erlbaum and Associates.

Orr, J. E. 1990, 'Sharing knowledge, celebrating identity: Community memory in a service culture', in Edwards, D. and Middleton, D. (eds), *Collective Remembering: Inquiries In Social Construction*, pp.169-89. London, Sage Publications.

Port, R. F. and van Gelder, T. 1995, *Mind As Motion : Explorations In The Dynamics Of Cognition*, Cambridge, Mass., MIT Press.

Rasmussen, J. 1988, 'A cognitive engineering approach to the modelling of decision making and its organisation in: process control, emergency management, cad/cam, office systems, and library systems', Advances in Man-Machine Systems Research, vol. 4, pp. 165-243.

Seddon, P. B. 1997, 'A re-specification and extension of the DeLone and McLean model of IS success', Information Systems Research, vol. 8, no. 3, pp. 240-53.

Seely Brown, J. 1986, 'From cognitive to social ergonomics and beyond', in Norman, D. A. and Draper, S. W. (eds), *User Centered System Design: New Perspectives on Human-Computer Interaction*, pp. 457-486. Hillsdale, NJ: Lawrence Erlbaum and Associates.

Sharda, R. M., Barr, S. H. and McDonnell, J. C. 1988, 'Decision support system effectiveness: A review and empirical test', Management Science, vol. 34, no. 2, pp. 139-59.

Silver, M. S. 1990, 'Decision Support Systems: Directed and non-directed change', Information Systems Research, vol. 1, no. 1, pp. 47-70.

Sprague, R. H. and Carlson, E. D. 1982, *Building Effective Decision Support Systems*, Englewood Cliffs, N.J., Prentice-Hall.

Sterman, J. D. 1989a, 'Misperceptions of feedback in dynamic decision making', Organisational Behavior and Human Decision Processes, vol. 43, no. 3, pp. 301-35.

Sterman, J. D. 1989b, 'Modelling managerial behavior: Misperceptions of feedback in a dynamic decision making experiment', Management Science, vol. 35, no. 3, pp. 321-39.

Thelen, E. and Smith, L. B. 1994, *A Dynamic Systems Approach To The Development Of Cognition And Action*, Cambridge, Mass., MIT Press.

Tversky, A. and Kahneman, D. 1974, 'Judgment under uncertainty: Heuristics and biases', Science, vol. 185, no. 4157, pp. 1124-31.

Umanath, N. S. and Vessey, I. 1994, 'Multiattribute data presentation and human judgment: A cognitive fit perspective', Decision Sciences, vol. 25, no. 5-6, pp. 795-824.

Venkatraman, N. 1989, 'The concept of fit in Strategy Research: Toward verbal and statistical correspondence', Academy of Management Review, vol.14, no. 3, pp. 423-44.

Vessey, I. 1991, 'Cognitive fit: A theory-based analysis of the graphs versus tables literature', Decision Sciences, vol. 22, no. 2, pp. 219-40.

Vessey, I. 1994, 'The effect of information presentation on decision making: An analysis using cost-benefit theory', Information and Management, vol. 27, pp. 103-19.

Vessey, I. and Galletta, D. 1991, 'Cognitive fit: An empirical study of information acquisition', Information Systems Research, vol. 2, no. 1, pp. 63-84.

Wand, Y. and Weber, R. 1990, 'Towards a deep structure theory of information systems', in DeGross, J. I., Alavi, M. and Oppelland, H. (eds), Proceedings of the International Conference on Information Systems, pp. 61-71. Copenhagen, Denmark.

Wood, R. E. 1986, 'Task complexity: Definition of the construct', Organisational Behavior and Human Decision Processes, vol. 37, pp. 60-82.

Zigurs, I. and Buckland, B. K. 1998, 'A theory of task/technology fit and group support systems effectiveness', MIS Quarterly, vol. 22, no. 3, pp. 313-34.

Are Routine Manual Systems Genuine Information Systems?

Reeva Lederman
Department of Information Systems, University of Melbourne
email: reevaml@unimelb.edu.au

Robert Johnston
Department of Information Systems, University of Melbourne
email: r.johnston@dis.unimelb.edu.au

Abstract

The information systems literature describes many systems — both computerised and manual — that are commonly accepted to be information systems (IS). However, there is also a group of systems found in the literature, which will be called routine, manual systems, that appear to provide participants with cues for action but which do not have the hallmarks of traditional information systems. These systems contain elements that are both stored and manipulated in ways that are different to what is observed in traditional data processing. This paper asks whether or not these systems in fact share common characteristics with traditional IS and which would allow us to call them information systems. It is found that, in using terminology from general systems theory and the semiotics literature, it is possible to find common ground between these systems and traditional IS, thus making the term 'information system' a legitimate label for such systems. Answering this question is an important first stage in a larger research project that examines what makes routine, manual systems function effectively.

Introduction

Information systems can be computerised or manual, with many manual information systems such as paper ledgers or Kalamazoo accounting systems being noted in the literature (Benson and Standing, 2002; Boddy et al., 2005; Land, 1987; Stair and Reynolds, 2003). However, examples of manual systems given in the literature are generally of systems where written data is stored on paper and there is a relatively simple translation to a computerised model (Checkland and Howell, 1998; Land, 1987). Descriptions of systems in the literature and also real world experience suggests, however, that there is a category of systems whose members support the performance of manual work but, because they do not always produce paper to file, or appear to store data in a conventional way, are not seen as information systems and do not fit well with traditional definitions of an information system. In these systems, tasks are completed manually through practiced routines and there is limited reliance on information stored in, and retrieved from, either fixed computerised databases or paper based files. These manual systems may include some paper artifacts (cards or tokens, rather than files) or have physical components often using tools such as whiteboards (Schmidt and Simone, 1996), cards or coloured magnets (Lederman et al., 2003; Mackay, 1999; Wong, 2000) as information resources. While there may be some written information on these artifacts, they do not function as traditional data stores. Instead, the meaning of these artifacts is contained, for example, in their colour or placement. Included among the socio-technical systems exhibiting these traits are some hospital scheduling systems, air traffic control systems and systems in small manufacturing concerns.

These manual systems support work that is relatively complex but largely repetitive and routine and many of the human activities in these systems appear to be performed in a largely non-cognitive way. They comprise forms of activity where participants use their tacit knowledge of work practices and various cues perceived directly from the work environment to routinely perform manual tasks. In these systems actors use cues embedded in the physical components of the system to deduce information on how to act to complete goals. For example, a magnet of a particular colour on a whiteboard might promote a particular response. While such systems have been discussed previously, the information systems literature does not consider to any significant degree how these manual artifacts provide signals or cues for behaviour, how system participants respond to these cues, or the role that manual artifacts play in providing information for routine (non-cognitive) action. Particularly, previous research does not focus on the extent to which these systems can be viewed as genuine information systems rather than simply as discrete tools or aides memoire. In this paper, such systems will be termed routine, manual systems.

This paper examines the legitimacy of regarding these routine, manual systems as information systems. Information in these systems is not defined in terms of our traditional understanding of it as processed data so conventional definitions of IS do not appear to suit these systems. However, this paper claims they can still rightfully be called information systems. Because these systems do not store or process data in ways commonly documented in the IS literature we seek a way of explaining how these systems conform to a definition of information systems that is broader than that commonly found in the IS literature.

The method we use is to firstly examine traditional definitions of the term 'information system'. From these definitions we extract four general concepts that we use to form the basis of a new definition: fact, transformation, signal and action. Then we present four example systems. The first is a conventional information system and is presented as an illustration of the type of system commonly regarded as an information system. This provides a basis for understanding why it may be difficult to also perceive a routine, manual system as an IS because, prima facie, they appear to be very different. However, we then describe three routine, manual systems and consider how the elements in our new definition of an information system appear in all three of these systems. Then we reflect, using the literature and our own observations, on the answer to the question: Are routine, manual systems genuine information systems?

We find that the three routine, manual systems form a class with common characteristics that can conform to a broader definition of information systems than is currently commonly used. In answering the question of whether or not they are information systems we stand to gain an important insight into their relationship to traditional information systems as well how they provide a source of information to their users in informing action.

Definitions of information systems

The information systems literature recognises that the term 'information system' is a broad one and throws up a number of different definitions. These definitions fall loosely into two categories: those that have computerised technology artifacts at the centre of the system and those where systems are not necessarily computer technology dependent. Definitions in the former category typically describe an information system as being 'any organised combination of people, hardware, software, communications networks and data resources that collects, transforms and disseminates information in an organisation' (O'Brien, 2003) or 'people, data/information, procedures, software, hardware, communications' (Benson and Standing, 2002). Those who subscribe to the second position include similar elements but without the idea of technology being an essential component. Stair and Reynolds (2003), for example, define an IS as a 'set of interrelated components that collect, manipulate and disseminate data and information to provide a feedback mechanism to meet an objective'. Similarly, according to Laudon and Laudon (2006), an IS is 'to support decision making and control in an organisation'. Most other approaches to information systems theory propose that all information systems exhibit certain basic features, notably input, processing (which produces output) and feedback. The input stage involves 'the gathering and capturing of raw data' (Stair and Reynolds, 2003), the output involves 'producing useful information' (Stair and Reynolds, 2003) from the processed input, and processing involves, 'converting or transforming data into useful outputs' (Stair and Reynolds, 2003). Finally, feedback 'is output that is used to make changes to input or processing activities' (Stair and Reynolds, 2003). In this way of thinking, a system that includes the interrelated components that perform these tasks is perceived as an information system. A common view also adds the idea of self containment in that users work with the system but without direct utilisation of the real world to which the system refers. Rather, they work through a model or abstract representation of the real world (Wand and Weber, 1995). So, for example a system participant can make a decision about action through reference to an inventory database and does not need to look at the stock on the shelf. Within the literature there are also definitions that stress the importance of overall goals and define information systems as systems that provide the impetus for activity (e.g. Goldkuhl and Agerfalk, 1988).

In comparing different types of systems such as traditional computerised information systems and routine, manual systems, implementation details are necessarily different. Consequently, in examining these definitions, we argue that it is valid to ignore those differences or variations that are concerned with implementation. However, four essential concepts remain common to other definitions: input and output, processing (which produces the output) and feedback.

Data inputs are the facts that are gathered and captured in the system. There are many definitions of data in the literature but they are all essentially about the projection, or communication of facts. As examples, data has been said to be 'facts, concepts or derivatives in a form that can be communicated and interpreted' (Galland, 1982) and a 'representation of facts, concepts or instructions in a formalised manner suitable for communication' (Hicks, 1993). Other definitions also include the idea of facts being available for processing (Laudon and Laudon, 2006; Maddison, 1989; Martin and Powell, 1992).

Processing is often considered to be the way data is manipulated, developed or built upon in some way that transforms it to create meaningful information. This is what is contained in the idea of a system itself. Systems theory, an umbrella theory within which information systems theory fits, considers the idea of transformation, which describes the structure of change in natural systems (Land, 1973). Land uses the term 'transformation' to describe how participants in a system negotiate meaning. Faced with signals from their environment, they define and redefine what to do next, repeating successful approaches. Thus, transformation incorporates the notion of processing.

When raw facts are transformed by system processing, output is produced that signals or communicates to participants in the system. Essentially, what defines output in its role as an information systems component is its indicative status, that it signals or projects itself to be acted upon in some way that has value to systems participants. It is the output signalling to users that leads to action. That is, participants react to processed facts and take action for as long as this approach is perceived to be goal attaining.

Feedback occurs when a user responds to the output in such a way that the system input is altered. In traditional information systems this may involve deliberation. In routine, manual systems, where there is a reactive response to the output, feedback can ensue without the cognitive activity that deliberation entails. Rather a routine response occurs, which has been learnt from earlier experiences. Either way the output triggers a response in the system participant as a guide and precursor to the feedback activity.

Where there is action it can be presumed that it has resulted as a response to output. It is this action and its effects on system inputs that is significant and keeps the system functioning. So while feedback is the traditional term used its significance in a system results from the action it promotes. The primacy of action in information system is reinforced within semiotics where it is claimed that 'Information systems should be conceived as ... systems intended for action' (Goldkuhl and Agerfalk, 2000). Information systems are also seen to 'exist to support directly those taking the action which results from the formed intentions' (Checkland and Howell, 1998).

This focus on 'those taking the action' is an important element of feedback in an information system. It is suggested that information systems have a 'social dimension' with problems they try to solve being 'people centred' and involving human participation (Benson and Standing, 2002). Also, many definitions of information systems include people and the procedures followed by people, as essential components (Benson and Standing, 2002; Boddy et al., 2005; Stair and Reynolds, 2003). This involvement of people in information systems feedback and activity is crucial.

In general systems theory, all systems include input, processing output and feedback, which creates a relatedness between the parts (von Bertalanffy, 1972; Donde and Huber, 1987). Complex systems such as control systems (for example a thermostat) include these elements. These systems are not, however, regarded as information systems since they do not involve a human or intentional agent who recognises the informational value of the output. In the systems literature there is much discussion of control systems, such as the flyball governor, a system developed in the late 18th century to automatically maintain steam engine speed despite changes in loads and steam supply. This system involves two balls connected to a shaft. The balls rotate in response to the steam supply, causing it to cut off the steam with increased speed and to open the valve as the shaft velocity slows. While this is an example of a system with input, processing producing output, and feedback, it is not an information system without a user to recognise the informational value of changes in the steam supply. Information systems provide information to someone or something; they are not just self-operating control mechanisms. In an information system, human involvement is evident. In traditional information systems the distinction between systems in general and information systems is more obvious because in the latter the informational aspects are separated off into the computer, which provides output reports or summaries or calculations for the user to respond to. In routine, manual systems many of the artifacts in these systems (such as magnets on a whiteboard) are not obviously sources of output information until they are placed in a certain way or set in a particular physical context. In these contexts, participants perceive the informational value of the artifacts and make a response to this value. This response requires some human perception of information content. Even where the action is routinised, it will have eventuated from a routine learnt through an earlier process where information was provided that imbued the routine with value for the human participant.

Considering all of these issues, we propose that, in deciding whether or not a system is an information system, the following test should be applied:

- Does it provide facts for the system to manipulate? These facts may be values in a data file or they might be the colours of magnets or the placement of flight strips on a table. A fact is an element that avails itself for transformation.
- Does it exhibit some sort of transformative activity? That is, does it take up the facts and manipulate them in some way that changes the state of the system?
- Does this transformation result in a signal for a system participant to react to? This signal might be a value in a table or a change in the arrangement of an ambulance card in an ambulance allocator's box. A signal is an indicator that presents itself for action.
- Is it a system where action results (through traditional feedback by users or some other type of response) leading to the fulfilment of goals?

In deciding whether or not routine, manual systems are information systems, through examining them alongside traditional systems, we extract examples of elements from both types systems to populate Table 1 below. In this table, the four common elements — fact, transformation, signal, and action — that we claim to be characteristic of all information systems, are provided in the second row. In the rest of this paper, traditional and routine manual systems will be examined in order to populate rows four and five, which are those aspects of the two systems that manifest themselves as facts, transformation, signals, and action. Row five will contain examples of this manifestation as they are uncovered.

All information systems								
	Fact		Transformation		Signal		Action	
	Traditional	Routine	Traditional	Routine	Traditional	Routine	Traditional	Routine
	?	?	?	?	?	?	?	?
Examples	?	?	?	?	?	?	?	?

Table 1: Elements in all information systems

Descriptions of systems

In this section four different systems will be described. The first is a conventional information system and the remaining three, routine manual systems. The nature of data processing and feedback in traditional systems will be examined after the first system is described and again for the three routine, manual systems after they are described.

Causeway Cash Receipts System: a traditional information system

The literature records many traditional systems, both computerised and manual (or a combination of both), that are universally considered to be information systems. One such system, used to process cash received from credit sales (Gelinas and Sutton, 2002), is described in detail below. This system typifies a widely used process for recording cash receipts:

> Customers send checks (sic) and remittance advice to Causeway. The mailroom clerk at Causeway endorses the checks and writes the amount paid and the check number on the remittance advice. Periodically, the mail room clerk prepares a batch total of the remittance advices and sends the batch of remittance advices to accounts receivable, along with a copy of the batch total. At the same time, the clerk sends the corresponding batch of checks to the cashier.

> In accounts receivable, the clerk enters the batch into an online terminal by keying the batch total, the customer number, the invoice number, the amount paid and the check number. After verifying that the invoice is open and the correct amount is being paid, the computer updates the accounts receivable master data. If there are any discrepancies, the clerk is notified. At the end of each batch (or at the end of the day) the computer prints a deposit slip in duplicate on the terminal in the cashier's office. The cashier compares the deposit slip to the corresponding batch of checks and then takes the deposit to the bank.

> As they are entered, the check number and the amount paid for each receipt are logged on disk. The event data is used to create a cash receipts listing at the end of each day. A summary of customer accounts paid that day is also printed at this time. The accounts receivable clerk compares these reports to the remittance advices and batch totals and sends the total of the cash receipts to the general ledger office (Gelinas and Sutton, 2002).

Qualities of traditional systems

The common, defining characteristics of systems such as the one above have been distilled from observation and presented in previous work (Lederman et al., 2003). The features of such systems are those that clearly exhibit the hallmarks of the classical definitions of information systems listed earlier: systems that collect data and process it in conventional ways. Data in these systems has the following qualities:

- Firstly, in such systems data is represented in symbol/object form, where symbols stored in a table correspond to objects in the real world, generally shown as records within fields, and indicate or signal potential manipulations that can be done in the real world. In a system such as Causeway, a table of customers would exist where a customer number and description of a customer forms a symbolic representation of a real customer that exists in the world and that can, for example, be given a new credit rating or a new account balance.
- The representation of data is persistent. That is, such systems display stable data structures. This is seen in Causeway where there are fixed fields with stable meanings, and multiple tables each with fixed record structures. This leads to data being processed in a conventional way where records are transformed but a stable structure remains.
- A third feature relates to the nature of processing. Users in such systems use these stable representations to determine the state of the world and then select the appropriate action. In Causeway, for example, a user might find a credit limit in a table and make a decision about allowing a customer credit. Change then occurs in the customer record as it is transformed to a new state.

Processing proceeds without significant consideration of the physical and social environment outside of the system but rather results from feedback within the system. The environment is not considered important for action. Nonetheless, action clearly proceeds and is significant to the rationale for the system.

The depiction of an information system presented in the Causeway example contains the idea that information is produced by the processing of data through set, planned methods and that the data will have the qualities noted above. In this sense the Causeway system is clearly an information system in accordance with traditional definitions that look for data, processing and feedback.

However, in presenting this case, our aim is to consider whether it exhibits universal qualities that allow it to be compared to routine, manual systems and whether there are common characteristics to be found in both types of systems. Can what appears in Causeway as data being processed to produce output and the resultant feedback leading to activity, be found to have some shared qualities with the features of routine, manual systems?

Routine, manual systems

A description of three routine, manual systems is presented below.

Emergency ambulance dispatch

An Emergency dispatch system for ambulances is described by Wong and Blandford (Wong, 2000; Wong and Blandford, 2001; Wong and Blandford, 2004). Emergency dispatch occurs in a difficult and changing context where it is essential to the process that operators are aware of the goings-on in and around the area being covered by the ambulances and are aware of the capabilities of ambulance control to respond to possible eventualities. The system is divided into two functional areas: call taking and prioritisation; and command and control of emergency ambulances. There is a single control room where radio operators sit on one side and dispatchers on the other. The call takers (allocators) sit in the middle.

The activity begins when calls for ambulances are received by a call taker and are keyed into a Computer Assisted Design system. This system produces a printed ticket that includes details such as the type of emergency, address of the emergency, the priority of the condition (e.g. a heart attack has priority over a broken leg) and a map reference. From this point, the system becomes manual as tickets are first handed to a telephone dispatcher who contacts an ambulance crew at the station and dispatches it, and then to a radio operator who stays in touch with the ambulances on the road.

Once the ticket is printed any status changes, such as whether or not the ambulance is on the way or has arrived, are recorded by hand on the ticket. However, these can also be indicated by where the ticket is placed on the allocator's desk or by how the ticket is placed in the allocator's box since:

> management of tickets centres around the 'allocator's box'. This is a slotted metal box with each slot corresponding to a vehicle in the sector. The ticket assigned to a vehicle, representing the job to which it is currently assigned, is kept in the relevant slot. The ticket faces forward while the vehicle is on the call, and is reversed when the vehicle is returning to the station but available for dispatch. The box sits between the allocator and radio operator, where either may easily access it (Blandford et al., 2002).

In deciding which ambulance to dispatch, allocators often use cues from the placement and positioning of the tickets rather than the written information contained thereon.

Air traffic control

Airports have traditionally used a largely manual system for air traffic control (Mackay, et al., 1998). The system is still respected and used in many places, and has longevity despite the drive for high-tech solutions in many airports.

The activity of landing a flight begins with a printed, paper flight strip containing a small area to record basic flight plan information. This includes 'airline, flight number and type of aircraft as well as the requested and authorised flight plan (speed, level, route, with expected times for particular cross points)' (Mackay et al., 1998). The system is routine and has an air traffic controller seated in front of a table of such strips. The strips are generated either by computer or can be hand-written in the absence of a working computer system.

Each airport has several air traffic controllers controlling different parts of the air space around the airport. The controller's first task in the system is to remove the flight strip from the printer and insert it into a strip holder. Strips are continually picked up and put down, reordered, grouped, moved into columns, arranged and rearranged on the controller's table to denote different traffic conditions. Strips are often offset. Offsetting provides a fast way of 'indicating conflicts or setting reminders' (Mackay, 1999). The placement of the strips in various configurations in relation to each other provides the controllers with information regarding action additional to what is written on the strips.

Once a controller takes control of a flight strip the controller gradually adds markings to the typed strip. The markings allow controllers to look at a group of flight strips and quickly select the ones coming under their control as well as giving other information about how the activity is progressing. The layout of strips also gives a controller an immediate appreciation of the control situation (involving many flights), thus helping the controller to select the next action. For example, a controller can see at a glance that a strip holder is full, and can also see the strip holders of adjacent controllers and monitor their activities without interrupting them. As the landing progresses the flight strip passes from one controller to another by physical handover that by its nature is palpable for both controllers. Often controllers are side-by-side, thus facilitating handover to another sector by structuring the area to help the activity.

ICU ward management system

Our third routine manual system is in the intensive care unit (ICU) of a 360–390-bed acute tertiary referral hospital. The intensive care unit has 24 beds, including 20 Intensive Care beds and four High Dependency beds

The system is a resource allocation system that monitors the movement in and out of the ward, and condition, of ICU patients. The goal of the system is to allocate beds as well as to manage movement in and out of beds in the short term.

The utilisation of beds is recorded on a whiteboard, which operates in the highly dynamic environment of a busy public hospital with a constantly operating admissions procedure presenting patients to the system. The whiteboard displays a picture of the bed cubicles, some or all of which may be occupied by patients, and a set of artifacts including magnets and stickers that indicate and describe bed usage. The board is located in a central position in full view of the beds that it depicts. It is positioned in such a way that it can be viewed simultaneously by a number of staff.

The board is designed with a large rectangle in the middle representing the nurses' station and with blank rectangles drawn around it corresponding to the position of each bed relative to the nurses station. There are 24 positions on the board, each representing one cubicle, and a set of magnetic name cards that can have patient names written on them. These name cards are erasable and re-usable. The name written on a magnetic card placed on rectangle 21, for example, corresponds to the patient in bed 21. Patient names are written on the name cards with coloured markers. A name written in blue marker is a cardiac patient and a name written in black marker can be any other non-cardiac patient.

In addition to the name labels there are coloured plastic magnets in groups at the top of the board. These can be taken and placed on particular bed cubicles on the whiteboard. An orange magnet means possible discharge from ICU, a green magnet means definite discharge, a red magnet means incoming patient, and yellow means the patient will receive no further treatment. Patients with red magnets may not have yet been allocated a bed but may be placed on a name sticker set to the side of the board. If a bed is allocated, the name sticker may be half on and half off the designated cubicle.

Users of the board, having different functions such as doctor, nurse, physiotherapist or chaplain within the ward, gather around the board to respond, both collectively and individually, to what it displays. Colours such as the blue for a cardiac patient allow a cardio-thoracic physiotherapist, for example, to instantly carve off her/his list of patients; many green magnets, designating patients ready for discharge from ICU, tells the managing nurse to start finding beds in the general wards; many yellow magnets for palliating patients tells the chaplain to prepare for many families requiring support. The ease with which the magnets can be picked up and swapped around facilitates formulating the solutions to many of the problems being addressed and redesigning patient discharge scenarios.

Qualities of routine, manual systems

In these routine, manual systems elements manifest themselves in a very different way to that described in conventional information systems such as Causeway. In these systems the following qualities, which have been previously attributed to 'situated' systems (Lederman, et al., 2003), are evident where participants focus on 'situations' that only include features of the world that relate to the participants' purposes (Agre, 1997). For example, a system participant might be interested in how much stock they could see on a shelf at this moment and the specific meaning that conveys to the participant concerned.

In routine, manual systems:

- Representations depend on the situation in which they are used. So, for example, a card in an ambulance dispatch system may have a different meaning when placed one way in a dispatch box than when placed another way. These different meanings signal the need to manipulate other system elements and generate a response from the system that tells participants how to act.

- Situations relevant to goal attainment can be represented temporarily when they are transitory. So, for example, a whiteboard for bed management in a hospital ward may use coloured magnets to express a situation where a patient 'may' be discharged. We see this in the ICU ward with an orange magnet, or sometimes two orange magnets to say, 'maybe, maybe'. The data expressed is not binary — where a patient is either ready for discharge or not — but an aspect of a changing and transitory situation. The data is not crisp or permanent but is instead fuzzy. Yet it has a valuable place in indicating a need for some development, such as a bed re-allocation, to take place that transforms the state of the system.

- Situations are triggers for reactive rule-like responses. In such systems, situations can be perceived directly. This direct perception can be considered akin to processing, but does not require reading or significant cognitive activity where rules have previously been learnt. Consequently, a development in the system occurs where actors respond automatically to the positioning of items, such as tickets laid out on a desk or different coloured magnets placed on a whiteboard. This leads to further changes in the situation at hand, with such changes being part of the rationale for such systems. That is, these triggers manifest themselves to inform action, to tell participants what to do next.

- The structuring of the social and physical environment of the system is important. In typical information systems all the data required is contained within databases or files that form predefined components of the system and the outside environment is of minimal importance. In these systems, however, aspects of the environment contain cues that are instrumental in triggering activity leading to consequent transformation within the system. So, for example, in the air traffic system a number of controllers grouped together talking intently can tell another controller that there is a problem requiring action. What leads to a response or action is separate from the actual information written on the flight strips. Rather, situations such as the placement of the strips, the arrangement of people in the room, or the number of strips in the strip board is significant for action. Because of this, these systems have evolved in ways that facilitate the inclusion of such factors — with rooms designed, for example, in ways that system participants can see and take advantage of available cues.

These three systems, while very different to the Causeway system contain many situations that signal the need for action. These situations occur and are developed in some way through the manipulations of system participants, with these new developments promoting further responses. The term development is used here to refer to a stage of growth or advancement (Australian Oxford Dictionary) where a practice is made active by successive changes (Webster's Dictionary). Whereas processing is present in traditional systems, in these systems situation development is observed directly and leads to a subsequent response from system participants. So, for example, where an extra magnet is added to the ICU whiteboard there is a growth in the information value of the board in the same way that processing traditional data in a spreadsheet is said to produce information. Such changes, or developments, activate the new situation in a way that encourages response. However, while these systems are characterised by 'situation, development of situation, new situation, response' whereas in traditional systems it is 'data, processing of data, output, feedback' we suggest that these differences may be superficial. In the next sections we consider whether there are qualities in both types of systems that are universal and make it possible to unite all systems under a common definition.

Are all these systems information systems?

It has been suggested earlier in this paper that for a system to be considered an information system it needs to demonstrate that it contains facts that can be manipulated in ways that change or transform the state of the system. This transformation then results in a signal that functions as an alert and triggers a response or feedback action. This resulting action maintains the dynamism of the system and occurs where informational aspects of the system are relevant to participants' goals. These four elements, fact, transformation, signal, and action are required for the label 'information system' to be applied. This section will look at the narrative that has been provided about each of the four systems and the qualities extracted from them and reflect on whether or not the required indicators are present. We attempt to extract the overarching concepts that encompass the qualities of both types of systems; qualities that include elements that are like data and like processing and like output and like feedback yet are also understandable in the context of non-traditional systems.

Fact: the first universal element

Looking at both types of systems, it is observed that the basic elements of both the traditional system and the routine manual system have the characteristics of facts. In both types of systems elements stand for something within the community of the system. In the traditional system there is a credit limit in a table of customers, in the manual routine system there is the manner in which cards are placed in an allocation box. Both elements stand for something as well as establishing a rule determining how the element is understood. While the elements in the traditional system are easily called data, in the non-traditional system using the term data, which has previously been more closely associated with numbers, words, symbols or events, creates expectations of something different in the situations encountered. Facts however, can be understood as observable objects or events (Checkland and Howell, 1998) or even 'a situation that exists' (Oxford English Dictionary). In this, the term fact can include the data found in traditional systems or the situations found in routine, manual systems.

Transformation: the second universal element

Traditional information systems are said to contain data, which is then processed. In processing, data is altered by first selecting it and then in some way organising, manipulating or aggregating it. In a system like Causeway, data such as an invoice amount is selected in a deliberative manner from an invoice. The data is then inserted into the accounts receivable master file, which is updated. Thus, traditional numeric data is processed.

In routine manual systems, a course of action that is both similar and different to processing in traditional systems occurs. A situation in a system, such as the existence of a coloured magnet on a whiteboard, is perceived directly by a user and the user reacts by, for example, instigating a development such as moving the magnet to a different place on the whiteboard. At the end of this activity the board reflects a newly developed situation, not dissimilar to the updating of a master file, and further response can occur. While what happens to the whiteboard may not commonly be seen as processing, what is common to the two systems is the idea of transformation discussed earlier from the systems literature (Land, 1973), and also referred to in the semiotics literature (e.g. Liu, 2000). Transformation occurs when systems participants are faced with cues from their environment, which may be data or situations, and the participants then define and redefine what to do next, either processing data or developing a situation, altering the system each time to transform it to a state closer to the participants' goal or objective. When a fact from either type of system is presented for manipulation, a transformation can occur. Thus, transformation is common to both types of systems.

Signal: the third universal element

As stated previously a conventional understanding of output includes the kind of elements, such as customer information, cheque totals, and credit listings, seen in the Causeway system. It does not traditionally include elements such as the way a ticket is placed on a table, the busyness of a room, or the emptiness of a slot on a whiteboard. However, earlier in this paper output was also described as something that signals or projects processed facts. Based on this description, semiotics provides a possible bridge across both types of systems. It is argued that elements within systems transfer messages (signs or signals) and that this communication results in action based on the transferred sign. A sign is defined as 'anything that conveys information because it stands for something else within a community' (Stamper, 2001). The role of a sign 'is to establish a habit or general rule determining ... the way the sign is to be "understood" on the occasions of its use' (MacEachren, 1995).

What unifies the elements of both types of system is the appropriateness of the application to each of the term sign, or its further extension from the semiotics literature, signal. According to MacEachren (1995) 'when a sign token mechanically or conventionally triggers some reaction on the part of the receiver, it is said to function as a signal'. Signals are seen as containing 'pragmatic information' (Stamper, 2001) that has the potential to change action and, in this sense, 'signal' is a more appropriate term for what is evident in a dynamic system than is 'sign'.

Stamper (2001) suggests that actors learn to employ particular repertoires of behaviour and that particular signals come to stand for these repertoires. In the ICU Ward Management Case, for example, a coloured magnet of a particular kind might come to trigger a particular repertoire. In systems where concepts are perspectival, behaviours are triggered for individuals who process the information in a way that is significant to them. Similarly, the representation of situations that may be transitory provides a signal that assists in the navigation of a changing environment. A magnet indicating or signalling that a patient may be discharged creates a cue to initiate or prepare for action. Additionally, situations that no traditional interpretation of what constitutes an information system would consider to be output, such as the phenomenon of ATC controllers gathered round a table, can be seen as signals that can be transformed into information for action. These new situations that occur following the transformation of previous situations, signal action in the same way that a credit limit in a database provides a signal that can be acted upon.

In routine, manual systems whole situations with multiple aspects may be significant as signals. For example, the way a flight strip is placed is interpreted within the context of a flight strip holder, which is in turn interpreted within the context of a room full of flight controllers. In traditional systems, conversely, output is abstracted and de-contextualised and the importance of the broader context outside of a particular table or database is marginal. However, while the form and breadth of representation in both types of system are different, they are similar in providing a signal for action. Thus, the term signal is a term that encompasses both the output of traditional systems and the new situations, following previous situation development, found in routine, manual systems.

Action: the fourth universal element

Finally, the response to, or feedback resulting from, the signals in both types of systems provides the fourth element of an information system: an impetus for action. In all systems the signals produced provide the cues for action necessary to keep the system functioning as a goal attaining entity. In Causeway, for example, processed data brings the database to a new state providing the feedback for the next activity. In the ICU ward, for example, a situation indicating possible availability of a patient for transfer is developed into a new situation, a definite availability evoking a response from a staff member. In the two types of systems what happens after the signal is apparent is different. In traditional systems, output generally provokes a cognitive response, based on the information the new state provides. That is, the original data is manipulated in some way and the user thinks about the result of processing (the output) before acting. In the routine, manual systems, new situations are often perceived much more directly (Lederman et al., 2003) in the sense that a movement of a coloured magnet on a whiteboard is detected and responded to in a way that is largely reactive and non-cognitive, and quite different from the deliberative reading of a new value in a table. However, whether the fourth stage is a traditional cognitively based or a reactive response, both eventualities correspond to action, the fourth common feature of the two types of system. Thus action is a unifying feature found in both types of systems following the initial three elements.

The universal features of information systems

These ideas are expressed in Table 2 below, which provides the values missing in Table 1. Table 2 expresses what is common in both types of systems and unifies these common elements under a larger, universal heading. Where there is data input, such as a cheque amount in a traditional system, in a routine, manual system the input is a situation that occurs, such as a magnet placed on a board. Both of these elements provide facts to enter into the next stage in the system. In a traditional system the data is processed by, for example, adding or multiplying whereas in a routine manual system it is developed in some way that augments or diminishes its meaning such as moving the magnet across the board. In all cases a transformation occurs where the state of the system is now changed. In traditional systems this changed state is represented as output; in routine, manual systems it is represented as a new situation. However, in both cases what is evident is a signal for action by users. Finally, in the traditional system an item of data output such as a cheque total produces an action such as a confirmation of the total. Similarly in the routine, manual system the new situation cues a response such as a rearrangement of other magnets or a review of bed allocations. Both feedback and response are unified in the impetus for action that they provide.

Reviewing Table 2 our claim is that all of the systems discussed above exhibit the qualities of information systems. While the difference between the system elements are analytical in routine manual systems rather than clearly separated in space and time in the way that making a change in a database and producing a new report might be in a traditional system, a unified view of both types of systems can still be presented. It may be harder to identify an element such as an output in a routine, manual system than in a traditional system. However our claim is that such elements, although having a different form, have universal qualities that can be found and aligned across both types of systems. These universal elements include facts and transformation, which encompass the traditional concepts of information systems, data and processing, as well as the situations and situation development found in routine, manual systems. When transformation occurs a change in the system takes place creating data output or the evolution of a new situation. This elicits action and moves the system one step closer to goal fulfilment. Fundamentally, what makes a system an information system is the existence of four things: *facts* that can be *transformed* by users into *signals* which promote *action*. Thus, we argue that through these shared features all of these systems can rightfully take the same label: information system.

All information systems

	Fact		Transformation		Signal		Action	
	Traditional	Routine	Traditional	Routine	Traditional	Routine	Traditional	Routine
	Data	Situation	Process	Development	Output	New Situation	Feedback	Response
Examples	Cheque amount Invoice total Customer total owed	Coloured magnet on a board Placement of a flight strip on a table Position of a card in allocation box	Totalling of cheques Verifying amount on invoice Summarising customer accounts	Movement of a magnet Re-ordering of a flight strip on a table Turning of a card in allocation box	New Cheque total New invoice total New Customer total	Whiteboard changed Rearranged flight strip Repositioned Ambulance ticket	Compare totals Confirm totals Confirm summary	Review bed allocations Attend to flight descent Reallocate ambulance

Table 2: Elements in all information systems

Conclusion

The four systems described here illustrate the qualities required to make a system deserving of the appellation 'information system'. We have shown that while the hallmarks of traditional systems, data, processing, output and feedback may not be obvious in some non-traditional systems, using a wider terminology allows systems with apparently quite different qualities to be included under a broader definition of IS. Adopting the terms signal and transformation, taken from the general systems and semiotics literature, and adding the concept of action, we have proposed a common terminology that legitimises the label information system not just for traditional systems but also for the routine manual systems described. This approach makes a novel contribution to the IS literature and will assist IS researchers in classifying a wide variety of systems as within or outside the information systems category.

References

Agre, P. 1997, *Computation and Human Experience*, New York, Cambridge University Press.

Benson, S. and Standing, C. 2002, *Information Systems: A Business Approach*, John Wiley and Sons.

Boddy, D., Boonnstra, A. and Kennedy, G. 2005, *Managing Information Systems*, Pearson.

Checkland, P. and Howell, S. 1998, *Information, Systems, and Information Systems*, Chichester: John Wiley and Sons.

Donde, P. A. and Huber, G. P. 1987, 'The systems paradigm in organisation theory: Correcting the record and suggesting the future', The Academy of Management Journal, vol. 12, no. 4, pp. 607-21.

Galland, F. J. 1982, *Dictionary of Computing*, Chichester: John Wiley and Sons.

Gelinas, U. and Sutton, S. 2002, *Accounting Information Systems*, Cincinnati, Thomson Learning.

Goldkuhl, G. and Agerfalk, P. 1988, 'Action within information systems: An outline of a requirements engineering method', Proceedings 4th International Workshop on Requirements Engineering: Foundation for Software Quality, Pisa, Italy.

Goldkuhl, G. and Agerfalk, P. 2000, 'Actability: A way to understand information systems pragmatics', Proceedings of the Third International Workshop on Organisational Semiotics, Staffordshire, UK.

Hicks, J. O. 1993, *Management Information Systems: A User Perspective*, Minneapolis, West Publishing.

Land, F. 1987, 'Adapting to changing user requirements', in Galliers, R. (ed.), *Information Analysis: Selected Readings*, Addison-Wesley, pp. 203-35.

Land, G. 1973, *Grow or Die: The Unifying Principle of Transformation*, Random House.

Laudon, K. and Laudon, J. 2006, *Management Information Systems*, 9th ed., New Jersey: Pearson/Prentice Hall.

Lederman, R., Johnston, R. and Milton, S. 2003, 'The significance of routines for the analysis and design of information systems', Proceedings of the European Conference in Information Systems, Naples, Italy.

Liu, K. 2000, *Semiotics in Information Systems Engineering*, Cambridge University Press.

MacEachren, A. M. 1995, *How Maps Work*, New York, The Guildford Press.

Mackay, W. 1999, 'Is paper safer? The role of paper flight strips in Air Traffic Control', ACM Transactions on Computer-Human Interaction, vol. 6, no. 4, pp. 311-40.

Mackay, W. E., Fayard, A.-L., Frobert, L. and Medini, L. 1998, 'Reinventing the familiar: Exploring and augmented reality design space for Air Traffic Control', Proceedings of Computer Human Interation (CHI'98), Los Angeles, CA.

Maddison, R. 1989, *Information Systems Development for Managers*, London, Paradigm.

Martin, C. and Powell, P. 1992, *Information Systems: A Management Perspective*, London, McGraw-Hill.

O'Brien, J. 2003, *Introduction to Information Systems*, Boston, McGraw-Hill Irwin.

Schmidt, K. and Simone, C. 1996, 'Coordination mechanisms: Towards a conceptual foundation of CSCW systems design', The Journal of Collaborative Computing, vol. 5, pp. 155-200.

Stair, R. and Reynolds, G. 2003, *Principles of Information Systems*, 6th ed., Boston, MA, Thomson Course Technology.

Stamper, R. 2001, 'Organisational semiotics: Informatics without the computer', in Lui, K., Clarke, R., Andersen, P. and Stamper, R. (eds), *Information, Organisation and Technology: Studies in Organisational Semiotics*, Boston, Kluwer Academic.

von Bertalanffy, L. 1972, 'The history and status of General Systems Theory', The Academy of Management Journal, vol. 15, no. 4, pp. 407-26.

Wand, Y. and Weber, R. 1995, 'On the deep structure of information systems', Information Systems Journal, vol. 5, no. 3, pp. 203-23.

Wong, W. 2000, 'The integrated decision model in Emergency Dispatch Management and its implications for design', Australian Journal of Information Systems, vol. 2, no. 7, pp. 95-101.

Wong, W. and Blandford, A. 2001, 'Situation awareness and its implications for human computer interaction', Proceedings of the Australian Conference on Computer Human Interaction OzCHI 2001, Perth.

Wong, W. and Blandford, A. 2004, 'Information Handling in Dynamic Decision Making Environments', Proceedings of the 12th European Conference on Cognitive Ergonomics, York.

Representation

Extending the Scope of Representation Theory: A Review and Proposed Research Model

Jan Recker
Business Process Management Group,
Queensland University of Technology
email: j.recker@qut.edu.au

Michael Rosemann
Business Process Management Group,
Queensland University of Technology
email: m.rosemann@qut.edu.au

Peter Green
UQ Business School, University of Queensland
email: p.green@uq.edu.au

Marta Indulska
UQ Business School, University of Queensland
email: m.indulska@business.uq.edu.au

Abstract

This paper reflects on a popular and influential theory unique to information systems (IS), namely representation theory, which is widespread in research on conceptual modelling. We review scholarly work in this domain and discuss why and how studies using representation theory need to transcend their focus of research and link their findings to further consequential variables of interest. We propose an innovative research design that builds upon, and converges, representation theory and the established technology acceptance model as an example for an extended study. We conclude by discussing how the example of this research study may inspire IS researchers to overcome traditional theory boundaries and converge rather than diverge existing approaches to IS research in related domains.

Introduction

The information systems discipline is relatively new. It evolved at the intersection of historically well-established research fields such as management science, computer science, organisational theory and others (Vessey et al., 2002). Researchers studying in the IS area have mostly originated from one of these reference disciplines, bringing with them not only a range of methods and methodologies but also a diversity of underlying philosophical assumptions about research and, going deeper, regarding understanding and cognition of reality, language and truth. However, since we understand our discipline is concerned with 'the effective design, delivery, use and impact of information technology in organisations and society' (Avison and Fitzgerald, 1995), we feel that it is quite uniquely placed at the interface of technology and organisation, unlike some of its foundational or reference disciplines. That is, it addresses the interaction in human-machine systems (Lee, 2001).

The evolution of IS research since its inception has led to the consequence that most of the theories used stem from its reference disciplines. Overall, a wide range of distinctly different foundational theories is being used in IS research, leading to considerable diversity (Robey, 1996; Vessey et al., 2002; Benbasat and Zmud, 2003) and the coining of the term 'fragmented adhocracy' (Banville and Landry, 1989) as a description of it. This has also resulted in an ongoing quest for a *cumulative tradition*, in the hope of evolving a research discipline that builds on an existing body of knowledge, has an awareness of the remaining open challenges, and is guided by a methodological procedure in its future research efforts (Kuhn, 1962; Keen, 1980; Weber, 1997).

The ongoing debate about what constitutes the IS field has centred on the question of what are the core theories unique to information systems that define the discipline and, from a broader perspective, its body of knowledge (Benbasat and Weber, 1996). The argument used in this context is that a reliance on foundational theories from reference disciplines distracts from the main game — namely, identifying, articulating and foremost of all, researching core phenomena that give IS its identity (Weber, 1987). In other words, unless the IS discipline evolves based on a unique core that comprises topics, theories and methodologies, there is a danger of it remaining an intellectual convocation of individuals that pledge allegiance to other disciplines while studying phenomena nominally ascribed to information systems (King, 1993).

Looking at how to address this, Benbasat and Weber (1996) identify three types of diversity, these being diversity in the *phenomena* that are being studied, diversity in the *theoretical foundations* that guide such studies, and diversity in the *research methods* used to study them.

In this paper we reflect on progress in a dedicated subset of the IS field, addressing selected instances of these three types of diversity. We focus on *conceptual modelling* and its associated phenomena, an area that is widely regarded as inseparable from IS development (Kottemann and Konsynski, 1984; Karimi, 1988). It also has repeatedly been proposed as one of the core artifacts in IS research overall (Weber, 1997; Frank, 1999). In terms of theoretical foundations, we look at the emergence of a promising candidate for conceptual modelling theories, namely *models of representation* (Wand and Weber, 1990, 1993, 1995) that are referred to as representation theory. In terms of research methods we investigate the principles of *representational analysis* (Rosemann et al., 2004), also referred to as ontological analysis.

The aim of our paper is to *assess* the current state of research in this specific domain and to give guidance on how to *progress* this state. While models of representation and the process of representational analysis per se have been shown to result in interesting and relevant findings, there remains a need for these studies to transcend their current research scope. We argue that representation theory and associated research efforts can be further advanced to exert a wider influence on information systems if this stream of research is put into a broader context by studying the impact of the findings on further phenomena relevant to our research domain. We recapitulate existing scholarly approaches and then discuss a research design that aims at expanding the scope of representation theory and method of representational analysis by converging it with other IS-specific theories, in this instance, the technology acceptance model.

We proceed as follows. In the next section, the main principles of representation theory and previous work in this area are reviewed, with consideration paid to the scope and focus of the analyses. Following this, we present and discuss a research model that converges representation theory and the technology acceptance model and briefly outline the stages of our research. The paper concludes with a discussion of contributions and guidance on how fellow researchers may extend the scope of the theory and related method.

Conceptual modelling and representation theory

Models of representation and representational analyses

Significant attention has been paid to the role that *conceptual models* play in the process of information systems development (Wand and Weber, 2002). Most of the attention has been directed at the domain of information systems analysis and design (ISAD), which is concerned with the development and engineering of IS artifacts based on the identification, elicitation and documentation of certain domain requirements. In particular, the process of conceptual modelling, that is building a representation of selected phenomena in the problem domain for the purpose of understanding and communication among stakeholders (Kung and Sølvberg, 1986; Mylopoulos, 1992; Siau, 2004), is believed to be an inevitable part of requirements engineering (Kottemann and Konsynski, 1984; Karimi, 1988). The quality of conceptual models used in the requirements engineering phase of IS development processes has been shown to have a determining impact on the acceptability and usability of the final IS artifact that is built (Lauesen and Vinter, 2001). As the cost of fixing errors grows exponentially with the elapsed time to discovery during the implementation process (Moody, 1998), an adequate problem domain representation through conceptual models may reveal errors such as faulty requirements specifications in an early stage of the IS development.

Conceptual modelling, as such, is a well-researched subject in IS (Wand and Weber, 2002). However, the majority of past studies have focused on the development of new approaches to conceptual modelling (Punter and Lemmen, 1996; Galliers and Swan, 2000) rather than on the critical evaluation and improvement of existing approaches (Moody, 2005). Several researchers state that there is a need to shift academic resources from development to evaluation and to strive for progress in the field of theoretical foundations and quality frameworks for conceptual modelling (Oei et al., 1992; Punter and Lemmen, 1996; Galliers and Swan, 2000; Wand and Weber, 2002; Moody, 2005).

Researchers are evidently concerned that the lack of rigorous and mature theoretical foundations for conceptual modelling can result in the development of information systems that are unable to completely capture relevant phenomena in their real world domains (Wand and Weber, 1995). This concern stems from the observation that, during requirements engineering for information systems development, modellers are confronted with the need for a conceptual structure on which to base the representation of requirements. The criticism has always been the lack of theories that provide conceptual modelling activities with such structures. In fact, most of the existing approaches for modelling have been developed on the basis of practical wisdom rather than on a scientific theory (Bubenko, 1986).

Over time, a number of approaches have been proposed to present theoretical guidance for the development, evaluation and use of conceptual modelling (e.g. Siau et al., 1996; Falkenberg et al., 1998; Agerfalk and Eriksson, 2004; Rockwell and Bajaj, 2004). Most notable are the approaches based on theories of ontology (e.g. Milton and Kazmierczak, 2004; Guizzardi, 2005), and especially the work of Wand and Weber (1990, 1993, 1995) towards a theory of representation, derived from an ontology defined by Bunge (1977), that became widely known as the Bunge-Wand-Weber representation model.

Generally, ontology studies the nature of the world and attempts to organise and describe what exists in it, in terms of the properties of, the structure of, and the interactions between real-world things (Bunge, 1977; Shanks et al., 2003). As computerised information systems are representations of real world systems,

Wand and Weber suggest that ontology can be used to help define and build information systems that contain the necessary representations of real world constructs. Yet, the philosophical nature of theories of ontology and their terminology and overall scope are not very conducive to application in the context of information systems or, more specifically, conceptual modelling. Thus, it was Wand and Weber's (1990, 1993, 1995) adoption of an ontology defined by Bunge (1977) that facilitated the wider uptake of this theoretical model within the information systems community. The Bunge-Wand-Weber set of models actually comprises three models (Wand and Weber, 1995; Weber, 1997); the representation model, the state-tracking model and the decomposition model. However, it is mainly the representation model that has been used in IS research.

The BWW representation model (henceforth referred to simply as 'the BWW model') specifies a number of constructs for which conceptual modelling languages that purport to model information systems domains need to provide representations. Some minor model alterations have been carried out over the years by Wand and Weber (1993, 1995) and Weber (1997), but the key constructs of the BWW model can be grouped into the following clusters: things including properties and types of things; states assumed by things; events and transformations occurring on things; and systems structured around things (refer to Weber, 1997 and Rosemann et al., 2006 for a complete list of constructs and clusters).

The BWW model has over recent years achieved significant levels of scholarly attention and dissemination, as is indicated by well over one hundred publications drawing on it in contexts such as comparison of modelling languages (Rosemann et al., 2006), modelling language foundations (Wand et al., 1995), model quality measurement (Gemino and Wand, 2005) and method engineering (Wand, 1996). Aside from its demonstrated usefulness in studies of phenomena associated with conceptual modelling, the BWW model has also been used in related research domains, for instance in studies on information systems requirements engineering (Soffer et al., 2001).

Most notably, however, the BWW model is used as a reference benchmark for the *representational analysis* of conceptual modelling languages in order to determine their representational capabilities and deficiencies. In this process, the constructs of the BWW representation model (e.g. thing, state, transformation) are compared with the language constructs of the modelling language (e.g. event, activity, actor). The basic assumption is that any deviation from a 1-1 relationship between the constructs in the representation model and the corresponding constructs in the modelling language leads to a situation of representational deficiency in the language, potentially causing confusion for its users. Two principal evaluation criteria may be studied: *ontological completeness* and *ontological clarity*. The study of ontological completeness is the analysis of the extent to which a modelling language has a *deficit* of constructs mapping to the set of constructs proposed in the BWW representation model. The study of ontological clarity involves the analysis of the extent to which the modelling language constructs are deemed *overloaded* (i.e. they map to two or more constructs in the BWW model), *redundant* (i.e. two or more language constructs map to the same construct in the BWW model), or *excess* (i.e. they map to none of the constructs in the BWW model (see Figure 1).

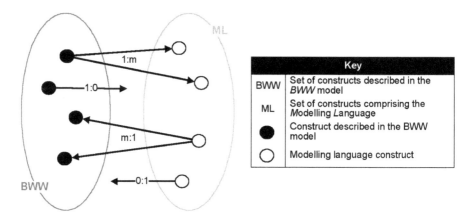

Figure 1: Types of potential representational deficiencies (Weber, 1997).

In terms of procedural guidelines, Rosemann et al. (2004) discussed how the method of representational analysis has, over time, been refined and revised to achieve higher levels of research maturity.

A research review: identifying the scope of analysis

Similar to the widespread acceptance of the BWW representational model in IS research, the research method of representational analysis has also gained wide-spread dissemination in studies related to conceptual modelling (Green and Rosemann, 2004). It has, in several instances, been shown to deliver insights into features and shortcomings of languages that purport to model real world domains. Due to space restrictions, we here limit our review of such studies to a discussion of selected examples of BWW-based studies of phenomena associated with various conceptual modelling languages.

Wand and Weber (1993) discussed the general applicability of the BWW model of the representational capability of conceptual modelling languages through their evaluation of the Entity-Relationship modelling language. The study comprised an analytical evaluation of the ER language constructs with respect to the achieved levels of ontological completeness and ontological clarity. From their analysis, Wand and Weber concluded that the BWW model provides the rudiments of a theory that can facilitate systematic insights into the nature and use of modelling languages.

Green and Rosemann (2000) used the BWW model to analyse the Event-Driven Process Chain (EPC) notation, focusing on both ontological completeness and clarity. Their findings have been empirically validated through interviews and surveys (Green and Rosemann, 2001). In a second iteration of their empirical study, Green and Rosemann (2002) identified the *modelling role* (e.g. business analyst, technical analyst), that the modelling subject occupies in the modelling initiative, as a contingency variable that moderates the perceived criticality of identified representational deficiencies. The role that the modelling subject occupies determines the views that he or she takes towards conceptual models. For instance, some interviewees questioned by Green and Rosemann (2002), who had a need for considering multiple modelling views (e.g. data, process, function, organisation) due to their role in the modelling initiative, perceived representational deficiencies with respect to construct redundancy as less critical than respondents that occupied a different modelling role. For them, seemingly redundant constructs provided the benefit of complexity reduction rather than being a deficiency.

Further empirical studies on the EPC notation with the help of the BWW model by Davies et al. (2004) found that the *modelling experience* also explains some of the variations between responses for each of the representational deficiencies explored. Less experienced modellers often have not yet encountered modelling scenarios in which certain representational deficiencies would induce problems in the use of the language. For instance, if a modeller has not used a potentially ambiguous language construct, he or she would not know how critically that deficiency would impact his or her modelling. Similarly, more experienced modellers often have an array of work-arounds for modelling problems they have encountered in their work and are thereby able to overcome deficiencies that may be critical without such work-arounds.

The same study found empirical support for the contingency effect of the *modelling purpose* that was earlier hypothesised by Rosemann and Green (2000) to also moderate the perceived criticality of representational deficiencies. Modelling purposes (e.g. workflow engineering, systems specification, business requirements documentation) determine representational requirements of a model. In the area of process modelling, for instance, workflow engineering has the requirements of sound and precise process models without deadlocks or starvation areas (Kiepuszewski et al. 2003). These requirements are, however, of less relevance to business requirements documentation purposes, which drive a different set of representation needs that a model has to meet.

The study of the BPMN language by Recker et al. (2006) found empirical evidence for the proposition that the *modelling tool* in which a modelling language is implemented can have the capacity to countervail some representational deficiencies. That is, the extent of tool support for a given modelling language can moderate the criticality of its representational deficiencies. For instance, Recker et al. (2006) found that deficiencies in BPMN with regard to the decomposition of models and processes were often not experienced as such due to support provided by the tool in the form of a model repository and object links.

In line with the findings of Davies et al. (2004), the study by Recker et al. (2006) further found that, in modelling practice, language users often do not use the modelling language in its original version. Instead of using a 'vanilla' specification of a language, organisations often follow a set of *modelling conventions* that restricts the set of language constructs to be used and sometimes even applies new meanings to particular constructs. Consequently, in cross-organisational studies, consideration has to be paid to the fact that modelling conventions may restrict or alter the original specification of a language, which in turn may have an impact on its representational capabilities and the way that language users perceive potential deficiencies.

The BWW model has also been used to explore representational deficiencies of object-oriented modelling languages such as OML (Opdahl and Henderson-Sellers, 2001) and UML (Opdahl and Henderson-Sellers, 2002). Both evaluations remain on an analytical level and investigated the completeness and clarity of the language specifications. Similar to Green and Rosemann (2001), Opdahl and Henderson-Sellers point out the moderating effect that different modelling purposes (e.g. representing a problem domain versus representing the proposed structure of information systems) may have on the criticality of a representational deficiency of the language.

As an example of work that explores representational deficiencies of modelling languages *in combination*, Green et al. (2004) analytically examined the ontological completeness of four leading standards for enterprise system interoperability, including BPEL4WS v1.1, BPML, WSC, and ebXML v1.1. A minimal ontological overlap (MOO) analysis (Wand and Weber, 1995; Weber, 1997) has been conducted in order to determine the set of modelling standards exhibiting the minimum number of overlapping constructs but having maximal ontological completeness (MOC) or, in other words, maximum expressiveness. Two different combinations of standards were identified that, when used together, allow for the most expressive power with the least construct overlap. These were ebXML and BPEL4WS, and ebXML and WSCI. The results of the analysis remain to be tested empirically.

Other analyses based on the BWW representation model include further evaluations of schema modelling languages (Weber and Zhang, 1996), structured analysis modelling languages (Rohde, 1995), process modelling languages (Recker et al., 2006) and interoperability choreography modelling languages (Green et al., 2005).

In summary, the usefulness of representational analysis is documented by over 30 applications (Green and Rosemann, 2004). However, our brief review shows that while previous findings based on representational analyses have been shown to be of relevance, the scholarly work has mostly focused on the representational capabilities of modelling languages. Capabilities and deficiencies have been identified, or the theorised effects of these deficiencies empirically explored or tested.

After more than two decades and a multitude of such studies, we believe that, in spite of the track record of demonstrated usefulness, the intense focus of previous and current representation theory based scholarly work on the capabilities of modelling languages induces an illusion of research progress when it comes to the building of a cumulative research tradition. Research progress cannot be achieved solely by the production of an abundance of papers more or less replicating the findings of previous representational analyses. In fact, we are concerned that the rich basis of representation theory may get lost in a rather inward looking research stream that retains a high focus on repeating studies using the same methodology for yet another phenomenon or language associated with conceptual modelling.

We do not, however, dispute that several conceptual modelling researchers have ventured beyond this traditional focus. Nevertheless, the majority of existing studies, while contributing to the impressive levels of maturity and dissemination of both theory and method, have remained within the narrow scope of language evaluation. Hence, we see a need for representational analysis to move beyond simply assessing modelling language capabilities. Figure 2 shows how the research scope of representational analysis may be extended beyond the focus of previous studies and also depicts potential dependant variables that may be studied.

The method of representational analysis in general provides a rich theoretical basis of propositions that may be used to study further consequential dependant variables of interest. Wand and Weber themselves saw this opportunity for further research:

> In general, future theoretical and empirical research on grammars should investigate their effectiveness or efficiency. ... Empirical work could now be done to determine the impacts, if any, that these deficiencies have on users of these grammars (Wand and Weber, 2002).

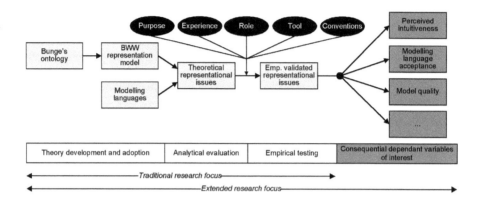

Figure 2: Research method of representational analysis and the quest for the dependent variables.

As an example of a study that addresses further dependant variables, outside of modelling language capabilities, Gemino and Wand (2005) investigated the effects of using optional versus mandatory properties in data models on the complexity and understanding of the resulting model. As another example, Recker et al. (2006) mention the possible need to consider how to derive modelling methodologies based on representational principles. This can, for instance, be achieved by initially modelling using a clear rather than complete set of language constructs to facilitate modelling with lower levels of complexity. In a second iteration this model could then be enriched with a second set of language constructs that add to its completeness, although perhaps at the cost of increased construct overload, redundancy or excess. As Figure 2 indicates, other interesting aspects to study are the effect of validated representational propositions (e.g. language constructs should not be overloaded) on the perceived intuitiveness of the resulting model, as well as factors arising from construct excess. In order to study the latter with respect to, for example, model quality (e.g. perceived understandability, effectiveness for problem solving or domain comprehension tasks), models that contain language constructs that the theory indicates to be unclear in nature and purpose (Weber, 1997) can be compared in laboratory experiments with models that do not contain excess constructs. Obviously, many other endogenous variables potentially contribute to the outcomes of such studies. The framework on conceptual modelling proposed by Wand and Weber (2002) that distinguishes the modelling language from the modelling method and the resulting model may be used as a starting point for identifying areas of evaluation in which potential causal relationships (e.g. language — model, language — method) have not yet been fully explored.

We see the potential to identify and integrate further related theories used in the information systems discipline in such studies. As a result, the state of research could be advanced by means of creative and novel theory adaptations and applications that have not yet been envisaged. In summing up, we observe that many stimulating research challenges stem from the principles of representation theory and representational analysis. In our own research we have sought to take on some of these challenges. In the next section we briefly outline a research model that is designed to study the consequences that representational capabilities have on the user acceptance of a modelling language.

A proposed research model

Stemming from Wand and Weber's (2002) comments on the need to study the impact of representational deficiencies on the effectiveness, usefulness and/or efficiency of a modelling language, we have sought to study the impact of ontological completeness and clarity on the perceived usefulness and ease of use of a language. As such, we have restricted our investigation in the sense that we do not consider other related phenomena such as, for instance, the quality of the model produced. We acknowledge that other areas of evaluation remain in which the consequences of representational deficiencies still need to be explored.

In this context of acceptance, the technology acceptance model (TAM) (Davis, 1986, 1989) postulates, and it has been shown in an extensive number of empirical studies, that perceived usefulness (PU) and perceived ease of use (PEOU) of an IS artifact directly influence an individual's intention to use that IS artifact (Davis, 1989; Davis et al., 1989; Moore and Benbasat, 1991). Such intention in turn has been found to accurately predict the actual use of the artifact (Davis et al., 1989; Venkatesh and Davis, 1996).

Hence, we see an opportunity to converge, if not amalgamate, two of the most influential approaches to IS research. The extensive amount of research related to TAM has reportedly made it one of the most influential and commonly employed IS models (Lee et al., 2003; King and He, 2006). Its advantages include the parsimony and explanatory power of the model (Venkatesh and Davis, 2000) and the well-researched and validated measurement inventory with high levels of reliability and validity of constructs and measurement scales (Davis, 1989; Segars and Grover, 1993). The large number of TAM studies will not be recapitulated here; instead the reader is referred to an annotated overview such as that given in, for instance, Lee et al., (2003). One interesting point, however, must be made. King and He (2006) found in their rigorous meta-analysis of TAM that, despite its recent adaptations to, for example, the method context (Moody, 2003), extensions such as the TAM2 model (Venkatesh and Davis, 2000), and revisions such as the UTAUT model (Venkatesh et al., 2003), the original model nevertheless is of high reliability, has good explanatory power and obtains high levels of robustness. We therefore deem TAM, in its original form, a suitable starting point for our line of investigation.

The interesting observation to be made with respect to representation theory is that TAM specifies a general model of IS acceptance that needs to be tailored to the specific research context (Fichman, 1992). As we, in our research, are concerned with conceptual modelling and the languages used for such efforts, we see an opportunity to link these two theories to study the acceptance of modelling languages. Along similar lines, Venkatesh and Davis (1996, 2000) argue that it is necessary to better understand the determinants of PU and PEOU since the generality of TAM, which allows for wide applicability, induces a lack of focus on the particular artifact under observation. Accordingly, we explicitly explore the determinants of PU and PEOU in the context of conceptual modelling languages by drawing on the principles of representational analysis.

Starting with PU, Moody (2003) argues that the original definition of PU (Davis, 1989) must be extended to reflect the objectives of the particular task for which the artifact is being used. Adopting this insight in the context of conceptual modelling, we can perceive PU as 'the degree to which a person believes that a particular language will be effective in achieving the intended modelling objective'. This definition reflects the notion of rational selection (Rescher, 1973), which states that, generally, those methods will be adopted that outperform others or are more effective in achieving intended objectives. Based on this understanding, we can argue that 'good' languages are those that contain all the constructs needed to produce *complete* representations of the relevant phenomena in a real-world domain of interest (Weber, 1997). Clearly, the notion of a *complete* language (without construct deficit) reflects the notion of an *effective* language with respect to the objective of conceptual modelling to *build a representation* of selected phenomena in the problem domain (Mylopoulos, 1992; Wand and Weber, 2002; Siau, 2004). Accordingly, we urge that *ontological completeness* is a determinant of the PU of a conceptual modelling language (see Figure 3), based on the argument that PU represents a perceptual judgment of an artifact's effectiveness (Rescher, 1973).

PEOU, adapting its original definition in Davis (1989) to the context of conceptual modelling, can be understood as 'the degree to which a person believes that using a particular language will be free of effort'. Modelling 'free of effort' means modelling without complexity (Gemino and Wand, 2005), which in turn provides another link to representation theory. Weber (1997) argues that, in addition to the question of 'what' can be represented, also the question of 'how' it can be represented is of importance. He says that the clarity of a language is determined by how unambiguously the meaning of its constructs is specified and thus how much effort is needed to apply desired real-world meaning to them. The notion of clarity embraces the three situations of construct overload, redundancy and excess. That is, a formative relationship exists between these sub-constructs and the overall construct of ontological clarity. Again, one can perceive a link between the notion of clarity of a language and PEOU of a language with respect to the aim of conceptual modelling to *facilitate communication and understanding* among stakeholders (Mylopoulos, 1992; Wand and Weber, 2002; Siau, 2004). Consequently, we argue that *ontological clarity* is a determinant of PEOU of a language (see Figure 3).

Aside from these primary constructs of the research model, in every scientific study it is necessary to identify and take into account endogenous variables that potentially impose a strong contingent effect on the 'independent variable — dependent variable' relationship. Moderating variables must be identified based on the context (Fichman, 1992). We draw on variables that have previously been identified, and validated, as having consequences for our particular research context. Previous representational analyses of process modelling languages (see above) have identified and explored the contextual factors of modelling role, modelling purpose, modelling tool, modelling conventions and modelling experience, all of which can moderate the perceived criticality of representational deficiencies, and which we therefore include in our model (see Figure 3).

Aside from these contextual factors, we also draw on one of the most frequently noted limitations of previous TAM studies, namely the impact of 'voluntariness' on adoption decisions. Moore and Benbasat (1991) first recognised that the acceptance behaviour of individuals may be influenced by a mandate from superiors, which is expressed as a moderating effect of a variable 'voluntariness'. This has been included in some studies (e.g. Venkatesh and Davis, 2000; Venkatesh et al., 2003). In the case of conceptual modelling, we note that in most cases the use of a particular modelling language is indeed mandated in organisations by superiors such as modelling coaches, consultants or other influential individuals. Accordingly, we argue that the extent of voluntariness impacts the causal relationship between the intention to use a modelling language and the actual usage of the language.

Figure 3 shows the overall research model, adapted to our selected research case of the BPMN modelling language. In previous work (Recker et al., 2006) we have identified and empirically tested representational deficiencies of BPMN with respect to construct deficit, redundancy, overload, and excess, and these results will now be used to derive measurement items for each representational deficiency.

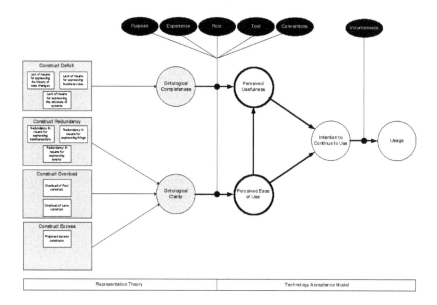

Figure 3: Proposed research model in the context of the BPMN process modelling language.

After the formulation of the research model we need to operationalise the hypotheses and measurement items contained in the model to create an empirical instrument with which to test it. The level of dissemination and maturity of TAM, and its measurement inventory, allows us to develop an appropriate instrument by adopting existing measurement scales to the context of process modelling languages. Nevertheless, this task still poses a number of challenges. Most significantly, several researchers have noted limitations related to the conceptualisation of 'usage' (DeLone and McLean, 2003) and the use of self-reported measurements (Lee et al., 2003). Also, the definition of 'intention to use' must be slightly modified to 'intention to continue to use'. This adaptation reflects the fact that only when a modelling individual has started using a language for modelling tasks is he or she able to explore its potential representational deficiencies and form an opinion about its usefulness and ease of use. Second, we will convert the measurement instrument to a web-based survey and distribute it to both actual and potential adopters of BPMN. In order to account for the fact that user perceptions and intentions may change over time (Lee et al., 2003) we will also add a longitudinal aspect to the study by measuring these quantities at two points in time: (a) in a period of early adoption and exposure to BPMN, and (b) in a later period of increased familiarity with the modelling language. This should allow us not only to counter the criticism of most acceptance studies that they are restricted to cross-sectional studies (Agarwal and Karahanna, 2000), but also account for, and further explore, the moderating effect of modelling experience on representational deficiencies and their impact on language acceptance. Also, it should allow us to study the impact of representational deficiencies not only on an individual's early *intention to start to use* a modelling language but also on the decision to *continue to use* it after a period of prolonged exposure. Finally, a web-based format of the instrument permits the gathering of data from a multitude of potential respondents across different regions and cultures, thereby overcoming the bias of restricted contextual settings and supporting potential cross-contextual analyses as well.

We would like to note here an obvious limitation of this proposed research. The presented study draws heavily on the principles of representation theory and TAM. Hence, the focus of study is restricted by the filtering lenses that these models employ. Accordingly, the research model may lack other, potentially relevant, endogenous variables that may also affect user acceptance of modelling languages. Nevertheless, the scope of the proposed model enables us to focus work on gaining insights into the expressiveness of the combination of the two theories, and to thereby avoid the necessity to translate findings from different theoretical bases.

Contributions and outlook

This paper has reviewed and discussed the state of progress of IS research using representation theory. We have argued that models of representation provide a mature theoretical basis for scholars researching conceptual modelling artifacts and activities. However, the state of progress in this particular area of research has mostly remained at the level of assessing various language capabilities and the argument in this paper is that the underlying representation theory provides a fruitful basis to transcend this level of investigation to study further phenomena of interest associated with conceptual modelling. In fact, it is time researchers moved outside the confines of traditional studies. Some prior research, such as the work by Gemino and Wand (2003, 2005), serve as stimulating examples for studies that use the richness of the theory to derive research hypotheses over and above the level of language capabilities. In our own research we aim to further transcend this research horizon and to progress the state of maturity and dissemination of representation theory and representational analysis. With this aim in mind, we have outlined an example of research that links propositions and findings from representation theory with other theories in our discipline, namely the issue of acceptance of IS artifacts.

In future work we aim to continue along two lines of investigation in particular. Firstly, we will continue our work on the acceptance of modelling languages. At present we are developing and testing a measurement scales inventory to conduct empirical studies on the adoption and acceptance of modelling languages in order to test the hypothesised relationships in our research model shown above. Secondly, in a related stream of research, we will continue our work on the effect of representational deficiencies on the quality of the models produced. As part of this work, we have evaluated and empirically confirmed representational deficiencies of a selected process modelling language and communicated our findings to the developers of that language in order to influence a revision of the language specification. After distribution of the revised process modelling language specification, we will, as a last step in the research, assess and compare the quality of business process models produced using the revised modelling language with those produced using the pre-revision version of the language.

As a concluding remark, we would like to add that we have found the research method of representational analysis very useful in understanding and exploring the challenges related to conceptual modelling and we expect this type of research to continue to give stimulating input to both academic and practical work in the area of conceptual modelling in the future.

References

Agarwal, R. and Karahanna, E. 2000, 'Time flies when you're having fun: Cognitive absorption and beliefs about information technology usage', MIS Quarterly, vol. 24, no. 4, pp. 665-94.

Agerfalk, P. J. and Eriksson, O. 2004, 'Action-oriented conceptual modelling', European Journal of Information Systems, vol. 13, no. 1, pp. 80-92.

Avison, D. E. and Fitzgerald, G. 1995, *Information Systems Development: Methodologies, Techniques and Tools*. London: McGraw-Hill.

Banville, C. and Landry, M. 1989, 'Can the field of MIS be disciplined?', Communications of the ACM, vol. 32, no. 1, pp. 48-60.

Benbasat, I. and Weber, R. 1996, 'Research Commentary: Rethinking "Diversity" in Information Systems Research', Information Systems Research, vol. 7, no. 4, pp. 389-99.

Benbasat, I. and Zmud, R. W. 2003, 'The identity crisis within the IS discipline: Defining and communicating the discipline's core properties', MIS Quarterly, vol. 27, no. 2, pp. 183-94.

Bubenko, J. A. 1986, 'Information systems methodologies — A research view', in Olle, T. W., Sol, H. G. and Verrijn-Stuart, A. A. (eds), *Information Systems Design Methodologies: Improving the Practice*, Amsterdam: North-Holland, pp. 289-318.

Bunge, M. A. 1977, *Treatise on Basic Philosophy Volume 3: Ontology I — The Furniture of the World*, Dordrecht, The Netherlands, Kluwer Academic Publishers.

Davies, I., Rosemann, M. and Green, P. 2004, 'Exploring proposed ontological issues of ARIS with different categories of modellers, *Proceedings of the 15th Australasian Conference on Information Systems*, Hobart, Australia.

Davis, F. D. 1986, 'Λ technology acceptance model for empirically testing new end-user information systems: Theory and results', Doctoral dissertation, MIT Sloan School of Management, Boston, Massachusetts.

Davis, F. D. 1989, 'Perceived usefulness, perceived ease of use, and user acceptance of information technology', MIS Quarterly, vol. 13, no. 3, pp. 319-40.

Davis, F. D., Bagozzi, R. P. and Warshaw, P. R. 1989, 'User acceptance of computer technology: A comparison of two theoretical models', Management Science, vol. 35, no. 8, pp. 982-1003.

DeLone, W. H. and McLean, E. R. 2003, 'The DeLone and McLean model of information systems success: A ten-year update', Journal of Management Information Systems, vol. 19, no. 4, pp. 9-30.

Falkenberg, E. D., Hesse, W., Lindgreen, P., Nilsson, B. E., Oei, J. L. H., Rolland, C., Stamper, R. K., van Assche, F. J. M., Verrijn-Stuart, A. A. and Voss, K. 1998, *A Framework of Information System Concepts. The FRISCO Report*, Web version: <http://www.mathematik.uni-marburg.de/~hesse/papers/fri-full.pdf>, International Federation for Information Processing WG 8.1.

Fichman, R. G. 1992, 'Information technology diffusion: A review of empirical research', *Proceedings of the 13th International Conference on Information Systems*, Dallas, Texas, pp. 195-206.

Frank, U. 1999, 'Conceptual modelling as the core of the information systems discipline — Perspectives and epistemological challenges', in Haseman, W. D. and Nazareth, D. L. (eds), Proceedings of the 5th America's Conference on Information Systems, Milwaukee: Association for Information Systems, pp. 695-8.

Galliers, R. D. and Swan, J. A. 2000, 'There's more to information systems development than structured approaches: Information requirements analysis as a socially mediated process', Requirements Engineering, vol. 5, no. 2, pp. 74-82.

Gemino, A. and Wand, Y. 2003, 'Evaluating modelling techniques based on models of learning', Communications of the ACM, vol. 46, no. 10, pp. 79-84.

Gemino, A. and Wand, Y. 2005, 'Complexity and clarity in conceptual modelling: Comparison of mandatory and optional properties', Data and Knowledge Engineering, vol. 55, no. 3, pp. 301-26.

Green, P. and Rosemann, M. 2000, 'Integrated process modelling. An ontological evaluation', Information Systems, vol. 25, no. 2, pp. 73-87.

Green, P. and Rosemann, M. 2001, 'Ontological analysis of integrated process models: Testing hypotheses', Australian Journal of Information Systems, vol. 9, no. 1, pp. 30-8.

Green, P. and Rosemann, M. 2002, 'Perceived ontological weaknesses of process modelling techniques: Further evidence', in Wrycza, S. (ed.), Proceedings of the 10th European Conference on Information Systems, Gdansk, pp. 312-21.

Green, P. and Rosemann, M. 2004, 'Applying ontologies to business and systems modelling techniques and perspectives: Lessons learned', Journal of Database Management, vol. 15, no. 2, pp. 105-17.

Green, P., Rosemann, M. and Indulska, M. 2005, 'Ontological evaluation of enterprise systems interoperability using ebXML', IEEE Transactions on Knowledge and Data Engineering, vol. 17, no. 5, pp. 713-25.

Green, P., Rosemann, M., Indulska, M. and Manning, C. 2004, 'Candidate interoperability standards: An ontological overlap analysis, Technical Report, University of Quneensland, Brisbane, Australia.

Guizzardi, G. 2005, *Ontological Foundations for Structural Conceptual Models*. Enschede, The Netherlands, Telematica Instituut.

Karimi, J. 1988, 'Strategic planning for information systems: Requirements and information engineering methods', Journal of Management Information Systems, vol. 4, no. 4, pp. 5-24.

Keen, P. G. W. 1980, 'MIS research: Reference disciplines and a cumulative tradition', in McLean, E. R. (ed.), Proceedings of the 1st International Conference on Information Systems, Philadelphia, Pennsylvania: ACM Press, pp. 9-18.

Kiepuszewski, B., ter Hofstede, A. H. M. and van der Aalst, W. M. P. 2003, 'Fundamentals of control flow in workflows', Acta Informatica, vol. 39, no. 3, pp. 143-209.

King, J. L. 1993, 'Editorial notes', Information Systems Research, vol. 4, no. 4, pp. 291-8.

King, W. R. and He, J. 2006, 'A meta-analysis of the Technology Acceptance Model', Information and Management, vol. 43, no. 6, pp. 740-55.

Kottemann, J. E. and Konsynski, B. R. 1984, 'Information systems planning and development: strategic postures and methodologies', Journal of Management Information Systems, vol. 1, no. 2, pp. 45-63.

Kuhn, T. S. 1962, *The Structure of Scientific Revolutions*. Chicago: Chicago University Press.

Kung, C. H. and Sølvberg, A. 1986, 'Activity modelling and behavior modelling of information systems', in Olle, T. W., Sol, H. G. and Verrijn-Stuart, A. A. (eds), *Information Systems Design Methodologies: Improving the Practice*, Amsterdam: North-Holland, pp. 145-71.

Lauesen, S. and Vinter, O. 2001, 'Preventing requirement defects: An experiment in process improvement', Requirements Engineering, vol. 6, no. 1, pp. 37-50.

Lee, A. S. 2001, 'Editor's Comments. MIS Quarterly's Editorial Policies and Practices', MIS Quarterly, vol. 25, no. 1, pp. iii-vii.

Lee, Y., Kozar, K. A. and Larsen, K. R. T. 2003, 'The Technology Acceptance Model: Past, present, and future', Communication of the Association for Information Systems, vol. 12, no. 50, pp. 752-80.

Milton, S. and Kazmierczak, E. 2004, 'An ontology of data modelling languages: A study using a common-sense realistic ontology', Journal of Database Management, vol. 15, no. 2, pp. 19-38.

Moody, D. L. 1998, 'Metrics for evaluating the quality of entity relationship models', *Proceedings of the 17th International Conference on Conceptual Modelling — ER '98*, Singapore: Springer, pp. 221-5

Moody, D. L. 2003, 'The method evaluation model: A theoretical model for validating information systems design methods', *Proceedings of the 11th European Conference on Information Systems*, Naples, Italy.

Moody, D. L. 2005, 'Theoretical and practical issues in evaluating the quality of conceptual models: Current state and future directions', Data and Knowledge Engineering, vol. 15, no. 3, pp. 243-76.

Moore, G. C. and Benbasat, I. 1991, 'Development of an instrument to measure the perceptions of adopting an information technology innovation', Information Systems Research, vol. 2, no. 3, pp. 192-222.

Mylopoulos, J. 1992, 'Conceptual Modelling and Telos', in Loucopoulos, P. and Zicari, R. (eds), *Conceptual Modelling, Databases, and CASE: An Integrated View of Information System Development*, New York, John Wiley and Sons, pp. 49-68.

Oei, J. L. H., van Hemmen, L. J. G. T., Falkenberg, E. D. and Brinkkemper, S. 1992, 'The meta model hierarchy: A framework for information systems concepts and techniques', Tech. Rep. No. 92-17, Department of Informatics, Faculty of Mathematics and Informatics, Katholieke Universiteir, Nijmegen, The Netherlands, pp. 1-30.

Opdahl, A. L. and Henderson-Sellers, B. 2001, 'Grounding the OML metamodel in ontology', Journal of Systems and Software, vol. 57, no. 2, pp. 119-43.

Opdahl, A. L. and Henderson-Sellers, B. 2002, 'Ontological evaluation of the UML using the Bunge-Wand-Weber model', Software and Systems Modelling, vol. 1, no. 1, pp. 43-67.

Punter, T. and Lemmen, K. 1996, 'The MEMA-model: Towards a new approach for Method Engineering', Information and Software Technology, vol. 38, no. 4, pp. 295-305.

Recker, J., Indulska, M., Rosemann, M. and Green, P. 2006, 'How good is bpmn really? insights from theory and practice', *Proceedings of the 14th European Conference on Information Systems*, Goeteborg, Sweden.

Rescher, N. 1973, *The Primacy of Practice*, Oxford, UK, Basil Blackwell.

Robey, D. 1996, 'Research Commentary: Diversity in Information Systems research: Threat, promise, and responsibility', Information Systems Research, vol. 7, no. 4, pp. 400-8.

Rockwell, S. and Bajaj, A. 2004, 'COGEVAL: Applying cognitive theories to evaluate conceptual models', in Siau, K. (ed.), *Advanced Topics in Database Research. Volume 4*, Hershey, Pennsylvania, Idea Group, pp. 255-82.

Rohde, F. 1995, 'An ontological evaluation of Jackson's System Development Model', Australian Journal of Information Systems, vol. 2, no. 2, pp. 77-87.

Rosemann, M. and Green, P. 2000, 'Integrating multi-perspective views into ontological analysis', Proceedings of the 21st International Conference on Information Systems, Brisbane, Australia, pp. 618-27

Rosemann, M., Green, P. and Indulska, M. 2004, 'A reference methodology for conducting ontological analyses, Proceedings of the 23rd International Conference on Conceptual Modelling — ER 2004, Shanghai, China, pp. 110-21.

Rosemann, M., Recker, J., Indulska, M. and Green, P. 2006, 'A study of the evolution of the representational capabilities of process modelling grammars', Proceedings of the 18th International Conference on Advanced Information Systems Engineering — CAiSE 2006, Luxembourg, Grand-Duchy of Luxembourg, pp. 447-61.

Segars, A. H. and Grover, V. 1993, 'Re-examining perceived ease of use and usefulness: A confirmatory factor analysis', MIS Quarterly, vol. 17, no. 4, pp. 517-25.

Shanks, G., Tansley, E. and Weber, R. 2003, 'Using ontology to validate conceptual models', Communications of the ACM, vol. 46, no. 10, pp. 85-9.

Siau, K. 2004, 'Informational and computational equivalence in comparing information modelling methods', Journal of Database Management, vol. 15, no. 1, pp. 73-86.

Siau, K., Wand, Y. and Benbasat, I. 1996, 'Evaluating information modelling methods — A cognitive perspective', Proceedings of the 1st Workshop on Evaluation of Modelling Methods in Systems Analysis and Design, Crete, Greece, pp. M1-M13.

Soffer, P., Golany, B., Dori, D. and Wand, Y. 2001, 'Modelling off-the-shelf information system requirements. An ontological approach', Requirements Engineering, vol. 6, no. 3, pp. 183-99.

Venkatesh, V. and Davis, F. D. 1996, 'A model of the antecedents of perceived ease of use: Development and test', Decision Sciences, vol. 27, no. 3, pp. 451-81.

Venkatesh, V. and Davis, F. D. 2000, 'A theoretical extension of the Technology Acceptance Model: Four longitudinal field studies', Management Science, vol. 46, no. 2, pp. 186-204.

Venkatesh, V., Morris, M. G., Davis, G. B. and Davis, F. D. 2003, 'User Acceptance of information technology: Toward a unified view', MIS Quarterly, vol. 27, no. 3, pp. 425-78.

Vessey, I., Ramesh, V. and Glass, R. L. 2002, 'Research in Information Systems: An empirical study of diversity in the discipline and its journals', Journal of Management Information Systems, vol. 19, no. 2, pp. 129-74.

Wand, Y. 1996, 'Ontology as a foundation for meta-modelling and method engineering', Information and Software Technology, vol. 38, no. 4, pp. 281-7.

Wand, Y., Monarchi, D. E., Parsons, J. and Woo, C. C. 1995, 'Theoretical foundations for conceptual modelling in information systems development', Decision Support Systems, vol. 15, no. 4, pp. 285-304.

Wand, Y., Weber, R. 1990, 'An ontological model of an information system', IEEE Transactions on Software Engineering, vol. 16, no. 11, pp. 1282-92.

Wand, Y., Weber, R. 1993, 'On the ontological expressiveness of information systems analysis and design grammars', Journal of Information Systems, vol. 3, no. 4, pp. 217-37.

Wand, Y., Weber, R. 1995, 'On the deep structure of information systems', Information Systems Journal, vol. 5, no. 3, pp. 203-23.

Wand, Y., Weber, R. 2002, 'Research commentary: Information systems and conceptual modelling — A research agenda', Information Systems Research, vol. 13, no. 4, pp. 363-76.

Weber, R. 1987, 'Toward a theory of artifacts: A paradigmatic basis for information systems research', Journal of Information Systems, vol. 1, no. 2, pp. 3-19.

Weber, R. 1997, *Ontological Foundations of Information Systems*, Coopers and Lybrand and the Accounting Association of Australia and New Zealand, Melbourne, Australia.

Weber, R. and Zhang, Y. 1996, 'An analytical evaluation of NIAM's grammar for conceptual schema diagrams', Information Systems Journal, vol. 6, no. 2, pp. 147-70.

Indexing Research: An Approach to Grounding Ingarden's Ontological Framework

John W Lamp
School of Information Systems, Deakin University, Geelong, Victoria
email: John.Lamp@deakin.edu.au

Simon Milton
Department of Information Systems, University of Melbourne, Melbourne, Victoria
email: smilton@unimelb.edu.au

Abstract

Attempts to produce an adequate and long-lived subject indexing system for information systems research have failed. In this paper we seek to address this by proposing an approach by which the terms expressed in research literature, such as those in the information systems literature, can be systematically and meaningfully categorised. The approach is significant in that it draws upon rigorous and philosophically compatible bodies of work in two areas. Firstly, we draw on work addressing the nature, existence, and categorisation of literary expression found in research papers (Roman Ingarden's ontological analysis of the scientific work of art). Secondly, we draw from qualitative research methods addressing how meaningful categories can be analysed from text and related to each other (grounded theory). The resulting approach has the potential to be applied in many scientific disciplines beyond information systems, and to form the intellectual core of an information tool in e-research.

Introduction

Roman Ingarden developed a number of conceptual and methodological frameworks for ontological analysis of texts, which are documented in his books *The Literary Work Of Art* (1965) and *The Cognition of the Literary Work Of Art* (1968). While Ingarden's primary focus was on mainstream literature, he also considered scientific works along with a number of other literary forms as borderline cases of the literary work of art. We are presently involved in a project, a significant aspect of which involves the analysis of papers reporting information systems research in academic journals. A broader description of this project and a discussion of the rationale for using Ingarden's frameworks can be found in Lamp and Milton (2003, 2004).

The issue of applying Ingarden's framework to scientific works is significant because, while his work has been extensively applied to mainstream literature (e.g. Thomasson, 1996), there are no reports in the archival literature relating to developing his ontological analysis of scientific works into a technique which can then be applied more generally.

A threshold matter that must be considered at this point is whether or not articles publishing information systems research can be considered to be scientific works in the sense intended by Ingarden in his analysis. Ingarden published in Polish and German and the versions of his work that we are using are translations into English published in the *Northwestern University Studies in Phenomenology and Existential Philosophy* series. As Ingarden himself comments about translating scientific works 'a "good" translation is not impossible, though it may often be difficult' (Ingarden, 1968). In this context the comments of Ingarden's translators are relevant:

> ... it must be noted that 'scientific' is used here in a much broader sense than usual, in connection not only with the natural sciences but also with any serious field of study, just as the German wissenschaftlich is used. (Ingarden 1968)

This interpretation is confirmed by *Cassell's German-English English-German Dictionary* (Betteridge, 1978), which offers 'scholarly, scientific, learned' as translations of *wissenschaftlich*. Accordingly, it can be validly asserted that articles publishing information systems research can be considered to be scientific works in the sense intended by Ingarden.

To illustrate Ingarden's framework based on scientific works, we use Broadbent et al (1999) as our exemplar. This paper is from the journal *MIS Quarterly*. While *MIS Quarterly* is often rated as the most significant information systems journal (e.g. Peffers and Ya, 2003; Katerattanakul et al, 2003a, 2003b; Bharati and Tarasewich, 2002; Mylonopoulos and Theoharakis, 2001; Walstrom and Hargrave, 2001), the choice of this particular paper is not significant; it was chosen simply because it was conveniently at hand. To provide a context and assist with understanding the analysis in the later sections, the abstract of the paper is reproduced here:

> Business process redesign (BPR) is a pervasive but challenging tool for transforming organisations. Information technology plays an important role by either enabling or constraining successful BPR. This paper explores the links between firm-wide IT infrastructure and business process change. IT infrastructure is the base foundation of the IT

portfolio, which is shared throughout the firm in the form of reliable services, and is usually coordinated by the IS group. IT infrastructure capability includes both the technical and managerial expertise required to provide reliable physical services and extensive electronic connectivity within and outside the firm.

Exploratory case analysis of four firms (two in retail and two in petroleum) was used to understand the ways IT infrastructure contributes to success in implementing BPR. The finding was that all firms needed a basic level of IT infrastructure capability to implement BPR. The firms that had developed a higher level of IT infrastructure capabilities, before or concurrent with undertaking business process redesign, were able to implement extensive changes to their business processes over relatively short time frames. The higher level of infrastructure capability was provided in the form of (1) a set of infrastructure services that spanned organisational boundaries such as those between functions, business units, or firms, and (2) the ability of the infrastructure to reach particular constituencies inside and outside the firm to transfer information and process complex transactions.

The more extensive business process changes were more innovative and radical, crossing business and functional unit boundaries, and resulted in more significant business impact. The practical implication of the study is that before embarking on any form of BPR, managers should complete a business audit of their IT infrastructure capabilities, as these capabilities have an important impact on the speed and nature of business process change.

Examining the abstract, one can see many features that are in common with many other works in the information systems literature. Specifically, the paper considers BPR, a strategic and tactical tool in which information systems play an enabling role, it applies both qualitative and quantitative techniques, it examines complex case studies in four organisations, and it discusses many infrastructural and organisational impacts on the success of implementing BPR and associated enabling technology. Consequently, we argue that by applying Ingarden's framework to this paper we will be able to gain insight into applying the methodology to other information systems literature.

Scientific works are asserted by Ingarden to consist almost exclusively of genuine judgements (1968), the most significant ontic items of which are:

- the states of affairs described;
- schematised aspects; and
- the represented objectivities.

In the following sections we examine the concepts in Ingarden's framework in some detail.

Genuine judgements and states of affairs

Ingarden (1968) asserts that literary works of art contain no *genuine* judgements, they contain *quasi*-judgements. The literary work of art concerns a portrayed world, in which assertions, or statements by portrayed persons, can only be considered within the context of the portrayed world. In contrast, he asserts that the role of the scientific work in the transmission of cognitive knowledge requires that its context is that of states of affairs in the real world. Consequently, because there is a real world to which judgements refer, he calls the judgements in scientific works *genuine judgements*.

Ingarden states that genuine judgements are assertions that may be true or false, but they lay claim to truthfulness. For example, a paper may report 'The management style of company A was undemocratic', which is a result perceived as true by that particular researcher, and yet a second researcher may report a different result. Despite their essential contradiction, both statements are genuine judgements. Ideally, genuine judgements allude to means of confirmation that may be found in experience, or are contained in literary proofs based on reasoning and written in conceptual language. Failure to provide means of confirmation weakens the paper and reduces its functional value (Ingarden, 1968). Broadbent, et al (1999) shows many examples of the first form of confirmation.

> From March to September 1992, a small team further examined process approaches concurrently with a detailed study of the capabilities of the firm's current systems and infrastructure.

This quote is a genuine judgement about the efforts of the CostCo business process reengineering team, as collected by the authors of the paper; that is, it reports events actually experienced by the person reporting to the authors of the paper, and therefore claims authority based on reporting an actual contemporary experience. On the other hand, consider:

> Business process redesign (BPR) is a pervasive tool for transforming organisations (Grover et al. 1993) and [is] ranked as one of the most important issues for information systems (IS) executives since the early 1990s (Brancheau et al. 1996; Index Group 1994; Watson et al. 1996).

This quote is a genuine judgement regarding the views of IS researchers on BPR; that is, it reports a state of affairs reported in the IS literature and therefore claims authority based on previous accepted research.

Genuine judgements whose authority is based on literary proofs are relatively unusual in information systems research and are not found in Broadbent et al

(1999). An example of this form of genuine judgement is the following definition from Smith (1998):

DD5 $\qquad$ $OS(x, y) :- x \leq y \wedge x \neq y \wedge \exists w(w \leq y \wedge \neg O(w,x) \wedge$
$SD(w,x)) \wedge \neg \exists w(w \leq y \wedge \neg O(w,x) \wedge SD(x,w))$

one-sidedly separability

Broadbent et al (1999) also contains questions such as those in the following extract:

> Important questions to consider include:
>
> To what extent does the firm have at least the 10 core infrastructure services (see Table 1) together with the seven boundary-crossing services in place?
>
> What is the reach in terms of who can be seamlessly connected?
>
> What range of services are available: only the ability to access information or the capacity to perform complex business transactions across multiple systems?

Such questions could be reworded as assertive statements, reporting evidence or argument supporting the affirmative or negative, and hence should also be considered genuine judgements (Ingarden, 1965).

Schematised aspects

Objects represented in a literary work are derived, purely intentional, objects projected by units of meaning (Ingarden, 1965). They are intentional because an author has written them with a purpose. For literary works of art, the purpose is to tell a story or generate a particular aesthetic effect; for scientific works, it is the transmission of cognitive results (Ingarden, 1965). In both cases the objects are derived, because we cannot enter the mind of the author. Finally, they are projected because it is only through language (in this case written language) that can we understand what is intended.

Consider the following extract, also from Broadbent et al (1999):

> CostCo has a robust network with numerous LANs in place at its head office, in large cities, and other major sites. 'About 2,000 PC users have whatever multihost connectivity is required for their business needs We have moved from computer-centric to network-centric computing', noted the CIO. Business units utilised these networks as a basis for a new distributorship, retail and electronic funds transfer, and point of sale (EFTPOS) systems.

This extract concerns the existence and nature of the network in place at CostCo — it describes one *aspect* of CostCo. The physical nature of the network is described along with the scope and purpose of the network and the attitude of management towards its use. An outline of the functionality offered by the network in place is also described.

However, what is represented by this extract does not stop at the network but extends further to linkages provided for EFTPOS, the retail activities of CostCo and other related activities, and the general management policy framework within which the specific network policy lies, even though none of this is directly given to us. This is also typical of scientific and other literary works because there is seldom enough room to *completely* describe a state of affairs. Equally, this description does not delve into the details of the precise networking protocols, hardware, operational requirements and other minutiae of CostCo's network. If this depth of analysis were provided, then the extract would no longer be talking about the network, but of the components of the network and how it was managed.

For these reasons, literary works necessarily consist of incomplete descriptions, termed *schematised aspects*, which contain fulfilled (explicitly described) components and unfulfilled components that, while not explicitly described, may not be indeterminate. The reader may fill these out from aspects held in readiness from previous experiences. Prompting the most appropriate aspect is influenced by the word choice and represented objectivities selected by the author. For example, by using two words identical in meaning, but different in word sound, the reader may be influenced towards different aspects (Ingarden, 1965). Substituting 'many' for 'numerous' in the preceding quote does not alter its meaning, but may influence the reader's choice of aspects between perceiving CostCo's LANs as an unordered collection or as an ordered and therefore managed collection.

Because these aspects are based in perception, and aspects of the same object that are experienced by different individuals must differ in various respects, it is not possible for the reader to actualise with complete accuracy the same aspects intended by the author (Ingarden, 1965). The degree of this type of perceptual error in a scientific work is reduced, as schematised aspects are intended only for assistance in the transmission of cognitive knowledge. The use of decorative or evocative aspects is unnecessary, and may hinder the essential aim of a scientific work — accurately transferring knowledge as intended by the author (Ingarden, 1965).

Represented objectivities

A literary work of art describes people, animals, lands, houses and other items. This represented world is not the real world — the represented objects within it may not exist in the real world or may behave differently to such objects within the real world. As a reader reads a passage of words and phrases (meaning units) containing a represented objectivity, he or she relates directly to the state of affairs that the represented objectivity is helping to clarify. Consequently, a particular represented objectivity within a scientific literary work causes us to direct ourselves to corresponding states of affairs. Because we are dealing with a scientific work rather than a literary work of art, this directional ray passes through the content of these represented objectivities so that they refer to objectively existing states of affairs, or to objects contained within them rather than to some fictional creation (Ingarden, 1965). See Figure 1 for a representation of this. It is through this directional meaning ray that the represented objectivities claim to determine objects in the real world as they are in themselves and thereby claim to be genuine judgements (Ingarden, 1968).

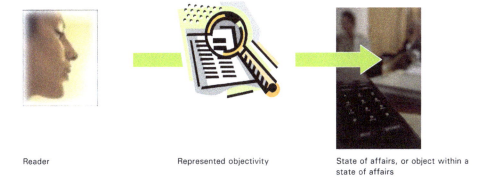

Reader   Represented objectivity   State of affairs, or object within a
                                                                             state of affairs

Figure 1: The directional meaning ray.

In a scientific work, clarity in writing directly affects the transparency of represented objectivities. Where readers have difficulty in relating to the state of affairs beyond the text then the represented objectivities are not 'clear'. Ideally the represented objectivities are transparent; that is, the way that they inform the reader regarding the particular state of affairs under discussion requires little conscious interpretation. In the extract above, the IT infrastructure (the state of affairs being discussed) is correlated with the represented objectivities 'computer-centric' and 'network-centric'. For readers of *MIS Quarterly*, these would be readily understood concepts and hence transparent. It should be noted that if that was not the case, and the authors went on to define the concepts, then the concepts would become states of affairs for which other, hopefully more transparent, represented objectivities could be found to describe them. In the absence of such explanation from the authors, the reader re-reads the sentences, concentrating on the word meanings and syntactic interconnections until the represented objectivities become clear and unequivocal (Ingarden, 1968).

Summarising, any scientific work will contain genuine judgements, states of affairs, schematised aspects, and represented objectivities. Effective subject indexing in any academic field requires the terms in these ontic categories be identified and the relations between them defined. The terms in these categories are meaningful to some group(s) of people and form the basis of the subject indexing. Clearly, there are potentially scores of specific terms that fit within each of the identified categories. Further, the relative importance of each term is not evident *a priori*. Thus, in order to operationalise Ingarden's high-level categories, we need an approach that captures the essence of the activity. We seek terms that (a) are meaningful to a group of people, (b) exhibit cognitive economy (Rosch, 1978), and (c) are discovered through a process that is repeatable. The principle of cognitive economy is that categorisation should provide a great deal of information about the item categorised with only minimal cognitive resources expended. In the following section we outline an approach based on both Ingarden's categories and the grounded theory method.

Developing a technique

In order to effectively apply Ingarden's framework, a technique must be developed for its application to the items being analysed. Information systems practice requires documenting and preparing specifications based on interviews with clients and textual material supplied by clients. Accordingly, information systems research has concerned itself with techniques for analysing text. One technique that has attracted a deal of interest is the grounded theory method (Glaser and Strauss, 1967). In this paper we propose to look at the use of this method for coding items in a text document and how this can be used for the identification and refinement of the categories of ontic items described by Ingarden.

Grounded theory method and its use in information systems

The grounded theory method provides a logically consistent set of data collection and analysis procedures that can be used in textual analysis. The original aim of the grounded theory method was to develop a research methodology that would systematically derive theories about human behaviour from empirical data. The grounded theory method seeks to discover *what is going on*. Typically, it is applied to texts obtained by interview, observation or other data collection methods. Explicit in the use of grounded theory is data collection from participants who may have different views of the phenomena being studied, and which must be accommodated in the development of theory. There is an apparent resonance here with Ingarden's concepts of schematised aspects held in readiness, and transparency of represented objectivities varying between individuals.

Since its original announcement, grounded theory has become an accepted qualitative research technique in information systems (Urquhart, 2001). Its adoption has probably been assisted by its originators' assertions that it is *'not bound* by either discipline or data collection' (Glaser, 1992). Grounded theory is concerned with the identification of categories, or properties of categories, as a major issue (Glaser, 1992). While grounded theory was described as having emerged from symbolic interactionism, Annells (1996) classified it as being ontologically based in critical realism. Glaser and Strauss (1967) state 'our position is not logical; it is phenomenological'. Grounded theory can therefore be considered to be framed from an ontological perspective that is not in conflict with the realism of Ingarden.

At this point it should be noted that, while we are seeking to develop a methodology where all components share a consistent philosophical perspective, the content of the papers being analysed would not be limited to this perspective. The nature of the philosophical perspective used and reported on by researchers in the papers studied would be a value assigned to a category in our analysis.

Reviews and examples of the use of grounded theory in information systems research can be found in Calloway and Ariav (1991), Pidgeon et al (1991), Hughes and Howcroft (2000), Urquhart (2001), Fernandez (2004) and Lings and Lundell (2005). Hughes and Howcroft (2000) review a number of uses and adaptations of the grounded theory method by information systems researchers. After considerable discussion of the implications of the way in which information systems researchers have applied grounded theory, and the views of the originators, Strauss and Corbin, Hughes and Howcroft (2000) argue against the rigid application of the grounded theory method in practice. They also note that '[i]f the research community is to mature then it would be of far greater benefit to tell the story as it were, and this should include the researcher's perspective, actual use of the method, and a reflective evaluation'. Further, they assert that 'the adoption and diffusion of the method should be welcomed since it represents its usefulness as a pragmatic tool for research'.

Urquhart (2001) provides considerable detail regarding an instance of using grounded theory method to examine client — analyst interaction and behaviour, and also lists a number of IS researchers using the grounded theory method. One instance where grounded theory was used (Orlikowski, 1993) received *MISQ's* Best Paper Award in 1993. Fernandez (2004) also provides a background discussion of the grounded theory method, plus a report of the experience of using the method. He agrees with many of the points made by Urquhart (2001). Fernandez (2004) employed the software package ATLAS.ti to assist with his analysis and makes some cautionary points about the limitations and negative aspects of software assisted coding, and in particular that the potential for automatic coding (e.g. coding all occurrences of a word or phrase) can have a negative effect in obscuring discovery by the researcher. This confirms the cautions given by Glaser about hiring coders and the use of automated systems, which remove the analyst from close contact with their data (Glaser 1978).

At this point it should be noted that grounded theory has come to include two divergent approaches. We now distinguish between those two approaches and the degree to which they suit the needs of this research.

In 1992 Barney Glaser published *Emergence vs. Forcing: Basics of Grounded Theory Analysis* (Glaser, 1992) in which he set out a comprehensive and vigorous attack on the contents of a 1990 book written by his original collaborator, Anselm Strauss, and Strauss' research partner, Juliet Corbin (Strauss and Corbin, 1990). Glaser considered their book 'distorts and misconceives grounded theory method, while engaging in a gross neglect of 90% of its important ideas' (Glaser 1992). In the years since this conflict, researchers have found both approaches useful since their different emphases make them more or less appropriate in specific research settings (Fernandez, 2004). The Glaserian approach is described as abstract conceptualisation, and the Straussian approach as full-description (Fernandez, 2004). This difference relates to a disagreement regarding the unit of analysis. The Straussian approach emphasises word by word analysis (Strauss and Corbin, 1990), while the Glaserian approach deals with units of meaning at the line or sentence level (Glaser, 1978). Strauss and Corbin give an example (1990) of taking an hour to discuss what an individual meant by the word 'once'.

Our purpose in undertaking this analysis is to discover what research is being reported in information systems journal papers. As described above, the purpose of such papers is the transmission of cognitive knowledge, a concomitant of which is for the papers to be written using represented objectivities that are, ideally, transparent. In this case then, there should be little need for extensive analysis of individual words and their possible meanings. Our aim is to abstract, rather than commentate. The Glaserian approach therefore appears to be more appropriate in this study.

Another significant difference in the two approaches to grounded theory, for our purposes, is the method of coding data. The Strauss and Corbin method requires that all data be coded against a single coding family — context, conditions, action/interactional strategies, intervening conditions and consequences. The Strauss and Corbin coding family is, however, clearly inappropriate for ontological analysis. This coding family was a variation of only one of eighteen coding families proposed as a significant part of the book *Theoretical Sensitivity* by Glaser (1978). Several of those coding families refer to ontological and mereological concepts (e.g. The Dimension Family, The Type Family, The Theoretical Family and The Conceptual Ordering Family — see Table 1). The list presented by Glaser is inclusive rather than exhaustive, and it is clearly intended that researchers using this method could derive their own coding families (Glaser, 1978) and this occurs in practice (Urquhart, 2001). Glaser expanded on his original list of coding families in two later books (Glaser, 1998, 2005).

Coding Family	Categories
The Dimension Family	dimensions, elements, division, piece of, properties of, facet, slice, sector, portion, segment, part, aspect, section
The Type Family	type, form, kinds, styles, classes, genre
The Theoretical Family	parsimony, scope, integration, density, conceptual level, relationship to data, relationship to other theory, clarity, fit, relevance, modifiability, utility, condensability, inductive-deductive balance and inter-feeding, degree of, multivariate structure, use of theoretical codes, interpretive, explanatory and predictive power, and so forth
The Conceptual Ordering Family	achievement orientation, institutional goal, organisational value, personal motivation.

Table 1: Selected examples of coding families (Glaser, 1978).

We propose to use Ingarden's ontological categories, defined in his framework, as the basis of a coding family for the grounded theory method coding technique. Further categories dealing with matters relating to publication, other than what is contained within the papers themselves (time to publication, reviewing status, intellectual property status) and which were suggested in Lamp (2002), may be added.

It should be noted that while this is not fully in accord with either the Glaserian or Straussian approaches, it draws on aspects of both. The unit of analysis and aim of conceptualisation tend towards the Glaserian approach. The use of a predetermined, rather than emergent, coding family is a Straussian feature, but the coding family is not that prescribed by Strauss. For the purposes of this research, we are seeking a technique that can be applied to discovering concepts within scientific works, and which is philosophically compatible with Ingarden's framework. The coding technique employed in grounded theory would appear to offer this, but we do not claim that what we are undertaking is grounded theory since it is not in accord with either the Glaserian or Straussian approaches. We appropriate the coding technique from grounded theory and adapt it to the ontological analysis of text.

The coding process: foundations of the technique

The process for coding where abstract conceptualisation is sought can be considered to consist of two phases: *substantive coding* and *theoretical coding*. Although described here sequentially, they are not executed in this way.

Substantive coding itself consists of two phases: open coding and selective coding. In open coding the analyst aims to 'generate an emergent set of categories and their properties which fit, work and are relevant for integrating into a theory' (Glaser, 1978). Units of meaning are examined and coded against as many categories as may fit. New categories emerge, and new units of meaning fit existing categories. In undertaking open coding the analyst considers three questions (Glaser, 1978):

- What is this data a study of?
- To what category or property of a category, or to what part of the emerging theory, does this incident relate?
- What is actually happening in the data?

The first question serves to remind the analyst that the data may not match any preconceptions held by the researcher. The second question serves to remind the analyst to consider codes already used. The third question serves to remind the analyst to consider whether a particular code might be a core category.

Selective coding occurs when the analyst identifies core categories and limits coding to 'those variables that relate to the core variable in sufficiently significant ways to be used in a parsimonious theory' (Glaser, 1978).

Theoretical coding uses the coding families, in our instance based on Ingarden's ontological categories, to ensure that the analyst works at the conceptual level, writing about concepts and interrelations, rather than being bogged down in the data. The coding families assist in ensuring that the analyst has not overlooked the dimensions of a particular approach to understanding the data. Coding continues until the main concern of the research can be accounted for and further coding fails to add significant value in categories or properties. At this point theoretical saturation is deemed to have been achieved.

Substantive theory: the product of the technique

It should be noted that while the description has necessarily been presented as a sequential set of steps, it is by no means this simple. Glaser (1998 *cit* Fernandez, 2004) describes it as a method that 'happens sequentially, subsequently, simultaneously, serendipitously and scheduled'. A model of the grounded theory method proposed by Fernandez (2004) is shown in Figure 2, and demonstrates this complexity. A detailed explanation of the Fernandez model is, however, beyond the scope of this paper.

Analysts applying this technique will use memos and other tools to aid the abstraction process and to provide a trail of decisions made while applying the technique. The output is expected to be a web of terms linked with high level categories. The terms will aid searching and be based on meaningful concepts that have a relationship with the texts making up the relevant body of work.

Two questions automatically arise. First, what is the group for whom the texts are meaningful? Second, how durable is the categorial scheme produced? Recall that we are interested in categorising scientific works based on the terms and concepts that exist in the work. Thus, we address these questions in that context.

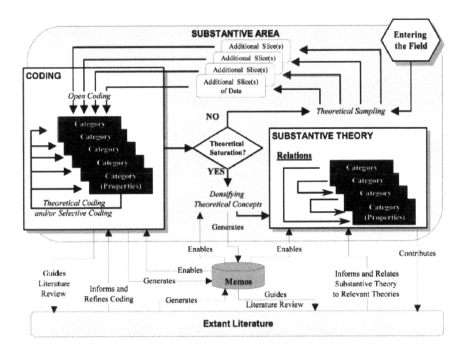

Figure 2: Grounded theory research model (Fernandez, 2004).

Regarding the first question, within a readership there may be several distinct communities of practice each of which brings different perspectives to reading the same works. The major influences are the different unfulfilled schematised aspects held in readiness by the readers from these groups. To adequately support such a heterogeneous readership, an application of the technique is required for each group. This would provide a consistent analysis reflecting the different perspectives of the readers. It could begin to capture the diversity of perspectives that exist in information systems. This is significant because it is accepted that the nature and scope of the information systems domain are diverse; the approaches to researching information systems are diverse; the approaches to teaching information systems are diverse, and there is a lack of any single clear theoretical basis underlying the study of information systems (Lamp and Milton, 2004).

With the second question, one can say that as disciplines mature and research progresses, our needs and readings of scientific works will change. For example, early theories about the structure of atoms are now largely historic and no longer have the currency they had when first published in the late nineteenth century. Clearly, however, the work itself does not change. What changes is the context of research and research theory, and also the needs and goals of the readership. Thus, the technique will need to be periodically reapplied to maintain durability.

Nevertheless, we can say that the approach is theoretically feasible. We say this because, firstly, we have the basis of a coding family based on a sound ontological theory of research texts. Secondly, we have a methodical well-respected qualitative research method designed to meaningfully analyse text to produce conceptual categories. Together, we therefore have an approach designed to produce terms (categories) that are meaningful, emergent, and relate to high-level ontological categories for research texts.

Conclusions

The motivation for this paper was the desire to undertake an ontological analysis of information systems research literature. The product of this analysis would constitute the starting point for a categorial scheme for that domain. In his books *The Literary Work of Art* (1965) and *The Cognition of the Literary Work of Art* (1968), Roman Ingarden developed a framework from a comprehensive high level ontological analysis of literary work, including scientific works. Our examination of the research literature failed to identify any efforts to develop a tool with which to rigorously apply his framework to scientific works and this paper has attempted to address that lack. Techniques from the grounded theory method have therefore been adapted to work with Ingarden's framework.

The grounded theory method and the adaptation of this method to information systems research has been successful over a number of years. The grounded theory method was considered appropriate in the context of the research discussed in this paper due to its similar philosophical heritage compared to Ingarden's ontological framework. They are both from the realist tradition and share assumptions about the world and the ways in which it may be understood. Importantly for this research, they both explicitly provide for the accommodation of differences in perception of states of affairs by individuals. The proposed tool therefore conforms to the definition of a method as a 'coherent and systematic approach, based on a particular philosophy' (Fitzgerald et al, 2002 *cit* Lings and Lundell, 2005).

The adaptation of the grounded theory method is expected to provide a number of additional benefits. The application of the method may be novel, but the method itself is approaching its 40th anniversary and, since it has had a presence in the information systems literature for the past 15 years, it should not be unfamiliar to information systems researchers. This last point is seen as significant because we see this tool as having applications beyond the immediate project for which we are developing it.

The use of this tool by a number of researchers for the purpose of this project would provide a consistent analysis that would reflect the intentionality of the researchers using it. This could begin to capture the diversity of perspectives that exists in information systems.

The tool may also be applicable for e-research in other interdisciplinary subject domains such as health informatics as well as other forms of literature intended for transmission of cognitive knowledge in the same way as scientific works (e.g. systems and user manuals, requirements specifications etc). Journal editorial boards could use it from time to time as a check on whether what was being published actually reflected their stated aims and scope.

What remains is to see if the approach is practically feasible. Hence, the next step is to apply the approach to a significant sample of papers from the top five information systems journals. We will then be able to comment on the practicality of the approach rather than simply addressing its theoretical feasibility, as we have done here.

References

Annells, M. 1996, 'Grounded theory method: Philosophical perspectives, paradigm of inquiry, and postmodernism', Qualitative Health Research, vol. 6, no. 3, pp. 379-93.

Betteridge, H. 1978, *Cassell's German-English English-German Dictionary*, London, Cassell.

Bharati, P. and Tarasewich, P. 2002, 'Global perceptions of journals publishing e-commerce research', Communications of the ACM, vol. 45, no. 5, pp. 21-6.

Broadbent, M., Weill, P. and Clair, D. S. 1999, 'The implications of information technology infrastructure for business process redesign', MIS Quarterly, vol. 23, no. 2, pp. 159-82.

Calloway, L. J. and Ariav, G. 1991, 'Developing and using a qualitative methodology to study relationships among designers and tools', in Nissen, H.-E., Klein, H. K. and Hirschheim, R. (eds), *Information Systems Research: Contemporary Approaches and Emergent Traditions*, Amsterdam: North Holland, pp. 175-93.

Fernandez, W. D. 2004, 'The Grounded Theory method and case study data in is research: Issues and design', in Hart, D. N. and Gregor, S. D. (eds) *Information Systems Foundations: Constructing and Criticising*, ANU E-Press, Canberra Australia.

Fitzgerald, B., Russo, N.L. and Stolterman, E. 2002, *Information Systems Development: Methods in Action*, McGraw-Hill, London.

Glaser, B. 1978, *Theoretical Sensitivity*, Mill Valley CA, Sociology Press.

Glaser, B. 1992, *Emergence vs Forcing: Basics of Grounded Theory Analysis*, Mill Valley CA, Sociology Press.

Glaser, B. 1998, *Doing Grounded Theory: Issues and Discussions*, Mill Valley CA, Sociology Press.

Glaser, B. 2005, *The Grounded Theory Perspective III: Theoretical Coding*, Mill Valley CA, Sociology Press.

Glaser, B. and Strauss A. 1967, *The Discovery of Grounded Theory*, New York, Aldine de Gruyter.

Hughes, J. and Howcroft D. 2000, 'Grounded Theory: Never knowingly understood', New Review of Information Systems Research, vol. 1, no. 1, pp. 181-99.

Ingarden, R. 1965, *Das Literarische Kunstwerk* (translated Grabowicz, G. G. 1973, *The Literary Work of Art: An Investigation on the Borderlines of Ontology, Logic and Theory of Literature*, Evanston, Northwestern University Press,) Max Niemeyer Verlag, Tübingen.

Ingarden, R. 1968, *Vom Erkennen des Literarischen Kunstwerks* (translated Crowley, R. A. and Olsen, K. R. 1973, *The Cognition of the Literary Work of Art*, Evanston, Northwestern University Press,) Max Niemeyer Verlag, Tübingen.

Katerattanakul, P., Han, B. and Hong, S. 2003a, 'Objective quality ranking of computing journals', Communications of the ACM, vol. 46, no. 10, pp. 111-4.

Katerattanakul, P., Razi, M. and Kam, H. 2003b, 'IS journal rankings versus citation analysis: Consistency and concerns', Proceedings of the 9th Americas Conference on Information Systems, Tampa, Florida.

Lamp, J. W. 2002, 'IS journal categorisation' <http://lamp.in-fosys.deakin.edu.au/journ_cat/> Accessed 18/05/2004.

Lamp, J. W. and Milton, S. 2003, 'An exploratory study of information systems subject indexing' *Proceedings of the 14th Australasian Conference on Information Systems*, Perth Australia, Edith Cowan University.

Lamp, J. W. and Milton, S. 2004, 'The reality of information systems research', in Hart, D. N. and Gregor, S. D. (eds) *Information Systems Foundations: Constructing and Criticising*, ANU E-Press, Canberra Australia.

Lings, B. and Lundell, B. 2005, 'On the adaptation of Grounded Theory procedures: Insights from the evolution of the 2G method', Information Technology and People, vol. 18, no. 3, pp. 196-211.

Mylonopoulos, N. A. and Theoharakis V. 2001, 'Global perceptions of IS journals: Where is the best IS research published?', Communications of the ACM, vol. 44, no. 9, pp. 29-33.

Orlikowski, W. J. 1993, 'CASE tools are organisational change: Investigating incremental and radical changes in systems development', MIS Quarterly, vol. 17, pp. 309-40.

Peffers, K. and Ya T. 2003, 'Identifying and evaluating the universe of outlets for information systems research: Ranking the journals', Journal of Information Technology Theory and Application, vol. 5, no. 1, pp. 63-84.

Pidgeon, N. F., Turner, B. A. and Blockley, D. I. 1991, 'The use of Grounded Theory for conceptual analysis in knowledge elicitation', International Journal of Man-Machine Studies, vol. 35, pp. 151-73.

Rosch, E. 1978, 'Principles of categorisation', in Rosh, E. and Lloyd, B. (eds), *Cognition and Categorisation*, Lawrence Erlbaum Associates, Hillsdale, pp. 27-48.

Smith, B. 1998, 'The basic tools of formal ontology', in Guarino, N. (ed.), *Formal Ontology in Information Systems*,. Amsterdam, IOS Press: 19-28.

Strauss, A. and Corbin, J. 1990, *Basics of Qualitative Research*, Sage, California.

Thomasson, A. L. 1996, 'Fiction and intentionality', Philosophy and Phenomenological Research, vol. 56, no. 2, pp. 277-98.

Urquhart, C. 2001, 'An encounter with grounded theory: Tackling the practical and philosophical issues', in Trauth, E. M. (ed.), *Qualitative Research in IS: Issues and Trends* , Hershey, Idea Group, pp. 104-40.

Walstrom, K. A. and Hargrave B. C. 2001, 'Forums for information systems scholars: III', Information and Management, vol. 39, pp. 117-24.

Using Protocol Analysis to Explore the Creative Requirements Engineering Process

Lemai Nguyen
Centre for Business Research, School of Information Systems,
Deakin University
email: lemai@deakin.edu.au

Graeme Shanks
Faculty of Information Technology, Monash University
email: Graeme.Shanks@infotech.monash.edu.au

Abstract

Protocol analysis is an empirical method applied by researchers in cognitive psychology and behavioural analysis. Protocol analysis can be used to collect, document and analyse thought processes by an individual problem solver. In general, research subjects are asked to think aloud when performing a given task. Their verbal reports are transcribed and represent a sequence of their thoughts and cognitive activities. These verbal reports are analysed to identify relevant segments of cognitive behaviours by the research subjects. The analysis results may be cross-examined (or validated through retrospective interviews with the research subjects). This paper offers a critical analysis of this research method, its approaches to data collection and analysis, strengths and limitations, and discusses its use in information systems research. The aim is to explore the use of protocol analysis in studying the creative requirements engineering process.

Creativity in requirements engineering

Requirements engineering (RE), an early phase in information systems (IS) development, has been commonly agreed to be one of the most crucial phases in the development process (e.g. Boehm, 1981; Loucopoulos and Karakostas, 1995; Nuseibeh and Easterbrook, 2000). RE is concerned with the elicitation, modelling and specification of user requirements for the new system to be built. Recently, creativity has been increasingly seen as playing an important role in RE (Nguyen et al., 2000; Maiden and Gizikis, 2001; Robertson, 2005; Nguyen and Swatman, 2006; Maiden and Robertson, 2005).

Creativity involves the *exploration of conceptual spaces* by people in order to produce an outcome that is both *novel and useful* for a specific context (Boden, 1991; Plucker and Beghetto, 2004; Sternberg, 2005). Based on this understanding of creativity, we see two strong supporting arguments for the role of creativity in RE: creating a vision for ICT-enabled future business practice and developing a requirements specification for an information system to enable the vision. First, creating a vision into future ICT-enabled business practice is crucial in order to develop a new system with an objective to leverage the competitiveness of the organisation and effectiveness of its business functions (Robertson, 2002; Robertson, 2005). Robertson has advocated that the requirements process should involve a creative discovery of requirements to invent business processes rather than passively eliciting requirements from business users as currently described in the RE literature because 'we won't make significant improvements to our software products by following a logical train of thought' (Robertson, 2005). Second, the RE process in its own right is not a purely deterministic, systematic process; it is an *exploration of conceptual spaces* involving cycles of structured and opportunistic insight-driven episodes (Nguyen et al., 2000; Nguyen and Swatman, 2003). Therefore, fostering and supporting creative thinking within the requirements gathering process is a key to effectively practice requirements engineering.

We argue that one major challenge in fostering and supporting creativity in RE is caused by the difficulty in obtaining a deep understanding of the creative cognitive process involved. For example, while all the practitioners participating in a focus group agreed that creativity was an essential requirement in all of their past requirements projects, they found it difficult to describe how the creative thinking process occurred (Cybulski et al., 2003). In their studies to select and integrate creativity techniques within RE, Maiden and Robertson (2005) criticised the fact that practitioners lack creativity theories and models to guide their creative process in RE. In response to this criticism, Nguyen and Shanks (2006) explored different facets of creativity, and especially different perspectives of creative processes in the creativity literature, and related them to creativity in RE. They concluded that an in-depth understanding of the creative cognitive process is required in order to effectively prompt and support creative thinking in RE.

In this paper, we explore the potential of protocol analysis, an empirical research method in cognitive psychology and behaviour analysis, for use in studying the creative RE process. The following section briefly describes different understandings of the problem solving process in RE and related fields to set a context for the following sections. After that, we describe and critically discuss the protocol analysis research method in terms of current approaches to data collection and analysis, and their benefits and limitations. Then we present a discussion of previous applications of protocol analysis in RE for different research purposes with a view to assessing its relevance to research into the creative requirements process. Finally, we summarise the paper and outline future research directions.

Understanding the creative RE process

Characteristics of the RE process

We view the creative process in RE as having both emergent and design characterisations.

First, RE has been described as an ill-structured problem solving process. The ill-structuredness of the requirements problem can be characterised through the open-endedness of the problem, poorly understood problem context, existence of multiple domains, complexity and dynamics of social interactions, organisation structures, business processes and technologies involved (Guindon, 1990b; Conklin, 2005; Nguyen and Swatman, 2006). In ill-structured problem solving, the understanding (and discovery) of the problem and structuring of the solution are intertwined. The problem solver (i.e. the systems analyst) moves between different problem areas in search of a possible solution, interacts and communicates his or her understanding with other stakeholders, and responds to the emergent situation. Therefore, both the problem space and the solution space progressively evolve as the systems analyst gains more knowledge and responds to the stimuli produced by the social, business and technical complexity and dynamics. This is similar to a description of the creative design process: 'The designer operates within a context which partially depends on the designer's perceptions of purposes, constraints and related contexts. These perceptions change as the designer explores the emerging relationships between putative designs and the context and as the designer learns more about possible designs' (Gero, 1996).

Second, RE should be seen as an art involving two different acts — articulating and documenting user requirements (i.e. describing the real world situation) as well as designing new business practice (enabled by a new system) by suggesting changes to the current situation. These acts are referred to, respectively, as analysing and modelling As-Is and To-Be requirements. However, the literature tends to focus on the former more extensively. Requirements elicitation, modelling and communication are fundamental activities (Nuseibeh and Easterbrook, 2000; Loucopoulos and Karakostas, 1995; Pohl, 1994). The first activity focuses on the acquisition and articulation of the user requirements. The second activity focuses on the representation and documentation of the requirements in various formats and perspectives. The third activity aims at requirements communication, negotiation and validating a correspondence between the requirements specification and the real world problem. We acknowledge that these fundamental systematic activities are still required in the development of To-Be requirements but we advocate that creative thinking plays a crucial role in envisaging and designing future information and communication technology (ICT) enabled business practice, especially if we aim at innovating in the business and creating new, significant added value through it. The invention of To-Be requirements, which is a largely missing activity in the current RE literature, is a key to envisaging and designing ICT enabled innovative business practice (Robertson, 2002, 2005). In addition, Simsion's (2006) investigation into data modelling in practice characterised data modelling as a creative design process although it is widely perceived to be a descriptive representation process.

Therefore, RE is a creative, emergent design process. In the next sub-section, we look at different views of the RE process and relate them to their counterparts in design studies and creativity research.

Views of the RE process

Nguyen and Swatman (2003, 2006) distinguished two views of the RE process that are held by members of the RE community:

The first view describes a systematic, structured and evolutionary process. Though detailed descriptions of the RE process may vary, essentially the requirements model is pictured as continually, incrementally structured and refined through a cyclic systematic process (e.g. Alexander, 1998; Loucopoulos and Karakostas, 1995; Kotonya and Sommerville, 1998).

The second view describes an opportunistic, constructivist process consisting of structuring and insight-driven restructuring of the requirements model. These opportunistic cognitive behaviours and insight-driven reconceptualisations of the problem space by the systems analyst are important in handling the emergent problem space and partial solutions (Guindon, 1990a; Visser, 1994; Khushalani et al., 1994; Nguyen et al., 2000; Robillard, 2005).

The existence of these two views of the RE process is reminiscent of the observation made by Dorst and Dijkhuis (1995) that there exist two views of the design process in the design studies community. The first view describes a rational problem solving process characterised by structured search and information processing in the problem space (Newell and Simon, 1972; Simon, 1969). The second view is constructivist and describes the design process as a reflective conversation with the situation (Schön, 1996).

Dorst and Dijkhuis (1995) have argued that the former characterisation describes the problem solving process for structured and fairly clear cut problems whereas the latter describes the conceptual design stage for ill-structured problems. Based on the discussion above, the latter matches the characteristics we attribute to the creative part of the RE process. We further note that these two descriptions of the design process are analogous to the two descriptions of the RE process.

We see this analogy as a manifestation of two 'forces' in RE: the enforcing of a systematic structured process to avoid a chaotic error-prone process, as opposed to the recognition and taking advantage of opportunistic cognitive behaviours and heuristics of professionals (in dealing with the emergent problem space). Both of these two forces are essential in RE problem solving; a good balance of them is required.

Boden (1991) has described the creative process as an internal process of exploration and transformation of conceptual spaces in an individual mind. However, understanding how this internal process, which actually happens in the individual mind, has long been a challenging topic in creativity research. There exist numerous models to describe the creative process. Shneiderman (2000) described three creative process models: inspirationalist, structuralist and situationalist.

The inspirationalist views the creative process as passing through four phases of preparation, incubation, illumination and verification, as in the model of Wallas (1926), and as unpredictable insight and associated restructuring of the problem space in Gestalt psychology (Mayer, 1992; Ohlsson, 1984). Common creativity enhancing techniques, such as lateral thinking, divergent thinking, six thinking hats, and free association, are often adopted to promote inspirational creativity.

The structuralist views the creative process as a more focused and structured effort to generate and evaluate ideas as in, for example, Osborn-Parnes' Creative Problem Solving CPS (Daupert, 2002; Osborn, 1979) and the Directed Creativity Cycle (Plsek, 1997). A cyclic process of divergent brainstorming and convergent thinking phases is included in these models to stress a balance between imagination and the analytical aspects of creativity.

The situationalist emphasises the social interactions between individual problem solvers and thus stresses the collaborative nature of the creative process. Three out of the four phases of collecting, relating, creating and disseminating in the creative process model of Shneiderman (2000) are designed to directly support collaboration and communication of information and ideas in the creative process. In this vein, a group of researchers at the University of South Australia extended CSCW (Computer Support Collaborative Work) theories in order to develop ICT-enabled supportive workplace for creative teams (Blackburn et al., 2005).

We have two observations. First, the inspirationalist and the structuralist tend to focus on the creative effort by individuals while the situationalist emphasises the collaboration between them. Second, the inspirationalist tends to focus on how the creative process actually occurs while the structuralist and situationalist tend to focus on how the creative process should be undertaken. Based on a synthesis of creativity models from creativity research and creativity research in RE, Nguyen and Shanks (2006) suggested integrating the different views through a collaborative process consisting of cycles of structured building up and opportunistic restructuring of the requirements model. This process needs to be further developed and refined. Overall, we conclude that the differences between different descriptions of the creative process that exist in the RE, design studies and creativity research communities manifest different styles of creative thinking and cognition. Our conclusion points to the need for, and difficulties in, integrating the different creative process views. It is therefore important to further explore creative thinking and cognition in the RE process and the question arises as to which research method(s) would be most appropriate to pursue this exploration.

To explore creative thinking and cognition, it is important to obtain data about the process and to reconstruct what happens in the mind of systems analyst. As highlighted earlier, a major challenge is that systems analysts can not describe accurately how they developed solutions for problems they faced (Lubars et al., 1993; Hofmann and Lehner, 2001). A similar challenge exists in design studies; designers 'cannot articulate what kind of expertise they use in designing and how' (Suwa et al., 1998). Researchers in design studies have been using protocol analysis, an empirical method in cognitive psychology, to examine the design process. In the next section, we describe and discuss the potential use of protocol analysis in exploring the creative process in RE.

Protocol analysis

Overview of protocol analysis

Researchers in the psychology of problem solving and design studies have recognised the importance of describing and understanding the cognitive process used by the problem solver. The belief is that a good understanding of the cognitive process would be useful to support and improve the problem solving and design practice and to effectively train practitioners. Protocol analysis is an empirical research method for studying the cognitive behaviours and thought processes used by problem solvers (Ericsson and Simon, 1993).

Protocol analysis usually takes place in a controlled environment. The research subject is a problem solver who is given a specific task and works individually on that task. Protocol analysis aims to collect as much detail as possible about the problem solving process, analysing the collected data and reconstructing what happens in the mind of the problem solver. On one hand, the controlled environment reduces 'noise' and allows the researcher to collect rich details and relevant data about the problem solving activities and artifacts produced during the experiment. On the other hand, shortcomings of this research method include a limited time period, a small problem, and the exclusion of social processes, teamwork and communication that often take place in everyday work.

There are different approaches to conducting protocol analysis. We discuss them in terms of data collection and data analysis.

Data collection approaches

There are two approaches to data collection in protocol analysis: concurrent and retrospective (Dorst and Dijkhuis, 1995; Ericsson and Simon, 1993).

Concurrent protocol

Concurrent protocols are generated when the problem solver verbalises their thoughts while working on a specific task. First, the problem solver is trained to verbalise his or her thoughts using a thinking aloud technique. Second, with a given task, the problem solver verbalises his or her thoughts while working on a given task. The process is video and/or audio taped, and transcribed. As a result, a thinking aloud concurrent protocol acts as the generator of the data source, which is then later coded and analysed.

Two assumptions underlie the validity of the verbalisation of thoughts process in concurrent protocols. The first is that the problem solving process has a conversational characteristic. Schön (1996) described design as a reflective dialogue of the problem solver with the materials of a problem situation. In developing a design rationale tool, Kaplan (1990) viewed the design process as a conversation-oriented activity, being either a monologue by one designer or conversations between different designers. The second is that the verbalisation of thoughts during the problem solving process will not affect the process. Ericsson and Simon (1993) describe three levels of verbalisation ranging from direct verbalisation without special effort to communicate thoughts, minimal intermediate processing to explicate the thought contents, and verbalisation with an explanation of thoughts, ideas and motives. Having reviewed empirical studies using these levels of verbalisation, Ericsson and Simon (1993) concluded that concurrent verbalisation does not alter the structure of thought processes. There is a disagreement about this conclusion. Lloyd et al. (1995) were concerned with the validity of concurrent protocols because thinking aloud may interfere with the problem solving process and, consequently, concurrent protocols may be incomplete and not reveal true insights into the actual problem solving process. A common view shared by the design studies research community is that concurrent protocols reveal a sequence of cognitive events and information processing stored in short-term memory (STM), thus providing rich details and opportunities for analysis to gain insight into the cognitive behaviours by the problem solver.

Retrospective protocol

Retrospective protocols conduct interviews with the problem solver after the problem solving process, usually immediately. During the interview, the problem solver is asked to recall his or her activities. Interviews are audio and/or video taped and transcribed. The generated retrospective protocols serve as data for later coding and analysis to reconstruct the problem solving process and gain insight into what happened during the process.

While both concurrent protocol and retrospective protocol approaches share a common position that collected data can be used to reconstruct the problem solving process, the latter is often seen as less intrusive to the process under observation (Lloyd et al., 1995). However, Ericsson and Simon (1993) have argued that, after the experiment session is complete, information processing details are no longer accessible from STM because they have been transmitted into Long Term Memory (LTM) from which it is harder to retrieve. Consequently, the reconstructed process based on a retrospective protocol may be incomplete and inaccurate. Retrospective protocols may not show the actual sequence of cognitive events, instead they may show a rationalised or theorised story of the problem solving process. To address this in design studies, Suwa et al. (1998) suggested videotaping the design experiment session and using the videotapes to assist the retrieval of the cognitive events stored in LTM after the experiment session. In addition, the contents (sketches and diagrams) can also be collected for analysis. Guindon (1990a) supplemented her concurrent protocols with retrospective interviews to obtain additional design rationale and to gain a deep understanding of the designer's cognitive behaviours and the design process.

Gero and Tang (2001) conducted an empirical study to examine similarities and differences between concurrent and retrospective protocols. They found that both types of protocol methods show a similar frequency of changes of design intentions and consistent structures of the design process. They also found that the number of segments in a retrospective protocol is larger than the number of segments in a concurrent one. They explain that, through a revision of sketches and rehearsed memory after the thinking aloud session, the retrospective protocol produced more details than the concurrent protocol (Gero and Tang, 2001). The authors concluded that concurrent and retrospective protocols lead to similar results and that the concurrent protocol is an efficient and applicable method in understanding the design process.

Kuusela and Pallab (2000) conducted a similar comparative study using an experiment set in a context of customer decision making. Although the problem solving contexts and coding methods in studies by Gero and Tang (2001) and Kuusela and Pallab (2000) are different, a common conclusion was reached, namely that both concurrent and retrospective protocols lead to consistent understandings of the problem solving process. In addition, Kuusela and Pallab (2000) suggest that concurrent protocols are more suitable for examining the process while retrospective protocols are more suitable for examining the outcome. Their conclusions support the potential use of protocol analysis to gain insight into the problem solving process in RE.

There are nevertheless two weaknesses with both concurrent and retrospective protocols. One of these is the well-known Hawthorne effect since both of these data collection approaches involve observation of a research subject who knows they are being watched. Other research approaches such as, for example, case study, action research and ethnography, also share this limitation (Neuman, 2003). Another weakness of protocol analysis is the difficulty in recruiting and training participants who are willing, capable and motivated to provide meaningful protocols. Previous successful applications of protocol analysis in design research have addressed this issue by explaining to participants the significance of the research and providing training that facilitates thinking aloud and articulating 'on the fly' thoughts.

Data analysis approaches

Data generated using either concurrent or retrospective protocols are coded (segmented) for the analysis and identification of cognitive patterns. First, the data is coded into segments. Often a change in the problem solver's intention, or the contents of their thoughts, signals a new segment. Second, the problem solving process is reconstructed as a sequence of coded segments. Finally, correlations between segments are identified. Based on the two views of the design process, rational problem solving and constructivist, there are two approaches to segmenting data: process-oriented and content-oriented (Dorst and Dijkhuis, 1995; Gero and Neill, 1998).

Process-oriented segmentation

The process-oriented segmentation approach aims at describing the design process as a sequence of problem solving activities, using a problem solving taxonomy such as, for example, problem recognition, goal setting, solution proposing, solution analysing, or top down vs. bottom up strategies. In this approach, the protocol transcriptions are often coded into segments by syntactic markers, such as pauses, intensity, intonations, phrases and sentences that then aggregate into cognitive units called design intentions or design moves, for analysis (Ericsson and Simon, 1993). Alternatively, protocols can be directly segmented by design intentions based on the problem solving taxonomy — for example, problem domain including abstraction levels, functions, behaviours, structures; and micro and macro design activities such as proposing solutions, analysing solutions, explicit strategies, top down, bottom up, opportunistic (Gero and Neill, 1998). The categorisation of design intentions is often determined before the segmentation of the protocol. Gero and Neil (1998) also suggest open segmentation of protocols to allow new categories to emerge during the segmentation process. The segments generated from the protocol are often quantitatively analysed to identify time spent on different types of design intentions, and to reconstruct a sequence of, and correlations between, them.

Benefits of process-oriented segmentation include: a design process described in the form of a sequence of design intentions and an understanding of correlations between design intentions, often presented in a graph form. Dorst and Cross's (2001) protocol analysis, involving an evaluation of nine creative designs in industrial design experiment, offered a refined model of a co-evolution of both the problem space and solution space. Their study supported Schön's (1983) argument that insight-driven problem (re)framing is crucial to the creative design process. Another example is a study by Guindon (1990a) involving eight designers in a lift control software design experiment. This study is often cited in the RE literature. Using a process-oriented segmentation method to examine concurrent protocols produced in this study, Guindon (1990a) observed significant deviations from a systematic structured process. She was amongst the first authors to propound opportunistic cognitive behaviours in high-level software design. Opportunistic behaviours and deviation from a structured process were also observed and reported in requirements engineering by Khushalani et al. (1994) and Nguyen et al. (2000).

Dorst and Dijkhuis (1995) have criticised the process-oriented approach on the basis that it fails to examine what designers see and think and what knowledge they exploit. This weakness can be addressed using the content-oriented segmentation approach.

Content-oriented segmentation

The content-oriented approach to protocol segmentation focuses on the cognition of the problem solver; that is, what he or she sees and thinks and what knowledge he or she uses (Suwa and Tversky, 1997; Suwa et al., 1998). There are two types of cognitive contents: visual contents (depicted elements and their spatial relations as drawn in the artifacts, and movements such as eye movement, moving pencils, etc) and non-visual contents (including thoughts and knowledge). A well defined classification of content-oriented segments (Tang and Gero, 2000) includes:

- Physical — depiction, looking, motion;
- Perceptual — perceiving depicted elements and their relations;
- Functional — assigning meaning to depictions/perception; and
- Conceptual — goal setting and decision making.

To study discontinuity and unexpected discoveries in the design process, design segments are indexed as being new, continual or revisited.

The content-oriented segmentation approach has been found to be useful in examining cognitive interactions between designer and artifacts. Using a content-oriented segmentation classification scheme, Suwa et al. (1998) found that sketches can seen as an external memory useful for subsequent inspections, visual cues for functional actions, and a physical setting for functional thoughts to be constructed on the fly in the emergent problem situation. The use of sketches was also investigated in a recent study (Bilda et al., 2006) using a revised content-oriented segmentation scheme. This study found that sketching or externalising may be useful but not necessary to design in terms of developing a network of ideas, pursuing cognitive activities and obtaining a satisfactory outcome. As systems analysts often use requirements models to represent and communicate requirements with each other and with other stakeholders, interactions between systems analysts and requirements models can be examined using content-oriented protocol analysis.

According to Tang and Gero (2000), there are two types of content-oriented segments and both are essential in the design process. Goal-driven segments reflect the rational problem solving process (Newell and Simon, 1972) and sensor-driven segments reflect the constructivist and reflection-in-action process (Schön, 1983). To us, this observation can be related to the description of catastrophe cycles in the requirements gathering process (Nguyen et al., 2000; Nguyen and Swatman, 2003).

In summary, the content-oriented and process-oriented segmentation approaches can both be beneficial. In RE, the invention or discovery of requirements and changes to requirements models should be studied in relation to associated cognitive behaviours to evaluate the creative requirements process and their impact on the creative outcome. There are, though, two common weaknesses from the point of view of RE in current segmentation classification schemes. First, both process-oriented and content-oriented segmentation approaches need to be adjusted to the RE knowledge domain, tailored, for example, to a particular requirements method and process. Second, segment classification should be linked to different types of creativity and creative thinking styles such as, for example, exploratory, combinatory, analogy, transformation, structured and unstructured (Boden, 1991; Ward and Finke, 1999; Sternberg, 2005).

Discussion

Protocol analysis is widely used in problem solving research, especially in design studies. As the debate about the strengths and weaknesses of protocol analysis continues, this research method evolves. In terms of data collection protocols, comparative studies tend to confirm that concurrent and retrospective protocols produce similar results (Tang and Gero, 2000; Kussela and Pallab, 2000). In terms of data segmentation and coding, segmentation schemes are developed to enable researchers to gain in-depth understandings of the process as well as the interaction between the designer and artifacts (Gero and Neill, 1998; Tang and Gero, 2000; Bilda et al., 2006).

Protocol analysis has also been adopted and adapted to studying thinking processes in teams. For example, Stempfle and Badke-Schaub (2002) recorded team concurrent communication and analysed the generated protocol sentence by sentence. They developed a new coding scheme to examine collective design actions. Amongst others, important findings concerned the structuring of group process and, a continual 'interweaving of content-oriented and process-oriented sequences', and a tendency to immediately evaluate new ideas by team members (Stempfle and Badke-Schaub, 2002). In our view, since the pseudo-concurrent protocol did not capture verbalised thoughts, the retrospective protocol may be complementary: a combination of intermediate artifacts, video tapes and retrospective interviews can be useful in reconstructing multiple cognitive processes and teamwork dynamics. Distributed cognition theories can be also adopted to investigate creative team processes.

It is interesting to observe that, between the 1990s and early 2000s, design studies and RE researchers have come up with similar observations about the creative, emergent problem solving process and the co-evolution of the problem space and the solution space. But researchers in design studies have used protocol analysis, and proactively invented new segmentation schemes to examine the creative design process while RE researchers have used other research approaches, as will be discussed below.

Discussion and conclusion

Applications of protocol analysis in requirements engineering

Protocol analysis has been applied to the study of the cognitive behaviours of software and database designers (Guindon, 1990a; Sutcliffe and Maiden, 1992) and systems analysts (Batra and Davis, 1992; Chaiyasut and Shanks, 1994). A majority of these studies focus on categorising cognitive behaviours exhibited by systems designers or analysts and/or examining similarities and differences between novices and experts.

Guindon (1990a) discovered that the ill-structuredness of the requirements problem was an important factor inducing the opportunistic behaviours of the software designer. The opportunistic behaviours are associated with inferences related to new, emergent details associated with the incompleteness and ambiguity of the ill-structured problem. Often, upon sudden discovery of such details, a designer tends to immediately develop new partial solutions and test and modify them, rather than continuing to work on their previous planned task at a higher abstraction level. Their traversal between different abstraction levels was not systematic.

Sutcliffe and Maiden (1992) analysed verbal protocols supplemented by retrospective questionnaires from the development of a requirements specification for a delivery scheduling system. They were able to categorise and model the cognitive behaviours as consisting of complex dependencies between information-gathering, assertions, conceptual modelling, planning, recognising goals and reasoning. According to these authors, the strongest associations were between information-gathering, assertions and conceptual modelling. These associations were explained as a representation of the analytical side of understanding the problem domain.

Batra and Davis (1992) examined similarities and differences between novice and expert database designers and concluded that novices focused on structuring requirements while experts' efforts were directed towards developing a holistic understanding of the problem, abstracting, categorising and representing. They noted cyclic movements between problem understanding and problem modelling by experts. With a focus on the data aspect, Chaiyasut and Shanks (1994) examined differences between data models produced by expert and novice data modellers. The authors categorised the cognitive process into six detailed types and noted that novices' models were developed 'literally' from the problem description while experts' models were more comprehensive, complete and held a holistic view of the problem.

Other studies using protocol analysis in requirements research are not related to the creative requirements process. For instance, protocol analysis was adopted as a research method in evaluating conceptual tools in modelling composites, data and properties (Shanks et al., 2003). More recently, Owen and his colleagues (Owen et al., 2006) criticised a lack of applications of protocol analysis in software engineering research and demonstrated benefits of protocol analysis as a research method in gaining valuable insight into how human factors influenced the interpretation and use of technical documentation by systems developers. Interestingly, protocol analysis was not only seen as a research method but also suggested as a way to observe and learn about the requirements problem context through users' work patterns and behaviours. Protocol analysis was also included as a technique in the ACRE framework, a framework to guide practitioners in requirements acquisition (Maiden and Rugg, 1996).

Can protocol analysis be used to study creative thinking and cognition in the requirements process?

We have reviewed various research approaches to studying the creative RE process and behaviours of the systems analysts. The table below summarises our findings in terms of their strengths and weaknesses.

Research method	References	Strengths	Weaknesses
Laboratory experiment	(Khushalani et al., 1994; Simsion, 2006)	More control over the process	Limited time and small tasks
		Gains insight into the process and outcome by individual in small tasks	Difficult to study collective creative problem solving process
Survey	(Simsion, 2006)	Investigates specific well-defined constructs and concepts	Difficult to explore new concepts and gain in-depth understandings of why and how
			Difficult to reconstruct non-verbal thinking processes and cognitive activities
Protocol analysis	(Guindon, 1990a; Sutcliffe and Maiden, 1992; Batra and Davis, 1992; Chaiyasut and Shanks, 1994)	Can be designed to have a more natural setting compared to lab experiments, similar to workshops.	Often limited time and small tasks
			Difficult to study situational collaborative creative process
		Generates rich data to gain insight into non observable thinking process by individual problem solvers	Difficulty to recruit and train participants
Workshop observation/ Positivist case study	(Khushalani et al., 1994; Maiden and Robertson, 2005)	More control of procedures and tasks, less control of interactions and group dynamics	Difficult to reconstruct non-verbal thinking process and cognitive activities
		May gain access to the situational collaborative process	Less control over the process, difficult to find host
		Useful to confirm or disconfirm hypotheses and explore and identify issues for further studies	Contextual, often limited time
Focus group	(Cybulski et al., 2003)	Good to explore/validate multiple view points through panel interviews	Difficult to reconstruct non-verbal thinking process and cognitive activities
			Group dynamics may be interfere with results, contextual
Interpretive case study/ Action research	(Nguyen et al., 2000; Dallman et al., 2005; Raisey et al., 2005)	May gain access to the situational collaborative process	Difficult to reconstruct non-verbal thinking process and cognitive activities
		Data-grounded and inductive	Less control over the process, difficult to find host
		Improving practice (action research)	Contextual

Table 1: Existing research approaches to studying the systems analysts' behaviours in RE.

As we have argued, cognitive behaviours are important in studying creative processes in RE. In obtaining data about the cognitive behaviours, a challenge faced by researchers is that creative thinking involves both verbal and non-verbal activities. While verbal activities (meetings, conversations, requirements workshops, and group brainstorming) can be observed directly to generate data, non-verbal activities (silent cognitive behaviours that occur in the mind of the systems analyst) are much harder to access. Therefore, protocol analysis can be a key research method to gain insight into cognition and creative thinking in the requirements process. Surprisingly, protocol analysis was used to study cognitive behaviours in RE in the early 1990s although it has not been used specifically in studying the creative requirements process.

We suggest two possible applications of protocol analysis: using it to examine creative thinking and cognition in the creative requirements process; and using it to evaluate different requirements processes that utilise creativity techniques (such as that of Maiden and Robertson, 2005) and that do not utilise creativity techniques (for example, UML in Dennis et al., 2002) in relation to assessing the creative outcome produced through using these different RE processes.

Protocol analysis comes with inherent limitations: limited generalisability to real commercial projects and weak suitability to study collaborative process. To address these, a combination of research methods can be useful. In fact, a number of authors adopt a combination of different research approaches. For example, Simsion (2006) used interviews, surveys and laboratory experiments in studying creativity in data modelling, and Khushalani et al. (1994) used workshop observations and laboratory experiments to examine opportunistic behaviours by systems designers. Protocol analysis can, we argue, potentially be used with other fieldwork research approaches and to study cognitive behaviours in the creative, emergent and collaborative process in RE in particular.

References

Alexander, I. 1998, 'Requirements engineering as a co-operative inquiry: A framework', Proceedings of the Conference on European Industrial Requirements Engineering CEIRE '98, London, UK.

Batra, D. and Davis, J. G. 1992, 'Conceptual data modelling in database design: Similarities and differences between expert and novice designers', International Journal of Man-Machine Studies, vol. 37, pp. 83-101.

Bilda, Z., Gero, J. S. and Purcell, T. 2006, 'To sketch or not to sketch? That is the question', Design Studies, in Press.

Blackburn, T., Swatman, P. and Vernik, R. 2005, 'Extending CSCW theories to model and support creative group processes', InSyL Working Papers, School of Computer and Information Science, University of South Australia.

Boden, M. A. 1991, *The Creative Mind: Myths and Mechanisms*, Basic Books.

Boehm, B. W. 1981, *Software Engineering Economics*, Englewood Cliffs, Prentice Hall.

Chaiyasut, P. and Shanks, G. 1994, 'Conceptual data modelling process: A study of novice and expert data modellers', Proceedings of the 1st International Conference on Object-Role Modelling, Magnetic Island, Queensland, Australia.

Conklin, J. 2005, *Dialogue Mapping: Building Shared Understanding of Wicked Problems*, John Wiley and Sons.

Cybulski, J., Nguyen, L., Thanasankit, T. and Lichtenstein, S. 2003, 'understanding problem solving in requirements engineering: debating creativity with IS practitioners', Proceedings of the 7th Pacific Asia Conference on Information Systems, PACIS'2003, Adelaide, Australia.

Dallman, S., Nguyen, L., Lamp, J. and Cybulski, J. 2005, 'Contextual factors which influence creativity in requirements engineering', Proceedings of 13th European Conference on Information Systems ECIS 2005, Regensburg, Germany.

Daupert, D. 2002, *The Osborne-Parnes Creative Problem Solving Process Manual*.

Dennis, A., Wixom, B. H. and Tegarden, D. 2002, *Systems Analysis and Design An Object-Oriented Approach with UML*, John Wiley and Sons.

Dorst, K. and Cross, N. 2001, 'Creativity in the design process: Co-evolution of problem—solution', Design Studies, vol. 22, pp. 425—37.

Dorst, K. and Dijkhuis, J. 1995, 'Comparing paradigms for describing design activity', Design Studies, vol. 16, pp. 261-74.

Ericsson, K. A. and Simon, H. A. 1993, *Protocol Analysis Verbal Reports as Data*, The MIT Press, Cambridge, Massachusetts.

Gero, J. S. 1996, 'Creativity, emergence and evolution in design: Concepts and framework', Knowledge-Based Systems, vol. 9, no. 7, pp. 435-48.

Gero, J. S. and Neill, T. M. 1998, 'An approach to the analysis of design protocols', Design Studies, vol. 19, pp. 21-61.

Gero, J. S. and Tang, H.-H. 2001, 'The differences between retrospective and concurrent protocols in revealing the process-oriented aspecs of the design process', Design Studies, vol. 21, no. 3, pp. 283-95.

Guindon, R. 1990a, 'Designing the design process: Exploiting opportunistic thoughts', Human-Computer Interaction, vol. 5, pp. 305-44.

Guindon, R. 1990b, 'Knowledge exploited by experts during software system design', International Journal of Man-Machine Studies, vol. 33, pp. 279-304.

Hofmann, H. F. and Lehner, F. 2001, 'Requirements engineering as a success factor in software projects', IEEE Software, vol. 18, no. 4 pp. 58-66.

Kaplan, S. M. 1990, 'COED: A conversation-oriented tool for coordinating design work', in Finkelstein, A., Tauber, M. J. and Traunmuller, R. (eds), *Human Factors in Information Systems Analysis and Design,* North-Holland, Elsevier Science Publishers, pp. 123-42.

Khushalani, A., Smith, R. and Howard, S. 1994, 'What happens when designers don't play by the rules: Towards a model of opportunistic behaviour in design', Australian Journal of Information Systems, vol. 1, no. 2, pp. 13-31.

Kotonya, G. and Sommerville, I. 1998, *Requirements Engineering: Processes and Techniques,* West Sussex, England, John Wiley and Sons.

Kuusela, H. and Pallab, P. 2000, 'A comparison of concurrent and retrospective verbal protocol analysis', American Journal of Psychology, vol. 113, no. 3, pp. 387-404.

Lloyd, P., Lawson, B. and Scott, P. 1995, 'Can concurrent verbalisation reveal design cognition?', Design Studies, vol. 16, pp. 237-59.

Loucopoulos, P. and Karakostas, V. 1995, *System Requirements Engineering*, New York McGraw-Hill.

Lubars, M., Potts, C. and Richter, C. 1993, 'A review of the state of the practice in requirements modelling', Proceedings of the 1st IEEE International Symposium on Requirements Engineering RE'93, San Diego, California, IEEE Computer Society Press.

Maiden, N. and Gizikis, A. 2001, 'Where do requirements come from?', IEEE Software, vol. 18, no. 5, pp. 10-2.

Maiden, N. and Robertson, S. 2005, 'Integrating creativity into requirements engineering process: Experiences with an air traffic management system', Proceedings of the 13th IEEE International Conference on Requirements Engineering (RE'05), Paris.

Maiden, N. and Rugg, G. 1996, 'ACRE: Selecting methods for requirements acquisition', Software Engineering Journal, vol. 11, no. 3, pp. 183-92.

Mayer, R. E. 1992, *Thinking, Problem solving, Cognition,* New York, W. H. Freeman and Company.

Neuman, W. L. 2003, *Social Research Methods: Qualitative and Quantitative Approaches*, Allyn and Bacon.

Newell, A. and Simon, H. A. 1972, *Human Problem Soving*, Englewood, Prentice-Hall.

Nguyen, L., Carroll, J. and Swatman, P. A. 2000, 'Supporting and monitoring the creativity of IS personnel during the requirements engineering process', Proceedings of the 33rd Hawai'i International Conference on System Sciences, HICSS-33, Maui, Hawaii.

Nguyen, L. and Shanks, G. 2006, 'Exploring creativity elements in requirements engineering', Forthcoming.

Nguyen, L. and Swatman, P. A. 2003, 'Managing the requirements engineering process', Requirements Engineering, vol. 8, no. 1, pp. 55-68.

Nguyen, L. and Swatman, P. A. 2006, 'Promoting and supporting requirements engineering creativity', in Dutoit, A. H., McCall, R., Mistrik, I. and Paech, B. (eds), *Rationale Management in Software Engineering*, Springer-Verlag.

Nuseibeh, B. A. and Easterbrook, S. M. 2000, *Requirements Engineering: A Roadmap*, IEEE Computer Society Press.

Ohlsson, S. 1984, 'I. Restructuring revisited: Summary and critique of the gestalt theory of problem solving', Scandinavian Journal of Psychology, vol. 25, pp. 65-78.

Osborn, A. F. 1979, *Applied Imagination: Principles and Procedures of Creative Problem-Solving*, New York, Charles Scribner's Sons.

Owen, S., Budgen, D. and Brereton, P. 2006, 'Protocol analysis: A neglected practice', Communications of the ACM, vol. 49, no. 2, pp. 117-22.

Plsek, P. E. 1997, *Creativity, Innovation, and Quality*, Quality Press

Plucker, J. A. and Beghetto, R. A. 2004, 'Why creativity is domain general, why it looks domain specific, and why the distinction does not matte', in Sternberg, R. J., Grigorenko, E. G. and Singer, J. L. (eds), *Creativity: From Potential to Realisation*, American Psychological Association (APA).

Pohl, K. 1994, 'Three dimensions of requirements engineering: A framework and its application', Information Systems, vol. 19, no. 3, pp. 243-58.

Raisey, D., Tan, K., Swatman, P., Blackburn, T. and Nguyen, V. 2005, 'An empirical study of the evolving dynamics of creative teams in action', InSyl Working Papers, School of Computer and Information Science, University of South Australia.

Robertson, J. 2002, 'Eureka! Why analysts should invent requirements', IEEE Software, vol. 19, no. 4, pp. 20-2.

Robertson, J. 2005, 'Requirements analysts must also be inventors', IEEE Software, vol. 22, no. 1, pp. 48, 50.

Robillard, P. N. 2005, 'Opportunistic problem solving in software engineering', IEEE Software, vol. 22, no. 6, pp. 60-7.

Schön, D. A. 1983, *The Reflective Practitioner: How Professionals Think in Action*, London England, Temple Smith.

Schön, D. A. 1996, 'Reflective conversation with materials', in Winograd, T. (ed.) *Bringing Design to Software*, New York, ACM Press, pp. 171-84.

Shanks, G., Tansley, E. and Weber, R. 2003, 'Using ontology to help validate conceptual models', Communictions of the ACM, vol.46, pp. 85-89.

Shneiderman, B. 2000, 'Creating creativity: User Interfaces for supporting innovation', ACM Transactions on Computer-Human Interaction (TOCHI), vol. 7, no. 1, pp. 114-38.

Simon, H. A. 1969, *The Sciences of the Artificial*, The MIT Press, Cambridge, Massachusetts.

Simsion, G. C. 2006, 'Data modelling: Description or design?', unpublished PhD thesis, Department of Information Systems, University of Melbourne, Melbourne, Australia.

Stempfle, J. and Badke-Schaub, P. 2002, 'Thinking in design teams — an analysis of team communication', Design Studies, vol. 23, pp. 473-96.

Sternberg, R. J. 2005, 'Creativity or creativities?', International Journal of Human-Computer Studies, vol. 63, pp. 370-82.

Sutcliffe, A. G. and Maiden, N. A. M. 1992, 'Analysing the novice analyst: Cognitive models in software engineering', International Journal Man-Machine Studies, vol. 36, pp. 719-40.

Suwa, M., Purcell, T. and Gero, J. 1998, 'Macroscopic analysis of design processes based on a scheme for coding designers' cognitive actions', Design Studies, vol. 19, pp. 455-83.

Suwa, M. and Tversky, B. 1997, 'What do architects and perceive in their design sketches? A protocol analysis', Design Studies, vol. 18, pp. 385-403.

Tang, H.-H. and Gero, J. S. 2000, 'Content-oriented coding scheme for protocol analysis and computer-aided architectural design', Proceedings of the 5th Conference on Computer Aided Architectural Design Research in Asia, CAADRIA2000, Singapore.

Visser, W. 1994, 'Organisation of design activities: Opportunistic, with hierarchical episodes', Interacting with Computers, vol. 6, no. 3, pp. 235-74.

Wallas, G. 1926, *The Art of Thought*, London England, Jonathan Cape.

Ward, T. B. and Finke, R. A. 1999, 'Creative cognition', in Sternberg, R. J. (ed.), *Handbook of Creativity*, New York, Cambridge University Press, pp. 189-212.

Poles Apart or Bedfellows? Re-conceptualising Information Systems Success and Failure

Dennis Hart[1]
School of Accounting and Business Information Systems,
The Australian National University
email: dennis.hart@anu.edu.au

Leoni Warne[2]
Defence Systems Analysis Division, DSTO
email: leoni.warne@dsto.defence.gov.au

Abstract

It is commonly stated that information systems continue to be plagued by persistently high rates of failure. However, we argue in this paper that the relationship between success and failure is more complex than usually assumed, and based in the different expectations that different stakeholders have of a development effort. The expectation failure concept of Lyytinen and Hirschheim is used as a starting point for discussion leading to the introduction of a new concept that we call 'defining characteristics'. We then proceed with a discussion of the implications of this new concept for ideas about success and failure and use a case study conducted by the second author to illustrate these ideas.

Introduction

Information systems success and failure have been much discussed in the literature for many years (e.g. Brooks, 1974; Davis et al, 1992; DeLone and McLean, 1992; Fortune and Peters, 2005; Lucas, 1975; Lyytinen and Hirschheim, 1987; McFarlan, 1981; Sauer, 1993). It seems, however, that the general assumption in all of these cases has been that the two concepts, success and failure, are inverses of each other. That is, a failure is by definition not a success and vice versa. While this appears natural enough and in accord with common sense, we argue against this view in this paper contending instead that the

---

[1] Previously of the Australian Defence Force Academy when this work was undertaken.
[2] Previously of the University of Canberra when this work was undertaken.

criteria that distinguish between success and failure are best regarded as being *independent* of each other. If this is admitted then it suddenly becomes possible for an information system or indeed any other project to be not only a success or a failure in the usually understood sense, but also both at once, or neither.

Contrary to common practice in much of the information systems literature dealing with this kind of topic, in what follows we take 'success' and 'failure' to be ground terms. We make no direct attempt to define them, for reasons that will become evident below. Moreover, information systems researchers are increasingly recognising the varying needs and expectations of different stakeholders in information systems development efforts (e.g. Seddon, 1997, 1999; Rai et al, 2002; Fortune and Peters, 2005) and, as we shall emphasise below, this has corresponding implications for their potentially disparate views concerning the eventual success or failure of these efforts.

We further argue that what is critical is to identify, for different stakeholders, the specific factors that will distinguish for them between success and failure. This is consistent with Seddon et al (1999) who say that in 'a world of conflicting human interests and vastly different systems, different sharply-focused measures of IS effectiveness are likely to be needed for different purposes'. Effective elicitation of these factors in the early stages of system development would, we contend, significantly assist developers by giving them an even better understanding than more traditional techniques provide, of what they should achieve, and also avoid doing, in their subsequent efforts.

Success and failure as independent dimensions

The view of success and failure as converses is commonly held. According to this picture, the two terms are antonyms (e.g. Allen, 1938); success is at one end of a spectrum and failure is at the other. They are 'poles apart':

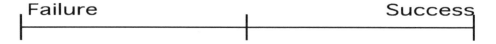

Figure 1: The success/failure spectrum.

However, we argue that a closer look reveals a more complex relationship between the concepts. For example, five different dictionaries, in their definition of the word 'failure', all include a reference to 'unsuccessful' or 'lack of success'. But in *none* of them does the definition of 'success' contain any mention of 'avoidance of failure' or the like. So, it seems, to be unsuccessful is to fail but avoidance of failure is not the same as success.

But even this does not appear to be adequate if we consider, for example, the concluding remarks of Bertrand Russell in his autobiography (Russell, 1975). In reviewing a long, rich and full life, he says:

My work is near its end, and the time has come when I can survey it as a whole. How far have I succeeded, and how far have I failed? ... To this extent I have succeeded. ... [but] ... In these [other] respects there was failure.

So, for Russell, his life and work was both a success and also a failure. It was not simply a case of one or the other for him, but *both*. However, in making such judgements and statements about success and failure it is manifestly important to be clear about the entity to which the judgement is being applied. For Russell, this entity was his work as a whole whereas of course in this paper our interest is in information systems. Other examples are easy to find or imagine. A person might be successful as (say) a parent and, at the same time, be a failure as a politician; a movie might be judged a critical success but also be a box office failure. Or, indeed, the entity concerned may be judged neither a particular success nor a failure on any count.

On this argument, then, with respect to success and failure there are four basic 'poles' for the entity of interest rather than just two. These are:

- Success and not failure (S and ~F);
- Failure and not success (F and ~S);
- Success and failure (S and F);
- Not success and not failure (~S and ~F).

Success and failure no longer face each other from the opposite ends of a linear spectrum containing intermediate possibilities, as in Figure 1, but may instead be present or absent independently of each other. A better picture of their relationship would, therefore, be that shown in Figure 2.

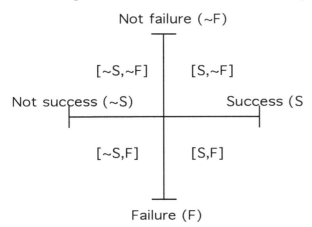

Figure 2: The success/failure matrix.

The picture of success and failure captured in Figure 2 has been introduced in general terms; our interest in what follows focuses on how this may be applied to information systems and their development.

Success, failure and stakeholder expectations

If the model of Figure 2 is accepted, the question then arises as to what differentiates 'not success' from 'success' and 'not failure' from 'failure'. Following Lyytinen and Hirschheim (1987), we contend that it is the expectations of the stakeholder concerned that provides this distinction. However, Lyytinen and Hirschheim's concept of expectation failure, which they define as '[an] inability of an IS to meet a specific stakeholder's expectations', does not, in our view, go far enough. We believe it is necessary to further distinguish between different types of expectation, both in their relevance to success or failure, as well as in their relative importance for the stakeholder concerned.

As an example, it is possible that for a certain information system development effort the IS department in an organisation (a stakeholder) expects that the project will be under its overall direction. If this expectation is not fulfilled, which would constitute an expectation failure in Lyytinen and Hirschheim's terms, then the development effort might well be perceived by the IS department as a failure, for them, *whatever* else happens. On the other hand, if the expectation is fulfilled then the project will not have failed (at least in the eyes of the IS department, and all other things being equal) but is unlikely to be said on this account alone to have succeeded. That is, the expectation of control of the project concerned, by the IS department, would in this case be one of the differentiators between failure and not-failure rather than between success and not-success. Of course there may be other differentiators too, and generally will be. A similar scenario may be painted for success versus not-success. For instance, suppose a particular user group is expecting expanded functionality in an area of their special interest. If the project and resulting information system provides it then they are very likely to regard it as a success, other things being equal. But if not — say only existing basic functionality is maintained — then does that mean it is a failure in their eyes or simply less than a complete success? If the latter, then their expectation of expanded functionality in their special area of interest is, for them, a differentiator between success and not-success and has no direct link to failure or not failure.

Positive and negative expectations

In most discussions of user requirements it seems to be implicitly assumed that requirements or expectations are of what we would call a 'positive' nature. That is, the system will *have* some characteristic or *provide* some feature or functionality. But we contend that expectations may also be *negative*. For example, a stakeholder may expect that a system will *not* use a particular operating system or should *not* affect their existing standard operating procedures in certain ways.

Now it could obviously be objected that the distinction being drawn here between positive and negative expectations is artificial and simply dependent on phrasing. From the point of view of a two-valued logic this is of course true. For example, one might argue that saying 'the characteristic of user friendliness must be present' is equivalent to saying that 'the characteristic of user unfriendliness must be absent'. But we are not dealing in simple two-valued logic. Instead it is the psychology and perceptions of stakeholders that are the issue here. The importance of the distinction between positive and negative characteristics lies in the psychological effect in the mind of the respondent. When asked for characteristics that should be present (positive expectations), the effect on the stakeholder is likely to be quite different from that produced when they are asked for characteristics which ought to be absent (negative expectations).

Defining characteristics

Lyytinen and Hirschheim (1987) as well as Seddon et al (1999) recognise that there are, in general, many stakeholder expectations and many of these may be unstated, vague, unformed or only partially formed, and, initially, even unconscious. This of course represents a practical difficulty for developers who are concerned with satisfying expectations, but even if this were not so, and more fundamentally, Lyytinen and Hirschheim (1987) omit to distinguish between expectations of differing importance and it is, we think, evident that not only may a stakeholder hold many expectations but also that some will carry much greater weight than others. Furthermore, in addition to explicit and well documented expectations, there may also be other implicit or pseudo-rational requirements that remain hidden. Leifer et al (1994) call these 'deep structures'. Hidden expectations could even be the most important from the stakeholder's point of view, and may, in the final analysis, critically affect their attitudes to success and/or failure. The question therefore arises: 'which, among all of the stakeholder expectation(s), are important enough to differentiate between success/not-success and failure/not-failure?'. This is unanswerable in general because expectations are so context and situation dependent. Instead, we use a concept called 'defining characteristics'.

The idea of information system 'defining characteristics' presented here is derived from a philosophical analysis of definition and meaning in language given in Hospers (1967). Discussing definition, Hospers asserts that it is necessary to:

> ... consider carefully which characteristics of a thing we consider to be
> *defining*. A defining characteristic of a thing ... is a characteristic *in the*

absence of which the word [under consideration] *would not be applicable to the thing.* (Emphasis in original).

Furthermore:

> ... the test of whether a certain characteristic is defining is always this: would the same word still apply if the thing lacked the characteristic? If the answer is no, the characteristic is defining; if the answer is yes, it is merely accompanying.

The simple example of a triangle is used: 'Being three-sided is a defining characteristic of triangles, since nothing would be ... a triangle unless it had three sides ... but being at least two inches in height ... is not a defining characteristic of a triangle ... since something can be a triangle ... and yet be smaller than this.'

This idea can be applied to information systems success and failure in four ways. (paraphrased from Hospers wording above). Firstly:

1. What characteristics would, if absent, prevent the system being classified as a success? Or, equivalently: What characteristics would, if present, make the system a success?

These are the positive expectations on the ~S...S dimension. There is nothing new here since these expectations may be equated to the traditional mandatory requirements. Now, secondly:

2. What characteristics would, if absent, prevent the system being classified as not a success? Or, equivalently: What characteristics would, if present, make the system not a success?

These are the negative expectations on the ~S...S dimension. In essence, this question is asking what must be *avoided* if the system is to be a success. Such a question seems, at least in our experience, to be not usually asked and may well cause the stakeholder responding to think in very different terms about the system under consideration and what it means to him or her. This difference of effect, of the question asked, on the respondent's thinking may be extremely important in eliciting a more complete picture of relevant stakeholder's views. Now, thirdly:

3. What characteristics would, if absent, prevent the system being classified as a failure? Or, equivalently: What characteristics would, if present, make the system a failure?

These are the negative expectations on the ~F...F dimension and are the things that must be avoided if a failure is to be averted; they are the absolute 'must not do's'. And lastly:

4. What characteristics would, if absent, prevent the system being classified as not a failure? Or, equivalently: What characteristics would, if present, make the system not a failure?

These are the positive expectations on the ~F...F dimension. The characteristics being identified here are similar to what are often called 'hygiene' factors in the theory of motivation (Herzberg et al, 1959). They must be present to avoid failure, but their presence is not of itself a guarantee of success.

This leads us now to a definition of 'defining characteristics' in an information systems success and failure context:

> A 'defining characteristic' of an information system is any characteristic that is held by a stakeholder to be of such importance that its presence (or absence) will differentiate between success and not success, or failure and not failure.

Presumably, for each individual stakeholder, the number of defining characteristics will be relatively few. However, no assumption is made about the clarity, awareness, breadth, or apparent triviality or otherwise of these characteristics in the perception of the stakeholder holding them. Like the dimensions of success identified by Seddon et al (1999), our concept of defining characteristics is firmly based in the expectations of the stakeholders, unlike any so-called general or objective list of specific system features or characteristics for defining success. Moreover, unlike the expectation failure idea of Lyytinen and Hirschheim (1987), our concept also takes account of the differences in importance of expectations, focusing specifically upon those both positive and negative that will determine overall system success/not-success or failure/not-failure, in the eyes of the stakeholders concerned.

Finally, it is necessary to note that we have presented our analysis of defining characteristics in terms of *a priori* stakeholder perceptions regarding success and failure and consequently painted a rather static picture of them. There is always the possibility, however, that stakeholder perceptions and therefore potentially also their defining characteristics for a system may change over time, perhaps because of the emergence of unanticipated benefits or disadvantages that were not evident initially. Analysis of stakeholder defining characteristics may therefore need to be a continuing or repeated process rather than a once-off exercise in a system development effort.

Multiple stakeholders

So far we have considered only a single stakeholder. But, of course, there are in general many stakeholders in an information system development effort. What effect does this have? Our answer is that we must construct a 2x2 success/failure matrix such as that shown in Figure 2, with its defining characteristics differentiating success/not-success and failure/not-failure, *for each stakeholder.* In effect each stakeholder has a different definition of the information system (Mathieson, 1993). Our diagram now becomes as shown in Figure 3.

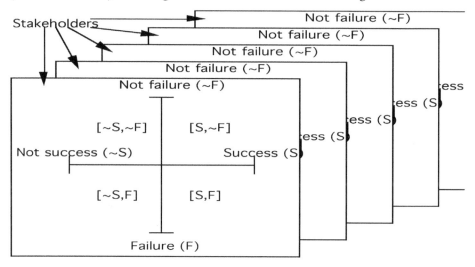

Figure 3: Multiple stakeholders.

Given a situation like that of Figure 3, what now of the prospects for success overall; that is, for 'success' and 'not failure' for all of the stakeholders? Clearly, this depends on the defining characteristics for each one and we may conclude that for overall success to even be possible requires that *none of the set of defining characteristics, across ALL of the stakeholders, be mutually exclusive of any other.* In a development effort with many stakeholders this is arguably unlikely and then the probability of success overall, by our definition at least, becomes correspondingly remote. Perhaps this represents a partial explanation of the notoriously high failure rates that characterise large information systems projects.

Seen in this light, it is clearly necessary for information systems developers to uncover and determine, at the outset, both the positive and negative defining characteristics for success/not success and failure/not failure, and to do this for all of the stakeholders of a proposed system. They must be prepared to ask questions like all of 1 to 4 above. However, in practice it would seem from our experience at least that only questions like 1 and 4 are asked in the requirements gathering process, and it may be that it is often the absence of questions like 2 and 3 that contributes to difficulties of understanding and resulting system implementation problems.

It is also possible that defining characteristics could apply not only to a delivered system but also to the development process or the project itself. For example, a particular stakeholder's defining characteristic for failure/not failure might be that a project should be constituted in a certain form, or a development process carried out in a certain way, and if it is not then *whatever* system is finally delivered (if any) may be deemed by them to be a failure regardless.

A case study

The authors were some years ago involved with a prematurely terminated information system project of substantial size, conducted in a large public sector organisation. Warne (1999) conducted a formal case study of the project. The project was originally intended to run for 9 years and deliver a final system costing some $250M, but only existed for 2.5 years and expended some $2.5M (not including the salaries of the developers). No working software was delivered by the project before its termination, although it did carry out considerable preliminary analysis work and produced large quantities of documentation. Further details regarding the project and case study results can be found in Warne (1999, 2002) and Warne and Hart (1996). A discussion and explanatory model concerning the reasons for its termination are also presented in Hart (1997).

In very broad terms (a finer breakdown is possible, but not necessary for our purpose here) the major stakeholders for this project may be identified as:

- End users
- Developers
- Middle/upper management (several subgroups)
- Corporate senior management.

Based on a document study, in-depth interviews with a number of participants in the project and quantitative and qualitative responses to a questionnaire, some of the defining characteristics of the project for these stakeholders can be postulated. It is not, however, possible from our data to identify with any certainty which of these defining characteristics relate to success/not-success or failure/not-failure. Nevertheless, the identified defining characteristics are:

End users

E1. Improved computer-based support at the operational level for personnel and pay related tasks.

Developers

D1. Development of an integrated system across the organisation as a whole.

D2. Freedom to proceed to project completion and delivery of a working system.

Middle/upper management (some groups)

M1. Improved computer-based support for managerial personnel and pay related tasks.

M2. No effect on existing organisational arrangements or power relationships.

Corporate senior management

C1. Better organisational efficiency in the personnel and pay management areas

C2. Value for money (favourable cost/benefit ratio).

Of these, most are positive defining characteristics. That is, they are characteristics that the project development process, or final system, should have. However, one (M2) is a negative defining characteristic. Note also that characteristics D1 and M2 were mutually exclusive in the context of the organisation concerned and therefore, according to our argument above, the project and the information system it was trying to develop *could not* succeed overall.

As defining characteristics are married to stakeholders' thoughts and perceptions, a selection of representative comments from project participants is included here to illustrate how the defining characteristics were derived from the case study data. Note also that the comments from one group are often revealing of the defining characteristics of another.

Comments from end users

'[The Case Study Project] could save [the Organisation] a lot of money, given that it could replace the individual [divisional] systems. For example, one leave system instead of three, one personal particulars system instead of three etc. etc. etc.' (E1)

'A project with great potential; the failure/termination of the project has left a "black hole" in critical management areas (career management, training, personnel data base, strength management, etc.) in terms of MIS.' (E1)

'[The Case Study Project] was a top-down approach at re-engineering a complex and politically sensitive system, fear of a [Central Division] take over and bad PR ensured the project would suffer a death from paralysis by analysis, a good idea, poorly nurtured.' (E1, M2)

'JAD [Joint Application Development] workshops were valuable from both users and developers' perspective. The commonality between [divisions] in personnel admin was (not unexpectedly) very high. The project was defeated by internal and high level politics and by not recognising and extolling the intangible benefits. If the business case was solely dollars/manpower savings driven for recognising benefits in the short term then it had to fail.' (E1, M2)

'Elements were leery of the validity of their data and unwilling to have it controlled and manipulated by outsiders. Differences of approach and tribal processes complicated the manpower management tasks.' (M2)

'The failure of [the Case Study Project] was due principally to vested interests by some elements within the Department who perceived a loss of influence if [the Case Study Project] were to have proceeded. This was to the detriment of some of the main intended beneficiaries' (M2)

Comments from developers

'A harmonious and focused development team in contrast with the short-sighted and divided interests of the traditional [Departmental] power structures. It failed for its political failings — not for technical reasons (or the complexity of the project) ... [the Department] has become less of an organisation in itself; the [different] programs have not developed a "corporate" philosophy, and seem to have difficulty agreeing on anything that has the potential to diminish their own power and control, even where there appears to be a clear business case.' (D1, E1, M2)

'Senior management essentially took no notice from the development team on realistic timing estimates of proposed tasks. The management staff made their own estimates on task timings (to best suit their agenda) and if the developers' estimates did not correspond, the developers' estimates were deemed inaccurate and unacceptable. As a result, task completion dates were continually extended. As it turned out, the original development team task timing estimates were accurate.' (D2)

'[The Case Study Project] threatened several user areas particularly the [Program 1] pay empire. Support was given for [the Case Study Project] by higher levels of user committee in its earlier stages but was later withdrawn at a critical stage in the project and hence [there was] no business case. Many user [groups] were reluctant to offer up savings as they perceived that this would infer that they had "excess" manpower ... Upper [departmental] management does not often have any idea of the real day-to-day IS problems (i.e. [in]accurate data, unfriendly systems etc.). [The Case Study Project] was trying to provide a more efficient, user friendly, integrated system for the [Department].' (D1, M2, E1)

'It could have worked, it should have worked, but it was beaten by vested interests amongst senior [Departmental] officers and their advisers who could not accept compromise, continually looked for *their* perfect solution and make the job of the developers impossible.' (D1, M2)

'It was a shame that [Departmental] politics and the hidden agendas of some Senior [Departmental] managers played such a large part in the demise of [the Case Study Project]. No doubt, it will be quite some time before the intended users will get the IT support they deserve, and it is highly unlikely that a project like [the Case Study Project] will ever be initiated again. However, if it did, and I had the opportunity to do it all again, I certainly would.' (E1, M2)

'Reasons for failure: vested interests; fear of loss of power; disagreement on savings which would have supported the business case; lack of support from senior user management (not senior [Departmental] management).' (M2)

Comments from middle/upper management (some groups)

'Implementation of [the Case Study Project] would have seen the control of a mission critical personnel management tool i.e. the personnel computing system, move from [Divisional] control to [Central Control]. This would have split the [Senior User Managers] from the management tools and threatened the achievement of their missions. If [the Case Study Project] were implemented, the whole personnel management structure of the [Department] would have had to change. In theory the structural change and the personnel computing change should have occurred simultaneously. Obviously the time was not fortuitous for a structural change, therefore the computing initiative was bound to fail.' (M1, M2)

'In my opinion, the major problem was the unwillingness of [the Departmental] management *at the most senior level* to embrace the need for IS functions and management to be devolved, involving *some* loss of functional control, but not of policy authority.' [respondent's emphases] (M2)

'There was a naive assumption that because [the Case Study Project] was being reasonably well project-managed that it would succeed. The era of highly centralised domineering IT systems is dead. Hopefully, [extant centralised Departmental project] is the last of its kind.' (M2)

'The whole project seemed to be set up to support [corporate headquarters] rather than the individual [divisional managers]. This led, from an early stage, to confrontation and hostility between developers and some of the user groups.' (C1, M2)

Comments from corporate senior management

'The Project was visionary and ambitious in that it was to be a catalyst to solve [Departmental] personnel information management deficiencies ... It was terminated because senior management were not committed to it nor to find/agree the savings, without that support [the Case Study Project] had no future and required termination.' (C1, C2)

'... reasons quite external to [the Case Study Project] and the whole [Case Study Project] debate also played a role. For example, the budgetary situation the Department faced. Even good prospects do not always get funded, and for time sensitive projects like IT, delay can be terminal.' (C2)

'A further problem was the unevenness of benefits across the [divisions] ... I also believe there was a lack of vision and this was driven by resource managers.' (C2, M2)

'The resource bill, both in terms of money and manpower, was much higher than any of the [divisions] could realistically afford at a time of substantial reductions in both areas ... project sponsors did not convince [Departmental] manpower planners and resource managers that the proposed system would produce any tangible benefit/utility for them.' (C2)

'[The Case Study Project] was always too large in scope and scale to ever be successful. The hardware and software costs would have been very high and the time-scale of the project would have meant we would get old technology and the old processes by the time it came into service.' (C1, C2)

'[The Case Study Project] had a lot going for it: a goal, high level support, a capable and dynamic project director a large project team, and a disciplined approach. Yet it failed. The reasons are complex, and many players had different reasons for either withdrawing their support or for seeking its demise. My own reasons for arguing against proceeding were very clear — the proposed approach was unlikely to be cost effective, and was high risk. There were other approaches more likely to be cost effective (but still not foolproof) and which were much lower risk. They also offered a much reduced service compared to [the Case Study Project], but not so reduced when compared to then existing and planned systems.' (C1, C2)

'I believe the costs were greater than the savings — it was a simple business assessment.' (C2)

Discussion

The final assessment of the project is a complex one based on the important expectations or, in our terms, the defining characteristics held by each stakeholder. The actions taken by each stakeholder regarding the project are easily understandable in the context of their defining characteristics. Of greatest interest is the case of the middle management. Their initial approach to the project was supportive based on their expectation of improved systems for personnel and pay management *without* significant impact on organisational power relationships. Once it became clear that implementation of the system as planned by the project would have involved such impact, they then worked to destroy it and pursued other options for system improvement. On the other hand, stakeholders without this defining characteristic (e.g. the developers) worked hard for the project to continue because this constituted the path to success from the perspective of their own defining characteristics.

Lastly, if the project management had realised what the defining characteristics were for each stakeholder, then care could have been taken to try to satisfy these. Or, if this proved impossible because of mutual incompatibility between them (as was the case), then perhaps the aims or nature of the project itself could have been modified to take this into account. For example, abandonment of at least some of the project's original aims might have permitted it to progress (Sauer, 1993). Or division of it into several separately controlled but related sub-projects could have avoided the problems that were actually encountered since it is well known that introducing an information system, especially a centralising one, can have unforeseen social and political impacts (Seddon et al, 1999). The importance of considering the stakeholder defining characteristics is, we think, evident.

Conclusion

Information systems and their development are complex organisational and social phenomena that are still not well enough understood. There is little doubt that this lack of understanding is a major contributor to the persistently high level of problems and failures that continue to plague information systems development projects. We have argued in this paper that the expectation failure concept of Lyytinen and Hirschheim (1987) is a useful starting point for progress in the analysis of failure, but the lack of differentiation between expectations of different importance is a weakness. The expectation failure concept, combined with recognition of the independence of the concepts of success and failure and also the fact that expectations may be negative as well as positive, is addressed in the discussion and definition of what we have called 'defining characteristics' for information systems.

The case study discussion not only illustrates the concept of defining characteristics but also shows, as is well known from previous studies (e.g. Saarinen, 1996; DeLone and McLean, 2002), that labelling an information system or project as a failure or success is not a simple matter. Indeed, we would argue that such labelling can be misleading and shallow. Our main point, however, is that for different stakeholders who view a project or information system through the different lenses of their own distinct defining characteristics, it may be both a success and a failure at one and the same time. The significance of our argument is that consideration during the requirements analysis process of stakeholder defining characteristics regarding *both* success/not-success and failure/not-failure, and particularly the negative defining characteristics that we believe are not usually addressed, has the potential to provide additional clues for developers regarding how they may need to modify either the approach taken by an information systems project, or perhaps the aims and constitution of the project itself, in order to increase the prospects for overall success.

References

Allen, F. S. 1938, *Allen's Synonyms and Antonyms*, Harper.

Brooks, F. 1974, *The Mythical Man Month*, Addison-Wesley.

Davis, G. B., Lee, A. S., Nickles, K. R., Chatterjee, S., Hartung, R. and Wu, Y. 1992, 'Diagnosis of an information system failure: A framework and interpretive process', Information and Management, vol. 23, pp. 293-318.

DeLone, W. H. and McLean, E. R. 1992, 'Information systems success: The quest for the dependent variable', Information Systems Research, vol. 3, no. 1, pp. 60-95.

DeLone, W. H. and McLean, E. R. 2002, 'Information systems success revisited', Proceedings of the 35th Hawaii International Conference on System Sciences.

Fitzgerald, J. and Fitzgerald A. 1987, *Fundamentals of Systems Analysis*, 3rd ed., John Wiley and Sons.

Fortune, J. and Peters, G. 2005, *Information Systems: Achieving Success by Avoiding Failure*, Wiley, Chichester.

Hart, D. 1997, 'Modelling the political aspects of information systems using "Information Wards"', Failures and Lessons Learned in Information Technology Management, vol. 1, no. 1, pp. 49-56.

Herzberg, F., Mausner, B. and Synderman, B. 1959, *The Motivation to Work*, John Wiley and Sons.

Hospers, J. 1967, *An Introduction to Philosophical Analysis*, Revised ed., RKP.

Leifer, R., Lee, S. and Durgee, J. 1994, 'Deep structures: Real information requirements determination', Information and Management, vol. 27, pp. 275-85.

Lucas, H. C. 1975, *Why Information Systems Fail*, Columbia University Press.

Lyytinen, K. and Hirschheim, R. 1987, 'Information systems failures — A survey and classification of the empirical literature', Oxford Surveys in Information Technology, vol. 4, pp. 257-309.

Mathieson, K. 1993, 'Variations in user's definitions of an information system', Information and Management, vol. 24, pp. 227-34.

McFarlan, W. 1981, Portfolio approach to information systems', Harvard Business Review, vol. 59, no. 5, pp. 142-50.

Rai, A., Lang, S. S. and Welker, R. B. 2002, 'Assessing the validity of IS success models: An empirical test and theoretical analysis', Information Systems Research, vol. 13, no. 1, pp. 50-69.

Russell, B. 1975, *Autobiography*, Unwin.

Saarinen, T. 1996, 'An expanded instrument for evaluating information system success', Information and Management, vol. 31, no. 2, pp. 103-18.

Sauer C. 1993, *Why Information Systems Fail: A Case Study Approach*, Alfred Waller.

Sauer C. 1993, 'Partial abandonment as a strategy for avoiding failure', in Avison D., Kendall J. E. and DeGross J. I. (eds), Human, Organisational, and

Social Dimensions of Information Systems Development, IFIP Transactions A-24, pp. 143-67.

Seddon, P. B. 1997, 'A respecification and extension of the DeLone and McLean model of IS success', Information Systems Research, vol. 8, no. 3, pp. 240-54.

Seddon, P. B., Staples, S., Patnayakuni, R. and Bowtell, M. 1999, 'Dimensions of information systems success', Communications of the Association of Information Systems, vol. 2, no. 20, November <http://cais.is-world.org/>, Accessed 14 August 2007.

Warne, L. 1999, 'Understanding organisational learning in military headquarters: Findings from a pilot study', Proceedings of the 10th Australasian Conference on Information Systems (ACIS), pp. 1144-58.

Warne, L. 2002, 'Conflict and politics and information systems failure: A challenge for information systems professionals and researchers', in Clarke, S. (ed.), Socio-Technical and Human Cognition Elements of Information Systems, Hershey, PA, Idea Group.

Warne L. and Hart D. 1996, 'The impact of organisational politics on information systems project failure — A case study', Proceedings of the 29th Annual Hawai'i International Conference on Systems Sciences IV, pp. 191-201.

Reality

An Action-Centred Approach to Conceptualising Information Support for Routine Work

Vivienne Waller
Department of Information Systems, University of Melbourne
email: vivienne.waller@unimelb.edu.au

Robert B Johnston
Department of Information Systems, University of Melbourne
email: robertj@unimelb.edu.au

Simon K Milton
Department of Information Systems, University of Melbourne
email: smilton@unimelb.edu.au

Abstract

In this paper, we continue our long-term project of developing a situated information systems analysis and design methodology, and present it as a radical alternative to conventional information systems analysis and design. Taking a situated approach entails focusing on action and a situated analysis and design methodology aims to increase efficiency and effectiveness through supporting routine action. We suggest that, as well as improving effectiveness and temporal efficiency, applying the situated methodology will result in less wasted human effort expended in search of information. We discuss the implications of an action focus for our conception of what an information system should be, and illustrate the application of the methodology with examples from a case study.

Introduction

Conventional information systems attempt to represent the real world (Weber, 1997). As the real world changes, the information system is updated. In other words, the information system enables tracking of state changes in the real-world system. As Weber points out:

> ... building, operating, maintaining, and observing the states of the information system must be less costly than observing the states of the

real-world phenomena. Otherwise, there is little point to building the information system. We might as well observe the real-world phenomena directly (Weber, 1997).

In this paper, we present the case for a situated system, a radically different type of information system designed to support action in the world. Rather than attempting to represent the real world, the situated system informs actors when to do something and what to do without the need for recourse to a representation of the state of the world; the information is located 'in' the world and can be observed directly.

In previous publications (Johnston and Milton, 2002; Johnston et al., 2005) we have identified what we call the deliberative theory of action, which assumes that an actor uses a mental model of the world to decide what to do next. We have critiqued this theory of action, arguing that in routine action, actors respond directly to structures in the environment in order to attain goals. This alternative theory of action, the situated theory of action, informs our long-term project to develop an analysis and design methodology for situated information systems.

This paper is a conceptual output from the long term project of developing an analysis and design methodology based on the situated theory of action (Johnston and Milton 2002; Johnston et al., 2005; Milton et al., 2005). This program of research has proceeded by means of case studies. Two case studies have been conducted to inform the development of the methodology. These case studies have provided an opportunity to test our ideas and reflect on their practical application. The first case study is reported in Johnston et al. (2005), while the second case study is reported in Waller et al. (2006). Between the publications, there has been a gradual evolution in our understanding of the nature of the appropriate abstraction. Whereas the previous iteration of the methodology involved abstraction from work practices to goals and constraints, the methodology now focuses more explicitly on analysing action at multiple levels of abstraction. Hence, while reflection on the conduct of the case studies has helped refine our concepts, the concepts that we present are developed from a theoretical starting point rather than being entirely generated from or grounded in empirical data. Vignettes from the second case study are included to illustrate the theoretical points and to give examples of practical application of the methodology. Although these vignettes are from a case study conducted in a clinical setting, the methodology is for use to support routine action in any type of organisation.

We advance the project of developing situated systems by showing how a situated approach to systems analysis and design demands a focus on action. We then show how a focus on action leads to a different understanding of how best to provide information support. We explain how restructuring the environment and providing situated information to actors can enable routine conduct of actions, with lighter-weight information systems and increased efficiency and effectiveness. We draw on our insights into the nature of action and routine action to produce a new kind of information system analysis and design methodology, and we outline the principles of this situated systems analysis and design methodology as well as illustrate its application with examples from a case study. The methodology will be useful to organisations by allowing them to increase efficiency and effectiveness through supporting routine action. Unlike conventional information systems, as well as increasing temporal efficiency, situated systems also aim to increase human efficiency; in particular, to reduce wasted human effort expended in search of information. They can also increase effectiveness by preventing incorrect actions.

Understanding actions

The theory of actions underpinning our methodology is somewhat unconventional, drawing inspiration from the philosophical thinking of Johansson (1989) and Searle (1983). In the field of information systems, through the concept of a transaction, actions are traditionally conceptualised as causing changes in state, with the desired outcome being achievement of the goal state. We, however, eschew this idea that change can be understood as like a film strip of states of the world with action joining each frame. Instead we view the world through the dynamic lens of action itself and regard every action as simultaneously having both purposive (goal-like) and performative aspects.

The following expands on this understanding of actions. Of particular importance for the methodology are the following three properties of actions: that they are always situated in the environment, that they are multi-scale in nature and that they are dependent on the execution of other actions for instantiation as part of the action system. These properties are illustrated using material from the second case study of the project, conducted in a chemotherapy ward in a large hospital.

The environment in which actions occur

Structured information systems analysis and design methodologies tend to ignore the environment in which actions occur, representing actions as if they occur in a virtual space. In contrast, it is crucial to our analysis of action to take account of the environment in which actions occur. Consistent with our focus on action, we conceptualise the environment as all the actions available to an actor, that is, as the *action possibility space*. This means that if two different environments allow the same set of actions, they are equivalent for our purposes.

We analyse the environment in terms of *structures* in the environment that constrain or enable action. Gibson (1979) gave the name 'affordance' to the opportunities for action that structures in the environment provide to a particular class of actor. For example a chair affords sitting to a person; a hollow log may afford shelter to a small animal. Whereas Gibson focused on physical structures, the idea of affordance can be extended to temporal and organisational structures too. Physical structures include space, things and the arrangement of things. Organisational structures include roles and norms.

Every action is conducted by an actor in time and space, making use of resources. We define the actor, location, time and resources associated with an action as the *action context*. In other words, the action context is the particular dimensions of the environment in which a particular action occurs. The specifics of the action context mean that particular actions are constrained and enabled, depending on the affordances of the environment in which the particular time, place, actor and resources are located. The actors in whom we are most interested are human actors, although an organisation itself can be conceived as a macro actor performing actions.

Table 1 shows some of the actions undertaken as part of the administration of chemotherapy and the particular action context in which they occur. From the table it can be seen that a blood test can be taken in an external pathology lab, the hospital pathology lab, or the chemotherapy ward. It can be taken by pathology staff or a nurse using particular equipment to draw a sample of blood from a patient. Implicit in this is the idea that there are locations which are *not* suitable for taking blood, resources which can *not* be used to take blood, and actors who can *not* take blood. In other words, the action context indicates constraints on where, how and with what, blood can be taken. The action context also can provide clues about what action is to occur.

Action	ACTION CONTEXT			
	Location	Actor	Resources	Time
a. Sign chemotherapy order	Hospital	Doctor	Chemotherapy order pen	All of these are to be done before patient appointment.
b. Approve chemo orders	Hospital	Pharmacist	Chemotherapy order	Actions a. and b. need to be done
c. Prepare treatment	Pharmacy	Pharmacy staff	Compounds, lab, etc	sufficiently before
d. Assess patient as well enough for treatment	Hospital	Nurse	Blood results Patient observations	patient appointment to allow treatment preparation
e. Give blood test	External pathology lab Hospital pathology lab Chemo Ward	Pathology staff Nurse	Syringe, etc Patient	
f. Check blood test results have arrived	Hospital	Hospital staff	Information system	
g. Analyse blood results	Hospital	Nurse	Blood results	
h. Take observations	Hospital	Enrolled nurse	Thermometer, blood pressure meter, etc	
i. Couch made available	Treatment ward	Previous Patient	Couch	
j. Patient is in ward	Chemo Ward	Patient	Transport to hospital	

Table 1: Actions and their context

Multi-scale nature of actions

Actions are multi-scale in nature. This means that both actions and the action context can be specified at different levels of detail or grain size. Another way of saying this is that an action can be expanded into a set of lower level actions that occur in valid particularisations of the context of the higher action. For example, compare the following descriptions of the same action from Table 1:

> 'Gave a blood test'

> Nurse applied the tourniquet to the patient's arm, spoke some words of reassurance to the patient, and inserted a syringe into a vein in the patient's arm. He raised the plunger of the syringe, withdrew it from the patient's arm and transferred the blood into two vials which he then labelled.

Johansson (1989) shows that actions have the peculiar trait of being 'temporally inclusive'. Roughly speaking, this means that each action can only be instantiated in time if those other actions that make up the action at a smaller grain size are instantiated within the duration of this action. For example, the duration of the action in which a blood test was given includes the duration of applying the tourniquet and the duration of inserting the syringe into the vein and withdrawing it full of blood. We suggest that this is a particular case of the more general case of the contextual inclusiveness of actions. For example, each action can only be instantiated in space if other actions (those that make up the action at a smaller grain size) are instantiated within the space of this action. This situational inclusiveness means that an actor is always simultaneously engaged in actions at all grain sizes. While inserting a syringe into a vein in the patient's arm, the Nurse is simultaneously taking a blood sample and giving a blood test.

Action abstraction hierarchy

We can understand this contextually inclusive relationship between actions of different grain size (in this case, inserting a syringe into a vein, taking a blood sample and giving a blood test) using Johansson's (1989) notion of an action abstraction hierarchy (here the term 'abstract' refers to abstraction away from particularities rather than meaning less 'real').

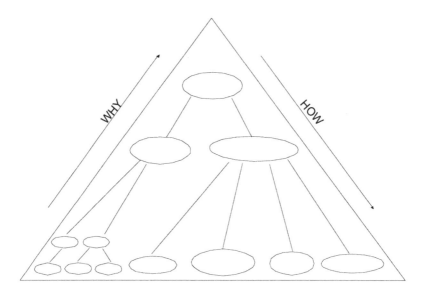

Figure 1: Action abstraction hierarchy: conceptual diagram of a system of actions.

The triangle in Figure 1 represents an action abstraction hierarchy in an action system, with the ellipses representing actions. Each action in the hierarchy refers to both the purpose and performance of action. Each action that is above other actions connected to it is the purpose of the action(s) below it; that is, it is *why* these subordinate actions are conducted. The collection of actions connected below the action is an elaboration of how the action is performed. This means that for any particular action, asking *why* that action is conducted moves one *up* the action abstraction hierarchy to more abstract levels. Asking *how* that action is conducted moves one *down* the action abstraction hierarchy to more concrete levels. The lower you go down the action hierarchy, the more is specified about the action context (that is, details of actor, location, time and resources). In other words, the action becomes more situated in a specific practice. By the same process, the implementation details of the higher-level action become specified more precisely as a set of more detailed actions.

As the hierarchy is ascended, the goal aspects of actions are emphasised; the performative aspects are emphasised in descent. In principle, each high level action could be specified with more and more precision as we move down the action hierarchy while the very apex of the triangle can be thought of as the ultimate purpose of the actions contained in the triangle. The triangle represents the domain space of all combinations of actions, actors, locations, resources and timing that will achieve the goal at the apex of the triangle. Note that the action abstraction hierarchy is an analytic device and the representation of it in two-dimensional space is indicative only rather than a precise rendering.

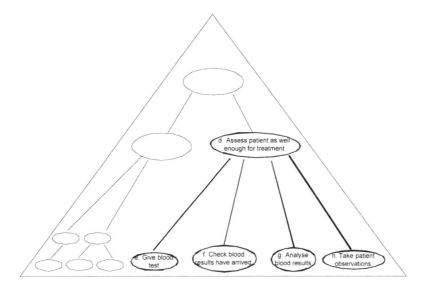

Figure 2: Action abstraction hierarchy: example from case study.

We can illustrate this abstraction/concretisation relationship between the actions listed in Table 1. For example, the actions, *e*. give blood test, *f.* check blood tests have arrived, *g*. analyse blood results and *h*. take patient observations, are all aspects of *how* the patient is assessed as well enough for treatment (action *d*). In turn, action *d* is an expression of *why* actions *e*, *f*, *g* and *h* are performed. This is depicted in Figure 2.

Action dependencies

An action dependency is another type of relation between two actions. It describes the case when one action is dependent on completion of another action for instantiation as part of an action system. Whereas the vertical relationship in Figure 1 was conceptualised as 'why-how', this horizontal dependency relationship can be conceptualised as 'depends on/condition for'.

Figure 3 shows in bold the action dependencies of some of the actions shown in Figure 2. Actions on the right are dependent on the completion of those actions on the left, to which they are joined, for instantiation in the action system. This means that the actions on the right occur later in time than those actions on their left, to which they are joined. Note that what we call an action dependency relates to the rules of practice and is not necessarily the same as logical dependency or feasibility. It is quite *feasible* that hospital staff could check whether blood results have arrived before a blood test has been given; these hospital staff may not know the timing of the blood test. However, for this action to be part of the action system being described, checking that blood results have arrived depends on the blood test being given. Similarly, there is no *a priori logical* reason why analysing the blood results is dependent on someone checking that blood results have arrived. It may seem more logical to bypass this step altogether, notifying the nurse who analyses the blood results of their arrival. The point is that, in the action system this diagram describes, analysis of blood results was dependent on hospital staff checking that blood test results had arrived.

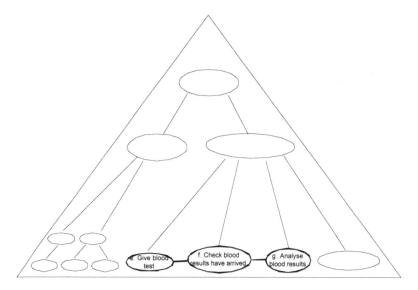

Figure 3: Action dependencies: some actions involved in administering chemotherapy.

Efficiency and effectiveness of actions

Having outlined our conception of actions, we now turn to what makes an action 'routine', relating routinisation of actions to increased efficiency and effectiveness. We start by defining what we mean by efficiency and effectiveness of actions.

Efficiency of actions

A common measure of efficiency is the minimisation of the expenditure of resources to achieve specified goals (Agerfalk and Eriksson, 2006). Bevan (1995) identifies three dimensions of efficiency. Although Bevan's work is about developing a measure for software quality, these dimensions are equally applicable to the characterisation of the efficiency of a system of actions. They are, firstly, temporal efficiency, or the minimisation of the expenditure of time; secondly, human efficiency, or the minimisation of mental or physical effort; and thirdly, economic efficiency, or the minimisation of financial cost.

One can measure the efficiency of the following three aspects of actions:

- What action is done?
- How is the action done?
- When is the action done?

Note that because each action is itself comprised of lower order actions, the answer to the question 'How is the action done?' gives answers to the question 'What action is done?' lower down the action abstraction hierarchy. For example, for the action 'Communicate account number', the answer to the question 'How is the action done?' may be 'Look up record and read out number over the phone'. This description of how, 'Read out number over the phone', is the answer to 'What action is done?' further down the action abstraction hierarchy.

Effectiveness of actions

A standard measure of the effectiveness of something is whether or not it leads to achievement of the intended goals. Two aspects of effectiveness mentioned in the international standard ISO 9241-11 are completeness and accuracy (Agerfalk and Eriksson, 2006).

> In the chemotherapy example four goals were identified, including administering chemotherapy and providing a high standard of patient care. High quality patient care included answering patient queries, and liaising with other health professionals involved in the patient's care, such as the dietician and social worker. Hence, in the chemotherapy example, completeness requires, not only that chemotherapy is efficiently administered, but also that nurses have time to attend to patients' other needs Accuracy entails correctly administering the correct dosage of the correct treatment to the right patient.

Routinising action

In order to act, an actor needs to select what to do next, how to do it, and when to do it. Another way of saying this is that in order to perform an action, an actor needs to know that action is feasible in the world (i.e. that they have the authority and skills to perform that action at the time, in the space, and with the resources at hand). The actor also needs to know that the action is possible now (i.e. that the action dependencies have been satisfied).

Routine action is characterised by the removal of discretion in the conduct of an action in one or more of the following aspects: *what* action is done, *when* the action is done and *how* the action is done. This is, however, removal of discretion at a meaningful grain size rather than the complete removal of discretion. Given a small enough grain size, there will always be some discretion in what, when and how an actor does something. For example, even if a doctor has to physically sign a chemotherapy order in order to authorise it, he or she has discretion over what sort of pen is used, how the pen is held, the exact form of the signature, and so on.

In later examples, we show how routinising action can improve the effectiveness and efficiency (economic, human and/or temporal) of action. Although temporal and human efficiency are related to economic efficiency, since time and people cost money, they are important aspects in their own right. Economic efficiency has always been an important driver of conventional information system design, and the importance of temporal efficiency is starting to be recognised (e.g. in JIT systems). However, the importance of human efficiency is often overlooked in conventional information systems. In situated analysis and design, we give explicit recognition to the cost of wasted human effort, including the human cost of unnecessary actions such as searching for information or resources.

Temporal efficiency is required for effectiveness in time-constrained environments; for example, a ward that has to administer chemotherapy to all patients during operating hours. Effectiveness is also increased by structuring the organisational and physical environment to limit the possibility for human error; that is, to avoid incorrect (and, in this case, possibly dangerous) actions.

A situated approach to enabling routine action with information

Conventional information systems provide information to actors through updating representations of states of the world. (Weber, 1997) As we have argued elsewhere (Johnston et al., 2005), this is because conventional information systems are based on the assumptions of a deliberative theory of action; that is, that an actor creates a mental model of the state of the world before acting. The conventional information system supplies information about the state of the world to inform the actor's mental model. The situated approach is based on our insights that information about the action context and the action dependencies are both necessary and sufficient for the actor to act routinely. Situated systems also use a form of representation to provide information to the actor but in their case it is the possibility for action that is represented in order to inform the actor about satisfaction of the action dependencies. However, whereas representation is the 'essence' of conventional information systems (Weber, 1997), situated systems enable routine action through manipulating the action possibility space to ensure that the action context is appropriate to the required action.

Signals: representing the possibility for action

We have shown that in an action abstraction hierarchy, the successful execution of an action is dependent upon the completion of the action or actions on which it is dependent. This means that in order to act, actors need to know that the actions on which their intended action is dependent have been successfully completed. Visual and/or aural information can indicate to the actor when this is so by representing the completion or result of the prerequisite action(s) or, more generally, by representing the possibility of the next action. For example, a green light may signal to an actor that they can proceed with an action.

Manipulating the action possibility space

We have discussed how the specifics of the action context mean that particular actions are constrained or enabled, depending on the affordances of the environment in which the particular time, place, actor and resources are located. Changing the affordances of the environment, through changing the physical, organisational, or temporal structures, can increase efficiency and can provide situated information to actors about what to do next and how to do it. It can also increase effectiveness by making incorrect and possibly dangerous actions impossible to perform.

For example, with regard to organisational structure, assigning a particular role to a particular class of actor circumscribes the actions available in a particular action context. In the workplace, this means that employees know that only certain types of employee can do certain things. It can also cause bottlenecks if the class of actor required to conduct a particular action is a scarce resource. Separating tasks into different time blocks is a way of structuring the temporal environment. This circumscribes the types of actions available in that time block and may increase human efficiency (Bevan, 1995) through reducing cognitive effort.

Parsimonious systems

The two approaches of representing the possibility of action, and manipulating the action possibility space, can be combined to yield lightweight information systems. For example, performing a network backup may require that all users have logged off but it is inefficient for the IT technician to have to make sure that each user has logged off. Instead, a temporal structure is imposed: users are told that they need to have logged off by 6pm. The clock striking six represents completion of logging off by all users. This is a signal to the IT technician that the backup can be performed.

Hence, structures in the environment such as particular divisions of labour, physical layout, provision of tools, and timetables can enable and constrain particular actions as well as provide situated information to actors about what to do next and when and how to do it. The signals can be quite simple, even binary, and can be conveyed by the mere presence or absence of a token (icon, card, tone, light) in the environment.

We suggest that these situated systems are more compatible than conventional information systems with the human efficiency requirements of time-constrained environments. Simplifying the environment can reduce an actor's cognitive load as well as the physical effort of searching for information. As well as being parsimonious, we suggest that these systems are more reliable than conventional systems since the potential for human error is reduced.

A methodology for situated analysis and design

We have explained how restructuring the environment and providing situated information to actors can increase efficiency and effectiveness by enabling routine conduct of actions. Now we show how these insights can be combined to produce a new kind of information system analysis and design methodology. This methodology aims to increase efficiency and effectiveness through supporting routine action; in particular, by reducing wasted human effort in search of information.

The domain of the situated analysis and design methodology

What actions can be routinised?

Not all actions systems can be routinised in order to improve efficiency and effectiveness. It is a separate project to define exactly what the necessary conditions are, but basically we need to be able to describe the action dependencies. For example, it would not be possible to design a system of routinised actions to cure patients of cancer. This is because we do not know what set of actions will reliably cure patients of cancer. In other words, we cannot describe the action dependencies that will lead to a patient being cured of cancer.

What actions should be routinised?

Whether or not an action should be routinised is not evident from the description of the action, any more than whether or not an action is useful is evident from the description of the action. For example, even as apparently creative an activity as writing a song can be routinised through use of a template and formulas; indeed, many popular 'hits' have been written this way. Similarly, lecture preparation can be approached either as a routine or as a creative activity.

While the purpose of routinising an action is to increase efficiency or effectiveness or both, a good system takes account of more than this. The ISO standard criteria for usability of *products* (ISO 9241-11) are the effectiveness, efficiency and satisfaction with which users can achieve their goals. We will apply these criteria to the quality of *systems*, replacing the notion of 'user' of a system with that of 'actor' in the system. This means that, although the purpose of routinising an action is to increase efficiency or effectiveness, this needs to be weighed up against the effects on actor satisfaction. Returning to the previous examples, there are writers who do not want to approach song writing in a formulaic way. Similarly, there are lecturers who prefer to have complete discretion over how they prepare and present a lecture, perhaps even eschewing established conventions.

In any organisation, choosing which actions are to be routinised is a matter of negotiation between stakeholders, rather than being evident *a priori*. The issues at stake in deciding whether to routinise something are efficiency, effectiveness and actor satisfaction. Actors who gain satisfaction from relying on their professional skill and judgement to carry out particular actions may not wish to see these actions routinised. Which actions should be routinised also depends upon the specifics of the workplace. If routinisation does not significantly improve the efficiency or effectiveness of the action, then there is no reason to introduce a routine system simply for the sake of it. On the other hand, routinisation has the potential to greatly improve efficiency and effectiveness, particularly through reducing actions such as unnecessary searches for information.

Applying the situated analysis and design methodology

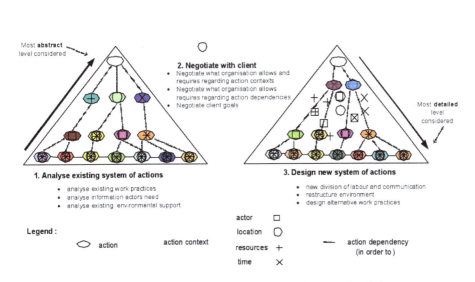

Figure 4: Applying the situated analysis and design methodology.

In this section, the principles of the methodology are outlined and illustrated using examples from the case study. Figure 4 is a conceptual depiction of the situated analysis and design methodology. As before, conceptually, each triangle represents a particular system of actions designed to achieve the goal(s) near the apex. The three stages in the methodology (represented as the triangles in Figure 4) are elaborated in the following sections.

Analysing the existing system of actions

Analysis involves both description and evaluation. The existing system of actions is described in order to identify what is currently being achieved; at the same time, the efficiency and effectiveness of the existing system of actions is evaluated. There are three conceptually distinct aspects to the analysis of the existing system of actions: analysis of existing work practices, analysis of information actors' needs, and analysis of existing environmental support. In practice, these analyses may occur concurrently.

Analysing existing work practices

In principle, and as discussed above, each action could be specified with more and more precision as we move down the action hierarchy. In actual analysis we need only go down to the level of detail that is natural and makes sense to actors when describing what they do. Of course, the situated information system is only concerned with providing information about non-discretionary action. Those actions that are not to be routinised (because, for example, they depend on an individual's judgement and skill) are treated as black boxes in the analysis.

A variety of tools to describe action systems already exist (e.g. Peterson, 1981) and the choice of tool is not important to the methodology. Our emphasis is not on modelling tools but on conceptualising the processes of changing the existing system.

The basic principle is that existing work practices need to be analysed in terms of actions and their context; that is, what happens, when and where, who does it, and with what (see, for example, Table 1). These actions also need to be described in terms of their action dependencies (see, for example, Figure 3) and the purpose of each action needs to be established (see, for example, Figure 2). This last aspect goes beyond simple notions of modelling processes. It involves ascending the action abstraction hierarchy (asking 'why' questions) in order to understand, in increasingly general terms, the purpose of each documented action. At the same time, the particulars of the action context are also increasingly generalised.

Describing the action system in this way makes it possible to identify whether the sequence of actions (what), and the division of labour, use of resources, timing, and location (how) is efficient in terms of human effort and time. The analysis assists in identifying whether any actions are redundant and whether there is a need for better coordination (i.e. coordination of actions by particular people or things) as well as making explicit exactly where any delays are occurring.

The following example from the case study demonstrates an inefficient division of labour that resulted in a bottleneck.

Case study example 1: inefficient division of labour

Before the pharmacy could prepare the treatment for a patient (individualised dosage of a drug), the patient's blood results needed to be checked and marked as OK on the chemotherapy orders. The liaison nurse had the job of checking the blood results and obtaining the chemotherapy orders for all patients to be treated for that day. However, the nature of the liaison nurse's job (liaising with doctors, nurses, patients, their carers, the pharmacist and other hospital staff) meant that she was constantly interrupted. This, in combination with the sheer numbers of patients to be checked meant that the liaison nurse tended to be a bottleneck in the process of chemotherapy preparation.

Analysing information actors' needs

In a system of actions, in order to act at the right time, actors need to know that the prior actions on which their action is dependent have been successfully completed. Analysis of the action dependencies reveals what information actors need in order to act. Both the human and temporal efficiency of actions can be improved by minimising the effort spent by actors looking for information; either information that required actions have been completed or information regarding which action is next. We return to the case study for an example where the existing system did not provide actors (nurses) with the information they needed at the time and place where they needed it.

Case study example 2: information nurses need in order to administer chemotherapy to a patient

In order to administer chemotherapy to a particular patient, nurses needed to know whether the patient had arrived, whether a treatment couch was available, whether the chemotherapy treatment had been prepared, and whether the patient was well enough for chemotherapy treatment. However, nurses were required to be physically by the side of the patients they were currently treating. While it was immediately (visually) obvious to a nurse when a treatment couch became available, information about whether the other conditions were met could only be obtained by leaving the side of the patient. A disproportionate amount of time was spent seeking this information, at the expense of attending to patient needs. The information sources that nurses used to find this information included the hospital mainframe computer system, inspection of the treatment table (where the chemotherapy treatments were brought after being made up in the pharmacy), visiting the waiting room and talking to the ward clerk. This meant that, while treating patients, nurses had to regularly walk into the treatment preparation room to check the treatment tables, walk to a computer to check the hospital computer system, or walk to the reception area to ask about particular patients, or to page a doctor.

A further difficulty was that a patient might arrive just after a nurse had looked up the mainframe computer system, the treatment might arrive just after a nurse checked which treatments were in the treatment preparation room, or the blood results might become available just after a nurse had looked up the relevant computer system. Each of these time lags between the condition being satisfied and the nurse knowing that the condition was satisfied, contributed to an avoidable delay in administering the treatment and placed severe limits on the quality of patient care delivered. That is, it hampered effectiveness. As well as being spatially remote, the necessary information was not accessed in a timely way.

Analysing existing environmental support

In analysing the action context, to what extent existing environmental structures (physical, organisational and temporal) support action becomes evident. Paying attention to the affordances offered by existing environmental structures makes apparent whether efficiency could be improved through, say, altering existing roles or changing the spatial layout of the workplace or the temporal structure of the day. What follows is an example of how the physical location of a resource (the chemotherapy order) was not supporting routine action.

Case study example 3: missing chemotherapy orders

A patient's treatment and dosage was hand-written on a paper form called the 'chemotherapy order'. These chemotherapy orders were essential as an authorisation for treatment. They were kept in a sleeve inside the patient's paper history file, which frequently ran to several volumes. In theory, these histories for chemotherapy patients were meant to be brought up to the Chemotherapy Unit at least a day before the patients' chemotherapy treatments. In practice, some of these histories could not be located. If a patient had a downstairs clinic appointment before their chemotherapy appointment, the history (containing the chemotherapy orders) would be downstairs in the clinic and the patient would be expected to carry their history up to the Chemotherapy Unit after their clinic. On almost every day of the field research, there was at least one history that could not be located or chemotherapy orders were otherwise missing. Finding missing chemotherapy orders was a frustrating task involving much running around by clerks and nurses.

Negotiations regarding the new system of actions

In traditional information systems analysis and design, a requirements analysis is conducted to determine client needs in situated analysis and design, a negotiation phase occurs based around aspects of action; broadly, what is to be done and how it is to be done.

Negotiation of the action context and action dependencies

Organisational constraints are those constraints to do with the specification of the action context and action dependencies; specifically, what is allowed and what is required by the organisation. Note that the constraints we refer to here are not the same as the structures in the environment that constrain or enable particular actions. Here we are referring to what is allowed and what is required by the organisation. What is allowed by the organisation is basically the set of actors, locations, times and resources that can be associated with action. A subset of these is what is required by the organisation. What is required by the organisation may be a reflection of the organisation's preferred way of operating or may be a response to outside pressures such as legislation. The organisation may have requirements regarding the action context. For example, the organisation may require that certain actions be conducted by a particular type of actor (e.g. a doctor), a particular instance of a type of actor (e.g. Doctor Jones), in a particular type of location (e.g. a hospital ward), a particular instance of a type of location (e.g. the chemotherapy ward), using a particular type of resource (e.g. expandable patient record), or a particular resource (e.g. written patient record), or any combination of these. The time may also be constrained. For example, chemotherapy treatments that take more than four hours to administer may have to be begun in the morning.

The organisation may also have some requirements regarding action dependencies; in other words, regarding the order of actions. For example, the organisation may require that treatment that has a short expiry is not prepared until chemotherapy orders are approved.

Nevertheless, some of what the organisation allows or requires will be negotiable, especially as some of the perceived requirements will simply be the way things have always been done. It is only in the negotiation phase that the analyst can identify which constraints are 'hard' (Johnston et al., 2005); that is, those that the organisation cannot or is unwilling to see changed. These 'hard' constraints are those constraints that necessarily govern aspects of any redesigned system; they are not negotiable with the client.

Negotiation of client goals

The client's goals for the system can be viewed as another type of 'hard' organisational constraint. Describing the existing system of actions included establishing the purpose of existing work practices. In other words, in terms of Figure 4, it involved moving up the action abstraction hierarchy. We make a pragmatic decision to move up the action abstraction hierarchy until we reach those actions the client considers are the goals. As well as describing the purpose of what is done, these higher-order actions become constraints on what is done.

For example, through analysing the system of actions in the chemotherapy ward we identified four main goals in its day to day work. These are delivering chemotherapy treatment, providing a high level of patient-centred care, participating in clinical trials and nursing research and fulfilling the organisational administrative requirements. Each of these is a higher-order action performed by the client's organisation and is recognised by them as a goal. However, these are not necessarily the highest (most abstract) actions. We could use 'why' questions to move even further up the abstraction hierarchy. For example, chemotherapy is administered in order to treat a patient's cancer, in order to improve their health and so on. However, administering chemotherapy was a hard constraint in how the organisation treated a patient's cancer. This meant that there was no scope for us as analysts to consider other treatments such as, for example, alternative therapies.

As Figure 4 indicates, in the design phase, all organisational constraints that have been identified through negotiations as 'hard' are taken as given aspects of the new system of actions.

Designing a new system of actions

Designing a new system of actions involves taking account of hard constraints and making use of the action possibilities of the mix of possible actors, locations, resources and temporal ordering. In terms of Figure 4 this means moving down from the agreed goals, through the fixed context and dependency constraints and designing a new set of actions, dependencies and contexts that satisfy the agreed goals. The action possibility space is also deliberately manipulated to constrain and enable particular actions. The purpose is to increase efficiency and effectiveness through routinisation of action. Working within the hard constraints, use may be made of the affordances offered by existing environmental structures or the existing environmental structure may be changed in order to routinise the action.

Providing information to support routine action is also of key importance. Information is conveyed through representation of the possibility for action. This information assists actors not only to know *what* to do next but also gives them the information they need that allows them to *do* the next thing. In designing a new system, the action system need only be specified with enough precision so that actors know what they have to do.

The following example from the case study describes how a change in organisational structure and representation of the possibility for action supported routinisation of action.

Case study example 4: redesigning a new system of actions

The proposed new system of actions included the following three solutions to problems identified in the analysis stage.

Change in organisational structure

As described earlier, analysis of existing work practices revealed that the liaison nurse tended to be a bottleneck in the process of chemotherapy preparation. A change in the organisational structure (division of labour) was recommended. Rather than having the liaison nurse check the blood results and obtain the chemotherapy orders for all patients, each treatment nurse was to check blood results and obtain chemotherapy orders for their own patients. This patient information was then in manageable parcels for each treatment nurse and it made sense that the treatment nurses obtain the information given that they were the ones who needed to use it. The shifting of more responsibility for patients to the treatment nurses was also welcomed by both the liaison nurse and the treatment nurses.

Representation of the possibility for action

Earlier in this section we described the wasted effort and delays caused by nurses having to seek out the information about whether the prerequisites for treating another patient were satisfied. The proposed solution was that Nurses carry devices to alert them in real time about the satisfaction of the prerequisites for patient treatment; that is when their patients arrive, when their patient's blood results arrive, and when the chemotherapy treatment is ready. In other words, the devices represented the possibility for action (the action of administering chemotherapy to a patient). Providing this information to nurses in the time and place in which they needed it, increased temporal and human efficiency.

Stabilisation of the physical environment (Hammond et al., 1995)

Again, earlier in this section, we described the wasted time and effort involved as clerks and nurses ran around trying to find missing chemotherapy orders. The proposed solution was that chemotherapy orders be taken out of the history files and stationed in DayWard. This greatly reduced the time spent searching for them.

Relation to existing literature

This section situates the approach taken in this paper in the relevant literature. Firstly, there are the theories of action that inspire the methodology. Accordingly, we summarise the relevant literature on action and the role of environmental structures.

Also relevant is the literature on other methodologies, with which situated analysis and design can be contrasted. We show that although situated analysis and design has some points of similarity with other ISAD methodologies, it is paradigmatically different from conventional methodologies, including business process reengineering. Situated analysis and design has more in common with less conventional methodologies such as soft systems methodology (SSM), Multiview, ETHICS, and cognitive work analysis. However, as the last part of this section shows, it is still quite a distinctive approach.

Theories that situate action in the environment

Our project draws theoretical inspiration from diverse areas of scholarly inquiry. The initial inspiration for a situated approach to information systems analysis and design came from Heidegger's existential phenomenology of being-in-the-world (Heidegger, 1961). Winograd and Flores (1986) explicitly drew on Heidegger to outline a new approach to design, as did Dreyfus (1999) in his critique of GOFAI (Good Old-Fashioned Artificial Intelligence). Both of these seminal works assisted in the conceptualising of an alternative kind of information system that did not require recourse to a representation of the world.

Although not necessarily using the term 'deliberative theory of action', the idea of situated action underpins work undertaken in artificial intelligence (Agre, 1997), robotics, (Brooks, 1991), distributed and situated cognition (Lave and Wenger, 1991; Hutchins, 1995; Clancey, 1997), animal behaviour (Hendriks-Jansen, 1996), and situated action itself (Suchman, 1987). All of this work is based around the idea that, in routine action, actors respond directly to structures in the environment to achieve their purpose. Within ecological psychology, the concept of affordance (Gibson, 1979; Heft, 2001) has provided a fuller account of the role of the environment in action, and more precisely, the role of environmental structures.

Studies of manual systems have also inspired the thinking behind the design of situated systems. For example, Mackay et al. (1998) describe how air traffic controllers use paper flight strips for landing planes. In this case the air traffic controllers use the flight strips to represent the possibility for action. Kanban is another type of manual system widely used in the automotive industry for the activity of replenishing parts for production (Schonberger 1987; Womack et al., 1990). In this case, Kanbans act as signals, with the meaning of the Kanban depending on its physical location. See Lederman and Johnston (2007) for other examples of manual systems that use signals and manipulation of the action possibility space to support routine action.

Paradigmatic differences with structured ISAD methodologies

Like situated analysis and design, business process reengineering (Hammer, 1990) pays attention to performance measures other than direct cost saving. In some ways, the situated analysis and design approach subsumes the approach of business process reengineering in providing a more general conceptual framework to identify opportunities to improve the efficiency and effectiveness of action.

However, business processes are not the same as actions. Data flows and processes do not refer directly to actions but rather the information consequences of actions. The concepts 'data flow' and 'process' are used in IS to refer to a whole cluster of ideas in the conventional approach, as articulated by (Weber, 1997), which are paradigmatically different to the situated approach. These ideas differ from the situated approach in two ways; the underlying theory of action and the underlying ontology.

The action-centred approach assumes that routine actions are a more or less direct response to the situations in which they occur. As argued previously, conventional approaches to ISAD are informed by a different theory of action that assumes that humans act after deliberation upon a mental model of the world (Johnston and Milton, 2001). In that tradition, processes are conceived in informational terms and what are essentially movements of data are taken to stand for the actions that create them. This is how processes are depicted in data flow diagrams (DFDs), for example. Situated analysis and design attempts to represent action directly whereas conventional descriptions of dataflow and processes are at one remove from the actual action.

Conventional tools such as DFDs are organised on the assumption that for every activity or action there is some sort of data flow. In other words, only activities that involve data flows really need to be modelled. However, in the situated approach, actions that do not involve data flows may still be important in describing what happens. For example, it was described in Case Study example 2 how nurses wasted a lot of time and effort checking whether blood results and the chemotherapy treatment had arrived. It was critical to the situated analysis and redesign to take account of these actions of checking, even though no data flows were involved. A conventional tool such as a DFD or process view would most likely model the presence or absence of the data (the data being the information consequence of blood results or chemotherapy treatment arriving). However, conventional tools may not capture the need to eliminate the effort of checking that the data had arrived.

With regard to the underlying ontology, according to the conventional view processes are manifest in data flows that convert inputs to outputs (Melao and Pidd, 2000). These data flows enable transition from one state of the world to another, with the aim being attainment of a particular goal state. According to the situated (and action-centred) view presented here, goals are the purpose of actions, and different actions can be grouped (and arranged in an action abstraction hierarchy) if they have a common purpose.

Relationship with other ISAD methodologies

Checkland and Holwell (1998) have described soft systems methodology (SSM) as 'a set of principles of method rather than a precise method'. Situated analysis and design also fits this description and shares, with SSM, a broad concern with providing information in support of action. However, whereas situated analysis and design is concerned with routine action, SSM is concerned with ill-defined problem situations. Although the terms appear similar, the 'activity systems' of SSM are quite different from the 'action systems' of Situated Analysis and Design. The activity systems of SSM are conceptual and may bear little relation to actions in the real world (Checkland and Holwell, 1998). In contrast, the action systems of situated analysis and design are descriptive of the actions actually undertaken in the organisation.

The ETHICS methodology of Mumford (1983) entails a participatory design approach to systems analysis and design, with particular attention paid to job satisfaction. Situated analysis and design shares, with ETHICS, an appreciation of the importance of implementation issues as well as the view that technology must be appropriate to the organisation. The two approaches are not incompatible and it is conceivable that situated analysis and design could be conducted within an ETHICS framework. While ETHICS focuses on the organisational processes involved in systems analysis and design, situated analysis and design focuses on the analytic processes. In order to conduct situated analysis and design using an ETHICS framework the former would be conducted using the organisational process of participatory design. Job satisfaction would be negotiated as a 'hard' constraint.

Like situated analysis and design, Multiview (Avison and Fitzgerald, 2002) also explicitly includes attention to implementation issues and the relationship between the social and the technical. However, Multiview presupposes a computerised solution. Moreover, the analysis techniques used in Multiview (i.e. both Multiview 1 and Multiview 2) are quite different from the situated analysis and design focus on situated action. Multiview 1 analyses information needs using conventional data flow and entity models while Multiview 2 uses Object-Oriented analysis.

Finally, in some respects the abstraction action hierarchy used in situated analysis and design is similar to that advocated in cognitive work analysis (Rasmussen and Pejtersen, 1995; Vicente, 1999). Both involve abstraction away from the details of existing work practices to goals in order to facilitate redesign. However, situated analysis and design is more explicitly centred around action and the intention of situated analysis and design is to support routine operational activity whereas cognitive, decision-making activity is typically the focus of cognitive work analysis. Cognitive work analysis involves reengineering the physical surroundings; no consideration is given to altering the organisational or temporal environment.

Conclusions

The purpose of this paper has been to outline what a methodology for analysing and designing information systems would look like if it were focused on action. We have identified the following three important aspects of actions and these form the basis of our intervention.

- Actions are multi-scale in nature.
- Actions are always performed in an action context; that is, actions are conducted by an actor in time and space, making use of resources.
- Actions are dependent on the execution of other actions for instantiation as part of an action system.

In order to act, an actor needs to know what to do next, how to do it and when to do it. Another way of saying this is that in order to perform an action, an actor needs to know that the action is feasible in the world (i.e. that they can perform that action at the time, in the space, and with resources at hand). The actor also needs to know that the action is possible now (i.e. that the action dependencies have been satisfied). Hence, information about the action context and the action dependencies are both necessary and sufficient for the actor to act routinely.

Our approach to information system design makes use of these two points of leverage. We manipulate the action possibility space to ensure that the action context is appropriate to the required action. By representing the possibility for action, we inform the actor about satisfaction of the action dependencies and signal that they can act now. Our approach leads to a different view of what information is and how best to support action. This points the way to future work on a precise definition of what constitutes an information system.

We suggest that the methodology will be useful to organisations by allowing them to increase efficiency and effectiveness, through supporting routine action, which is generally marginalised in conventional IS methodologies. Unlike conventional information systems, as well as increasing temporal efficiency, situated systems also aim to increase human efficiency; in particular, to reduce wasted human effort expended in search of information. They can also increase effectiveness by making incorrect and possibly dangerous actions impossible to perform. Through the designs we have produced in the project case studies (Johnston et al., 2005; Waller et al., 2006), we have already provided evidence that systems designed using the situated analysis and design methodology are likely to be more lightweight than those designed using conventional methodologies.

As well as being of practical significance, the methodology is theoretically important as it articulates for the first time what many experienced practitioners know tacitly: it is necessary to be sensitive to the importance of action. In addition, the situated analysis and design methodology provides theoretical support for the practical application of ubiquitous computing and this is something that we will be investigating further in future research.

References

Agerfalk, P. and Eriksson, O. 2006, 'Socio-instrumental usability: IT is all about social action', Journal of Information Techology, vol. 21, pp. 24-39.

Agre, P. 1997, *Computation and Human Experience*, Cambridge, Cambridge University Press.

Avison, D. and Fitzgerald, G. 2002, *Information Systems Development: Methodologies, Techniques and Tools*, 3rd ed., England, McGraw Hill.

Bevan, N. 1995, 'Measuring usablity as quality of use', Software Quality Journal, vol. 4, no. 2, pp. 115-50.

Brooks, R. A. 1991, 'Intelligence without representation', Artifical Intelligence, vol. 47, no. 1-3, pp. 139-59.

Checkland, P. and Holwell, S. 1998, *Information, Systems, and Information Systems'*, Chichester, John Wiley and Sons.

Clancey, W. J. 1997, *Situated Cognition: On Human Knowledge and Computer Representation*, Cambridge, Cambridge University Press.

Dreyfus, H. L. 1999, *What Computers Still Can't Do: A Critique of Artificial Reason*, Cambridge, MIT Press.

Gibson, J. 1979, *The Ecological Approach to Visual Perception*, Boston, Houghton Mifflin Company.

Hammer, M. 1990, 'Reengineering Work: Don't Automate, Obliterate', Harvard Business Review, vol. 68, no. 4, pp. 104-12.

Hammond, K., Converse, T. and Grass, J. 1995, 'The stabilisation of environments', Artificial Intelligence, vol. 72, pp. 305-27.

Heft, H. 2001, *Ecological Psychology in Context: James Gibson, Roger Barker, and the legacy of William James's Radical Empiricism*, New Jersey, Lawrence Erlbaum Associates.

Heidegger, M. 1961, *Being and Time*, New York, Harper and Row.

Hendriks-Jansen, H. 1996, *Catching OurselvesiIn the Act: Situated Activity, Interactive Emergence, Evolution, and Human Thought*. Cambridge, The MIT Press.

Hutchins, E. 1995, *Cognition in the Wild*, Cambridge, The MIT Press.

Johansson, I. 1989, *Ontological Investigations: An Inquiry into the Categories of Nature, Man and Society*, London, Routledge.

Johnston, R. B. and Milton, S. K. 2001, 'The significance of intentionality for the ontological evaluation of information systems', Proceedings of the 7th Americas Conference on Information Systems, Boston, MA, pp. 1980-6.

Johnston, R. B. and Milton, S. K. 2002, 'The foundational role for theories of agency in understanding of information systems design', Australian Journal of Information Systems, vol. 9, Special Issue, pp. 40-9.

Johnston, R. B., Waller, V. and Milton, S. K. 2005, 'Situated information systems: Supporting routine activity in organisations', International Journal of Business Information Systems, vol. 1, no. 1/2, pp. 53-82.

Lave, J. and Wenger, E. 1991, *Situated Learning: Legitimate Peripheral Participation*, Cambridge, Cambridge University Press.

Lederman, R. and Johnston, R. B. 2007, 'Are routine manual systems genuine information systems?', in Hart, D. and Gregor, S. (eds), *Information Systems Foundations: Theory, Representation and Reality*, ANU E-Press.

Mackay, W. E., Fayard, A.-L., Frobert, L. and Medini, L. 1998, 'Reinventing the familiar: Exploring and augmented reality design space for Air Traffic Control', Proceedings of Computer Human Interation (CHI'98), Los Angeles, CA.

Melao, N. and Pidd, M. 2000, 'A conceptual framework for understanding business processes and business process modelling', Information Systems Journal, vol. 10, pp. 105-29.

Milton, S. K., Johnston, R. B., Lederman, R. M. and Waller, V. 2005, 'Developing a methodology for designing routine information systems based on the situational theory of action', Proceedings of the13th European Conference on Information Systems, Regensburg, Germany.

Mumford, E. 1983, *Designing Human Systems for New Technology: The ETHICS Method*, Manchester, Manchester Business School.

Peterson, J. L. 1981, *Petri Net Theory and the Modelling of Systems*, New Jersey, Prentice-Hall.

Rasmussen, J. and Pejtersen, A. 1995, 'Virtual ecology of work', in Flasch, J., Hancock, P., Caird, J. and Vicente, K. (eds), *Global Perspectives on the Ecology of Human-Machine Systems*. Hillsdale, NJ, Lawrence Erlbaum Associates, pp. 121—156.

Schonberger, R. J. 1987, 'The Kanban System', in Voss, C. A. (ed.), *Just-in-Time Manufacture*, IFS (Publications), pp. 59—72.

Searle, J. 1983, *Intentionality*, Cambridge, Cambridge University Press.

Suchman, L. A. 1987, *Plans and Situated Actions: The Problem of Human Machine Communication*, Cambridge, Cambridge University Press.

Vicente, K. 1999, *Cognitive Work Analysis: Toward Safe, Productive, and Healthy Computer-Based Work*, Mahwah, N.J, Lawrence Erlbaum Associates.

Waller, V., Johnston, R. B. and Milton, S. K. 2006, 'Development of a Situated Information Systems Analysis and Design methodology: a health care setting', Proceedings of the European and Mediterranean Conference on Information Systems, Alicante, Spain.

Weber, R. 1997, *Ontological Foundations of Information Systems*, Melbourne, Coopers and Lybrand.

Winograd, T. and Flores, F. 1986, *Understanding Computers and Cognition: A New Foundation for Design*, New Jersey, Ablex Publishing Corporation.

Womack, J. P., Jones, D. T. and Roos, D. 1990, *The Machine That Changed the World*, New York, Rawson Associates.

Emergent Conversational Technologies That Are Democratising Information Systems in Organisations: The Case of the Corporate Wiki

Helen Hasan
Information Systems, University of Wollongong
email: hasan@uow.edu.au

Charmaine C Pfaff
Central Queensland University, (CMS), Sydney International Campus
email: c.pfaff@syd.cqu.edu.au

Abstract

Conversational technologies such as discussion forums, chatrooms, weblogs (or blogs) and wikis have transformed the way information is exchanged and disseminated in civil society but their take up in corporations is slow. We contend that one reason for this is the way they democratise organisational information and knowledge, with consequential changes to the distribution of power, rights and obligations. In this paper, we discuss the opportunities and the threats associated with the corporate Wiki and the implications of this for the future of the field of information systems.

Introduction

Together with Personal Digital Assistants (PDAs) and mobile telephones, conversational technologies such as email, discussion forums, chatrooms, weblogs and wikis have been readily adopted in civil society and are transforming the way many of us access information. We now conduct transactions and connect with others anywhere and any time in our everyday lives. However, these transforming systems are often treated with suspicion by the organisations in which we work (frequently with outmoded ICT tools and limitations imposed by management on our social uses of email, telephone and the Internet in general). It is proposed in this paper that in the future the information systems (IS) discipline should pay increased attention to the adoption and impact of open cooperative technologies in the workplace. Since the 1970s, IS has endeavoured to take a distinctive scientific approach to representing the data and processes of large formal organisations in the design of computer based systems but we believe that IS cannot afford to get mired in issues to do with 20th century technology and must move on to a world where technology increasingly empowers the individual, with the potential consequence of democratising organisational information and knowledge.

Conversational technologies can be seen as tools to support work units and the individual knowledge worker. For this new breed of employee, it is as much part of their job to seek out, share and create knowledge as it is to perform work tasks. They need the skills, capabilities and authority, as well as Information and Communications Technology (ICT) support, to do this, thereby providing the firm with innovation and creativity. While this represents an obvious avenue for organisations to try to gain or increase their advantage over competitors, it also poses a challenge where employers and managers may have to relinquish some control in providing knowledge workers with appropriate resources, incentives and rewards. This is also a challenge for research and practice in the field of IS, which can no longer employ traditional analysis and design approaches to the new socio-technical organisational systems where knowledge workers may choose to use applications such as weblogs and wikis and develop them as end-users. This may be perceived as a threat to shift the core focus of IS research and practice but may rather be an opportunity for IS to re-invent itself to be more relevant for the 21st century.

In order to make this argument, we examine the issues, challenges and potential benefits arising from the prospect of implementing wiki technologies in corporate or government settings. Four cases are presented in which a wiki is being adopted or at least considered as a means to enable broad participation in knowledge management in a formal work setting. The cases are chosen to showcase a variety of corporate wikis in different developmental stages. The first case study records a failed attempt at setting up a wiki in a conservative organisation whose business is acquiring and transferring knowledge. The second case study examines the setting up a wiki for professionals in a state-wide government health department. The third case study explores the use of a wiki by a national Standards organisation for knowledge collection and dissemination among small businesses and, lastly, an evaluation is made of an existing wiki in the research division of a large private manufacturing organisation. The potential benefits and challenges in each case are described, leading to a general discussion of the democratising effect of wiki technology in the hands of individuals and the need for organisations to strike a balance between control and trust. The challenges and opportunities of this technology for IS practitioners and researchers are discussed in the following paragraphs.

Conversational technologies

Background

Wagner and Bolloju (2005) portrayed the three technologies, discussion forums, wikis, and weblogs (or blogs) as conversational technologies. Conversational technologies facilitate processes in which knowledge creation and storage is carried out through a discussion forum where participants contribute to the discussion with questions and answers, or through a blog that is typified by a process of storytelling, or through a wiki using collaborative writing. Constructivist learning theorists (Vygotsky, 1978; Leidner and Jarvenpaa, 1995) explain that the process of expressing knowledge aids its creation, and conversations benefit the refinement of knowledge. Cheung et al. (2005) maintains that conversational knowledge management fulfils this purpose because conversations, for example questions and answers, become the source of relevant knowledge.

It is our contention that new and exciting issues of information processing and knowledge management arise as a result of these conversational technologies infiltrating organisations. They are becoming almost ubiquitous in some circles but are raising controversies in others. However, studies of these phenomena are only now beginning to appear in the literature. An informative study of online discussion groups was undertaken by Timbrell et al. (2005), drawing out the particular language and associated behaviour that has emerged in this arena, including things such as patterns of posting, the active core (about 30% of members), seeding of threads, self-imposed netiquette, moderation, lurking, etc. Such studies are made possible because these technologies leave a permanent and structured electronic record of the social phenomena being studied.

According to Semple (2006), blogs and wikis have dominated the scene because of their appeal to the wider community and their ability to disseminate knowledge. However, blogs are time indexed, set up by an individual, and tend to focus on the current topic. Comments and entries are usually made by one participant at a time. Holding a senior position as Head of Knowledge Management in the BBC, Semple introduced blogs and wikis into that previously conservative organisation to make the most of this wired-up world of work, and thereby learnt how businesses can prepare themselves for the challenges and the opportunities they represent. While he describes the obvious popularity of the General Manager's daily blog, it is the adoption of wikis for corporate knowledge management that is particularly compelling.

Issues of ownership and democratisation

Hart and Warne (2006), among others, argue that it is difficult to get different parties to share organisational data, information and knowledge. These authors propose that those who are reluctant or refuse to share data, information or knowledge with each other, can generally be identified with different sub-cultures within the organisation. Different value sets, beliefs, assumptions, norms of behaviour and so on, could be a source of power struggles, conflict and political activity concerning not only data, information and knowledge sharing but also in other areas of organisational activity. The culturally oriented view suggests that a lack of sharing of organisational data, information and knowledge is a behaviour that can be changed. People who are refusing to share can be encouraged or educated to see the benefits of sharing or the organisational culture changed. In contrast, the politically oriented view argues that sharing takes place only with those who want to share. Encouraging, educating or coercing sharing will not be successful, and can even be detrimental.

Traditionally, the channels of information have been controlled by those who have wealth or influence. The creation of the Internet has had a democratising effect on the availability and use of information. Many users who are active on the Internet are there because they are attracted to the equal access it allows, and its break from traditional media. Affordable e-commerce has provided an opportunity for individuals and small businesses to compete in the global market place, often more successfully than cumbersome multi-national companies. Democracy raises public awareness of issues such as openness, freedom of information and public accountability (Benkler, 2006).

The same democratising effect will be true of conversational technologies. A wiki represents the power of many and this power is distributed collectively to improve content quality. Each author is able to change the contributions of other authors, refining the quality of the knowledge asset.

A wiki can be a type of 'information commons' that is a common space where people can share experiences and have unanticipated, un-chosen exposures to the ideas of others. Sunstein (2006) argues that the on-line effort of joining together people with diverse talents and interests to achieve common goals might well provide the best path to infotopia. However, in order for that to happen, people must feel they have more to gain from coming together than from being independent. Scardamalia (2003) adds that symmetric knowledge advancement occurs when the participants in a network are able to advance their own knowledge-building agendas by helping other participants advance theirs.

The wiki phenomenon

A wiki is a web-based application that allows many participants to write collaboratively, where they can continue to add to or edit the content of documents and dynamically determine the relationships between sets of documents. Such documents can be anything supported by the Web, with hyperlinks to anywhere on the World Wide Web including text documents, images and video. This type of application is named after the Hawaiian 'wiki', meaning 'quick', 'fast', or 'to hasten' and which is symbolic of the quick changes to content enabled by the editing processes that characterise it (Leuf and Cunningham, 2005). A wiki is, therefore, a collection of interlinked HTML web pages and has cross-links between internal pages where each page can not only be easily edited but also a complete record of such changes can be kept. In addition, any changed page can be easily reverted to any of its previous states. A wiki can be accessed from any web browser and no other special tools are needed to create and edit existing pages.

A wiki can be said to be an evolving knowledge repository where users are encouraged to make additions by adding new documents or working on existing ones (Pfaff and Hasan, 2006). The wiki takes advantage of the collaborative efforts of all members of the organisation to create an effective library of knowledge. An organisation that wants to survive and grow in the global competitive marketplace needs to familiarise itself with 'organisational learning' (Argyris and Schön, 1996; Friedman et al., 2005) and how successful an organisation is at being able to acquire and deploy knowledge will have an important impact on its competitive advantage.

Wiki sites have been created using several development tools and languages. The original wiki, developed by Ward Cunningham in 1994, was written in HyperPerl. Many clones have since been written in other languages such as Python, Java, Smalltalk, Active Server Pages, Ruby, PHP and Visual Basic. Blake (2001) states that the open platform makes it versatile to create clones to support corporate or departmental intranets. Many public sites, such as wikispaces,[1] offer an area on their wiki that is either free (to the public) or available for a small annual fee if it is for private use.

The best known example of a wiki is the popular English language version of Wikipedia,[2] which was started in 2001 and now has nearly 900,000 articles. Wikipedias have been published in 200 languages and contain a total of more than three million articles. Contributions come from all over the world. It is estimated that 100,000 people have made contributions, which does not include the four million who have done editing work on the contributed articles. In fact, more people have visited Wikipedia than other popular sites such as the online New York Times and CNN.

As their uses have become more apparent, countless numbers of wikis have been created, mostly independent of formal organisations. A wiki provides an ideal collaboration environment that offers users the capability to co-create and co-evolve a knowledge repository. It therefore also offers corporations the option to consider adopting the wiki as a growing and living resource for knowledge

[1] www.wikispaces.com
[2] http://en.wikipedia.org

management. Central to the concept of a wiki is that a user does not need to have any technical (computing or Web-related) expertise to add, edit or delete a page. This means that even a novice user can contribute to the knowledge acquisition process in an organisation. A wiki allows sufficient flexibility for users to lend their own interpretation regarding a particular topic and it also avoids individual bias because the content is determined by all the users.

There are, however, social and legal issues that are militating against the easy uptake of wikis in corporations. If the wiki can legitimately be described as 'social software' (Swisher, 2004), then there are social factors that must undergo some changes before the wiki will be accepted as a way to improve an organisation's knowledge management. The informal network approach that is currently favoured in a wiki may make some companies believe that their data quality will be affected and that system errors will occur. However, a centralised and highly structured environment will make it difficult to adopt a 'community approach' towards knowledge acquisition. Knowledge management priorities are linked to organisational structure and, as Santoro and Gopalakrishnan (2000) argue, knowledge management priorities are affected by environmental structures.

A wiki is open to vandalism, as has been demonstrated in at least one well-known case. The Los Angeles Times experimented with a wiki editorial and invited readers to collaborate online to add facts or update information. This 'wikitorial' only lasted three days because a few readers had posted obscene photographs on the site. The newspaper had to put the website out of commission because they could not prevent future disruptions (Shepard, 2005).

There is no recognition of authorship in a wiki because pages can be freely written or edited by anybody. This goes against the innate need by workers for recognition, as well as a common belief that the source of contributions should be accurately reflected. The wiki software uses the 'contributors tag' for general name recognition of 'good' authors or editors. However, this might lead to disputes among the contributors that they have not contributed 'enough' to the article to be considered as one of the authors or editors.

There are also concerns about the quality of content that contributors make. As stated in Wikipedia (2006), it is the official policy of Wikipedia to adopt a 'neutral point of view' (NPOV) to prevent the infiltration of biased views by some authors. This is to appeal to the forbearance of the majority to be fair and conciliatory if there are conflicts in opinions. To maintain quality compliance standards, an organisation needs assurance that the information on a wiki is credible. There is a need to determine matters of responsibility and how to decide who is to be held accountable if the data is fraudulent. The principal dilemma of a wiki is that, while its anarchic nature is desirable for fostering open debate without censorship, it also raises questions about the quality of information available, which could inhibit its usefulness. Issues of quality control need to be thought through. However, an evaluation of knowledge quality is extremely difficult to achieve. Donabedian (1980) suggests that measures of process and structure can be used as indirect indicators of quality. For example, one must take into account the reliability of information, provision of context, qualification of authors, as well as the use or acceptance of this information by other employees.

Finally, there are legal concerns in the use of a wiki in a formal organisational setting. The ability to protect intellectual property is potentially undermined by the use of a wiki since it is difficult to determine the true source of authorship and because in general there will be many authors contributing to an item. Another example of legal concerns is demonstrated in the case of John Seigenthaler, a former assistant attorney general working under Bobby Kennedy, who was dismayed to find that a false Wikipedia entry listed him as having been briefly suspected of involvement in the assassinations of both John Kennedy and Robert Kennedy (Seigenthaler, 2005). However, legal experts assert that Section 230 of the Federal Communications Act (CDA) 1996 made Wikipedia safe from legal liability for libel, regardless of how long an inaccurate article stays on the site. Wikipedia is a service provider, not a publisher, and that fact makes them immune from liability for libel (Terdiman, 2005).

Cases of actual or potential wiki adoption

Four cases are now described in which a wiki is being adopted or at least considered for adoption to enable broad participation in knowledge management in a formal work setting. The cases describe a variety of corporate wikis in different developmental stages and are presented in order from least likely to most likely to be sustainable. The potential benefits and challenges of each are also addressed.

Case One: a failed attempt to set up a wiki in a knowledge institution

This research project was planned as a piece of action research in which the researchers would participate in the setting up of a wiki in the organisation and observe its contribution to knowledge management. When it became apparent that management support would not be forthcoming, the research plan was altered to identify and examine the reasons for the organisation's reluctance to proceed with the wiki project.

The organisation was a small educational institution with less than 200 employees. It had developed a centralised knowledge portal from which employees drew heavily, accessing previous reports and research papers, work plans, project schedules and best practices that were critical to customer support. The employees of the organisation perceived drawbacks with this system concerning the risk of information overload and deterioration of the quality of information.

It was also time-consuming to read everything that purported to be relevant information since the search engine yielded far too many hits or the keywords gave unanticipated meanings. Sometimes, a user might not get any hits at all if they did not know the precise keywords to use.

The institution had few resources to address the challenges posed by the knowledge portal, and could not afford an expensive knowledge management system. They initially welcomed the chance to set up a wiki as part of our study of the adoption of corporate wikis for knowledge management projects. The wiki was seen by some as a tool to cause a major transformation in the way the institution would manage knowledge resources, while keeping in mind its constraints. However, it was not long before management decided to cancel the project and reject the wiki concept outright.

Much of what has been discussed above regarding the merits of promoting an open democratic approach to knowledge sharing has been ignored by this organisation, which favours a traditional organisational structure. Management were concerned that the use of a wiki might flatten the organisational hierarchy, changing traditional and hierarchical communication channels (Stenmark, 2003) and, if knowledge is power, then senior executives were reluctant to share this power with their subordinates. The organisation did not offer cultural support such as reward and recognition programs for the sharing of knowledge.

It was noted that the organisation favoured a top down management approach, which can be seen as antagonistic to the democratisation of knowledge. There are a number of reasons for centralised control. In particular, the organisation maintained that its existing approach to documentation management offers better quality control with its formal editing opportunities, review and verification stages. Their implementation of specific objectives in this regard makes it a simple task to ensure local compliance and checking to see if these objectives have been met.

The potential for 'wiki vandalism' was another reason cited by the organisation for its reluctance to implement a wiki. Vandalism involves editing a wiki in a wilful and destructive manner to deface the website or change the content to include incorrect or irrelevant material. Since the wiki would have no internal organisational or social boundaries, the opportunities for vandalism might be overwhelming. The insertion of spam links and false or malicious content about groups or individuals were considered possible violations as well. Concern was expressed regarding how the organisation could be assured that the information on a wiki was credible and correct. However, what management overlooked was the fact that 'wiki vandalism' generally occurs on public wikis. They would not address matters of responsibility and accountability as expected from each employee.

Case Two: setting up a wiki for professionals in a state-wide government health department

This case was motivated by an ongoing project, in a central Coordination and Monitoring Unit for the Intensive Care Units (ICUs) of a State Heath System in Australia. More specifically, it was to develop a Web-based service to meet the information needs of administrators and clinicians in ICUs of their public hospitals. Material posted on the website was carefully developed and controlled by specially appointed expert committees. At the same time, the Coordination and Monitoring Unit started up an online discussion forum that grew in popularity with ICU professionals. Membership included clinicians from the state hospital and ICU professionals from hospitals in other states and countries. Discussions on this list included valuable information and advice on topics of immediate concern, but these were archived in a generic form and were difficult to access at a later date.

From time to time, the Coordination and Monitoring Unit considered the possibility of extracting text on given topics from the discussion lists and using it to produce formal material to be posted on the website. However using the current procedures, this would have involved constituting a relevant expert committee to edit and evaluate the material into a formal document that would pass the quality control demanded for posting on the website. Resources were not available to do this. An alternative suggestion was to install a wiki and allow members of the discussion groups to transfer suitable sets of postings into the wiki where members could edit it themselves into a document to go up on the public website. Although this solution was approved in principle, and technically could be set up quite quickly, progress in the near future is unlikely for reasons not dissimilar to those described in Case One. Government health departments are notoriously conservative and risk averse, and do not have the flexibility or agility to approve implementation of such a, to them, unknown technology without long deliberation.

Case Three: the use of a wiki by a national standards organisation for knowledge collection and dissemination among small businesses

The Business and Management Division of Standards Australia has recently produced descriptive standards in areas such as governance, knowledge management, risk management and so on. These have been readily adopted in large private and public organisations, but not by small businesses where they are seen as costly, inappropriate and irrelevant. A committee for Small Business was established to produce material to address this problem but did not have a clear direction or the necessary resources to do this because of the traditional approaches that were adopted. A wiki project was therefore suggested as a solution that could be implemented at low cost by a research student; it could be set up by the student and seeded with summary material from the various Business Standards. Suitable members of the small business community would be invited to add experiences, advice, and so on, to this material to build up a body of knowledge on topics having an appropriate focus on small business issues. The material could be monitored and edited by members of the committee and the result could then be made available at no cost to small business managers. This project is currently underway and has the makings of an ideal research endeavour in demonstrating the use of a corporate wiki.

Case Four: an existing wiki in the research division of a large private manufacturing organisation

This project investigates employee perceptions of the role and value of an existing wiki set up for knowledge management of the Research Division of a large multinational corporation. As typical knowledge workers, employees in this division were deemed to require new awareness and skills in knowledge management but their supervisors were not sure how to give employees the resources and authority for this. The wiki was established by the Research Division's Knowledge Management Officer to allow employees to access the Division's documents, plans, reports, and other resources, and enables them to create and share new knowledge on current and past work activities. However, the wiki is not being used as originally intended by the employees.

A team of researchers were invited to study the employees' use of, and attitudes towards, the wiki within the organisational reality of how they do their work, solve problems, and acquire new knowledge. The project brings together the expertise of investigators in information systems knowledge management and organisational learning and aims to develop a model in the context of an industry partner's whole knowledge management strategy. At this stage, research funding is being sought for this project and the authors intend to report in more detail on the progress of this project at a later stage.

Discussion

Lessons from the four cases

None of the four cases briefly described above presents a complete success story of a corporate wiki, although the level of achievement improves from Case One to Case Four. In Cases One, Two and Three we are dealing with traditional, conservative public sector organisations for all of which conversational technologies are relatively new and not well understood. The educational institution of Case One expressed most concern for the open nature of a wiki and rejected its use outright. The Health Department Unit of Case Two was receptive to the use of a wiki, perhaps because of positive results from its online discussion forum, but was still cautious about giving full consent to the wiki project without further deliberation. They could see benefits from the generated joint and voluntary collaboration that would enable them to capture and generate up-to-date professional knowledge but were wary of how they would ensure quality control of the output if they were to put it on their public website. Standards Australia, as discussed in Case Three, was concerned about developing a Knowledge Management System that would manage the exhaustive generation of the content and editing work that went with the presentation of its publications. Standards Australia managers were quite enthusiastic about the use of a wiki, both to collect content and to make it publicly available. However, they did not have the final responsibility for the knowledge that would end up in small businesses because the wiki would be hosted outside the organisation and ultimately be part of a research endeavour. They were, however, nevertheless prepared to have their organisation's name associated with the wiki.

It is from Case Four that most can be learnt about the benefits and challenges of the corporate wiki since it is already in operation. First, they have overcome resistance of management to having this type of technological system and the wiki was given senior level management support. In contrast to the concerns of the other cases, their main problem was to get employees to use it so that issues of the balance between control and trust have not yet been faced. Research has been commissioned by the wiki sponsor to analyse employees' ability and willingness to use and contribute to the wiki. There is some indication that the wiki may challenge management authority through the attempt to engage the knowledge worker in a more participatory knowledge management capability and environment. An action research approach will be used to determine the ability of the corporate wiki to drive and enable the democratisation of information and knowledge and where there is a change to a culture that says that knowledge management is the responsibility of all workers.

Drucker observes that '… fewer and fewer people are subordinates — even in fairly low-level jobs. Increasingly they are knowledge workers. Knowledge workers cannot be managed as subordinates; they are associates… This difference is more than cosmetic. Once beyond the apprentice stage, knowledge workers must know more about their job than their boss does — or what good are they? The very definition of a knowledge worker is one who knows more about his or her job than anyone else in the organisation' (Drucker, 1998). However, he goes on to say that, 'the productivity of the knowledge worker is still abysmally low. It has probably not improved in the past 100 or even 200 years-for the simple reason that nobody has worked at improving the productivity. All our work on productivity has been on the productivity of the manual worker. The way one maximises their performance is by capitalising on their strengths and their knowledge rather than trying to force them into moulds'. It could be that new ICT tools such as the wiki can both drive and enable changes to this effect within organisations.

The challenges and opportunities for IS

The characteristic of IS that distinguishes it from other management fields in the social sciences is that it concerns the use of 'artifacts in human-machine systems' (Gregor, 2002). Conversely, the characteristic that distinguishes IS from more technical fields, such as Computer Science and Information Technology, is its concern for the human elements in organisational and social systems. The field of IS emerged in the 1970s when there was a need to have more rigorous and scientific methodologies for building organisational computer-based systems that accurately represented the data and processes of the real world. Since that time IS research has drawn its significance from the uniqueness of computer-based information and communication tools and their place in shaping recent human, social and organisational history.

The information systems of the 20th century are now firmly entrenched as basic infrastructure in most organisations. However, in the 21st century computer-based tools will continue to change so advances in the IS field will only result from a better understanding of the latest types of applications; who is using them, how they are being used and for what purposes. Conversational technologies such as wikis can readily be set up and used effectively with no assistance or guidance from organisational IT service units. This poses a whole new set of issues of ownership and authority that challenges existing organisational cultures and power structures. We believe that this is an exciting time for IS to take on a whole new relevance for organisations and for a world where the technology increasingly empowers the individual, and consequently democratises organisational information and knowledge.

References

Argyris, C. and Schön, D. 1996, *Organisational Learning II: Theory, Method, and Practice*, Addison-Wesley.

Benkler, Y. 2006, *The Wealth of Networks*, <http://www.benkler.org/wealth_of_networks/>, Accessed 21 Aug. 07.

Blake, J. 2001, 'WikiWikiweb', Computerworld, <http://www.computerworld.com/printthis/2001/0,4814,56996,00.html>, Accessed 5 May 2006.

Cheung, K., Lee, F., Ip, R. and Wagner, C. 2005, 'The development of successful on-line communities', International Journal of the Computer, the Internet and Management, vol.13, no.1, pp. 71-89.

Donabedian, A. 1980, 'The definition of quality: A conceptual exploration', in *Explorations in Quality Assessment and Monitoring, Vol. 1: The Definition of Quality and Approaches to its Assessment*, Ann Arbor, MI, Health Administration Press.

Drucker, P. 1998, 'Management's new paradigms', Forbes, vol. 162, no. 7, pp. 152-77.

Friedman, H., Friedman, L. and Pollack, S. 2005, 'Transforming a university from a teaching organisation to a learning organisation', Review of Business, vol.26, no.3, pp. 31-6.

Gregor, S. 2002, 'A theory of theories in information systems', in Gregor, S. and Hart, D. (eds), *Information Systems Foundations: Building the Theoretical Base*, ANU Canberra, pp. 1-20.

Hart, D. and Warne, L. 2006, 'Comparing cultural and political perspectives of data, information and knowledge sharing in organisations', *International Journal of Knowledge Management*, vol. 2, no. 2, pp. 1-15.

Leidner, D. and Jarvenpaa, S. 1995, 'The use of information technology to enhance management school education: A theoretical view', MIS Quarterly, vol.19, no.3, pp. 265-91.

Leuf, B. and Cunningham, W. 2001, *The Wiki Way, Quick Collaboration on the Web*, Addison-Wesley.

Pfaff, C. and Hasan, H. 2006, 'Overcoming organisational resistance to using Wiki technology for knowledge management', Proceedings of the 10th Pacific Asia Conference on Information Systems (PACIS2006).

Santoro, M. D. and Gopalakrishnan, S. 2000, 'The Institutionalisation of knowledge transfer activities within industry—university collaborative ventures', Journal of Engineering and Technology Management, vol.17, no. 3—4, pp. 299—319.

Scardamalia, M. 2003, 'Knowledge Society Network (KSN): Toward an expert society for democratising knowledge', *Journal of Distance Education*, vol. 17 (Suppl. 3), pp. 63-6.

Seigenthaler, J. 2005, 'A false Wikipedia 'biography'', USA Today, 29 November.

Semple, E. 2006, Presentation to the NSW KM Society.

Shepard, A. C. 2005, 'Postings of obscene photos end free-form editorial experiment', New York Times, 21 June.

Stenmark, D. 2003, 'Knowledge creation and the Web: Factors indicating why some intranets succeed where others fail', Knowledge and Process Management, vol.10, no.3, pp. 207—16.

Sunstein, C. R. 2006, *Infotopia: How Many Minds Produce Knowledge*, Oxford University Press.

Swisher, K. 2004, 'Boomtown: Wiki may alter how employees work together', Wall Street Journal , Jul 29, pp. B1.

Terdiman, D. 2005, 'Is Wikipedia safe from libel liability?, CNET News.com, <http://news.com.com/Is+wikipedia+safe+from+libel+liability/2100-1025_3-5984880.html?tag=st.rc.targ_mb>, Accessed 21 February 2006.

Timbrell, G., Taule, O. and Lambe, P. 2005, 'Throwing pebbles into a dark cave: A study of participation and behaviours in the only act-km online community', *ActKM Conference*, Canberra, October.

Vygotsky, L. 1978, *Mind in Society*, Harvard University Press, Cambridge, MA.

Wagner, C. and Bolloju, N. 2005, 'Supporting knowledge management in organisations with conversational technologies: Discussion forums, Weblogs, and Wikis', Editorial preface", Journal of Database Management, vol.16, no.2, pp. 1.

Wikipedia, 2006, The free encyclopedia, 'Wikipedia: Neutral point of view', <http://en.wikipedia.org/Wiki/NPOV>, Accessed 22 February 2006.

A Road Less Travelled: Exploratory Practice-Driven Theory Development Opportunities in IS Project Management

Peter Reynolds
Australian Graduate School of Management,
University of New South Wales
email: peter.reynolds@agsm.edu.au

Philip Yetton
Australian Graduate School of Management,
University of New South Wales
email: phily@agsm.edu.au

Abstract

This paper reports on a high potential and under-utilised approach to developing theory to improve IS project performance, a significant and persistent problem for the IS discipline. It presents a multi-disciplinary approach to exploratory research, which is oriented towards solving problems in practice by developing new theory or adapting extant theory to a new milieu. This research approach is based on 'looking for a gap in practice and finding the theory in the gap'. It presents examples from a program of research that has provided a number of theories to improve IS project management performance. It shows that the IS field may require multiple theories to support the management of projects rather than a single theory of project management.

Introduction

This paper focuses on a high potential and under-utilised research approach to improve, through the development and application of new theory, IS project management performance. The development of theory to improve IS project management performance presents a major challenge to the IS discipline since IS project management has limited explicit theory (Shenhar, 1998; Williams, 2005) and delivers poor performance in practice with slow learning over time (Johnson et al., 2001; Standish Group, 2003, 2004).

This paper highlights the potential of 'exploratory practice-driven research', which builds on Kilduff's (2006) comments about the opportunities for deriving influential theories from the observation of real-life phenomena, and uses March's (1991) concepts of learning and knowledge creation.

Examples of solving problems in practice with new theory development are presented from an ongoing research program to improve IS project management. The research uses a multi-disciplinary research approach based on 'looking for a gap in practice' and 'finding the theory in the gap'. It shows that the IS field may require multiple theories to improve IS project management performance, rather than a single theory of IS project management.

The goal is to formalise a rigorous research approach, illustrated with examples, on which future research can build. We do not contend that exploratory practice-driven theory development is the only approach to improve IS project management performance. Rather, we highlight the research opportunities and describe an approach to improve performance.

The remainder of this paper is organised into four sections. First, we examine the available approaches to developing theory to improve IS project management, and describe the focus of this research. Next, we describe the research approach and theory development process. Following this, we present a number of examples and discuss the strengths and challenges of this approach when applied to IS project management. Finally, we present our conclusions.

Theory development motivated by practice

> Nothing is so practical as a good theory (Lewin, 1945)

Theories make sense of the observable world and can provide significant breakthroughs in the way that problems are conceptualised and addressed (Chalmers, 1999). Good theory advances knowledge in a scientific discipline, guiding research towards critical questions. Good project theory would also be practical, improving the professionalism of management (Van de Ven, 1989). This section presents the case for exploratory practice-led theory development to improve IS project management performance. We begin by outlining the poor state of IS project management performance and the limited theory that currently underpins it. We then provide a typology of research approaches, noting the limited efforts to develop practice-driven theory. Finally, we discuss the benefits of this practice-driven approach with a specific focus on IS project management theory development.

IS project management performance

> It must be considered that there is nothing more difficult to carry out nor more doubtful of success nor more dangerous to handle than to initiate a new order of things (Machiavelli, 1513)

This research adopts the commonly accepted definition of a *project* as 'a temporary undertaking to create a unique product' (PMI, 2000). The undertaking is temporary because it has defined start and end dates, and it is unique because its purpose is to fulfil a specific requirement. Its *performance* is typically measured on four dimensions: time, cost, quality and functionality (Kerzner, 1998; Schwalbe, 2002; Turner, 1993).

Based on these definitions, IS project performance to date has been poor. Table 1 reports the findings from a series of longitudinal surveys conducted by the Standish Group since 1994. So-called 'challenged' projects are defined as being over budget, over schedule, or under specification. It should be noted, however, that these measures are against *ex ante* estimates of project time, cost, quality and functionality, which are affected by other dimensions including the socio—technical complexities involved with major projects and the human ability to produce accurate predictions (Kahneman et al., 1982). The research program on which we draw in this paper is broad, including studies into IT planning and IT investment processes and the way in which project managers effectively decompose, structure and sequence project and business outcomes.

Year	Project Outcomes		
	Succeeded	Failed	Challenged
1994	16%	31%	53%
1996	27%	40%	33%
1998	26%	28%	46%
2000	28%	23%	49%
2003	34%	15%	51%
2004	29%	18%	53%

Table 1: IS project performance (Johnson et al., 2001; Standish Group, 2003, 2004)

The data in Table 1 show that there is a large disparity between achieved and projected performance, and that learning has been slow. This is consistent with other research on IS project success. For example, Field (1997) finds that about 40% of projects are cancelled before completion, and Ambler (1999) reports that some practitioners claim that, for large scale, mission-critical software projects, the failure rate has been as high as 85%.

IS project management theory

Much of the accumulation of practical knowledge in IS project management has been driven by practitioners, who have amassed their collective knowledge of 'successful' practices into Bodies of Knowledge (BOK) such as the US-based Project Management Institute's (PMI) Project Management Body of Knowledge (PMBOK) (PMI, 2000). However, these bodies of knowledge lack a strong explicit theoretical base. In addition, there is often little formal evidence of the success of the espoused practices.

In an analysis of the implicit theory underpinning these bodies of professional knowledge, Williams (2005) identifies three meta-theoretical assumptions that characterise the dominant discourse in current project management. Table 2 presents these assumptions.

Koskela and Howell (2002) review the theories that underpin project management as espoused in the PMBOK and that are frequently applied in practice. They show that the espoused practice rests on three theories of management: management as planning, the dispatch model of execution and the thermostat model of control. They conclude that these implicit and narrow theories are of limited value and explanatory power. They also note that they have already been superseded in the original management field from which they were imported.

In summary, practice dominates IS project management, with weak underpinning theory that could be developed, extended and enriched to improve project performance.

Assumption	Description	Authors
Project Management is rational and normative	Project management presents itself as self-evidently correct (and, therefore, presumably an explicit espoused strategy is not essential), providing a normative set of techniques.	Lundin (1995) Packendorff (1996)
The ontological stance is positivist	Reality is 'out there' and the 'facts' of a situation are observable. Further, the observer is independent of the fact under observation and can stand back and observe the 'real' world objectively.	Johnson and Duberley (2000)
Project management is particularly concerned with managing scope	Project management decomposes the total work effort into smaller chunks of work with sequential dependencies — giving rise to the standard decomposition models; work breakdown structures and project networks, for example.	Remington and Crawford (2004) Soderlund (2001) Koskela and Howell (2002)
	Further, project management assumes that tasks are independent (apart from sequence and resource relationships), tasks are discrete and bounded, uncertainty as to requirements and tasks is low, all work is captured by top-down decomposition of the total transformation, and requirements exist at the outset and can be decomposed along with the work.	

Table 2: Assumptions underpinning the dominant discourse in current project management (adapted from Williams, 2005).

A focus on exploratory practice-driven research

Kilduff (2006) argues that 'the route to good theory leads not through gaps in the literature but through an engagement with problems in the real-world that you find personally interesting'. He reiterates the observation of Hambrick (2005) that influential theories derive from the observation of real-life phenomena, not from 'scholars struggling to find holes in the literature'.

When motivated by a hole in the literature, researchers generally start with a problem within an existing theory, extend or refine it in some way, and apply it to a specific context (Kuhn, 1996). The nature of this learning and knowledge creation is 'exploitation' of the existing theory (March, 1991), including processes captured by terms such as refinement, choice, production, efficiency, selection, implementation and execution. Alternatively, researchers can address a gap in theory by starting with a new theory and testing it in a specific context. The nature of this learning and knowledge creation is 'exploration', including processes such as search, variation, risk taking, experimentation, play, flexibility, discovery, and innovation.

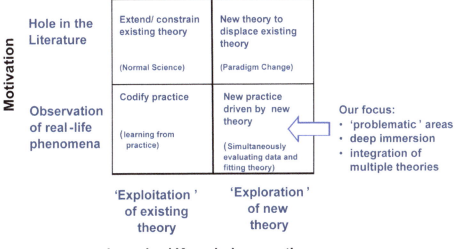

Figure 1: Theory development research typology.

When motivated by the observation of practice, the problem is practice-driven, framed by the phenomena rather than by a well defined research model (Zmud, 1998). By not adopting a well-defined research model *ex ante*, this approach acknowledges that the research team does not know, *a priori*, the solution or the theory to be developed. Practice-led research that uses existing theories to codify best practice is exploitative. This includes research that seeks to improve project performance by developing more methodologies, better execution and stronger governance. Alternatively, and the focus of this paper, the research can be exploratory, looking to solve problems by drawing on new theories, frequently borrowed from other research domains. Integrating the two categories of theory development motivation (Kilduff, 2006) and learning and knowledge creation (March, 1991), Figure 1 presents a framework with exploratory practice-driven research located in the bottom right-hand quadrant.

Progress typically involves a mix of research approaches from all of the quadrants in Figure 1. Kuhn (1996) outlines the importance of the existing paradigm for conducting 'normal science', with punctuated changes to the status quo involving 'paradigm changes'. March (1991) contends that maintaining an appropriate balance between exploration and exploitation efforts is necessary for system survival and prosperity. This paper argues that the research in the bottom right hand quadrant holds great potential for unlocking the intransigent problems of IS project management performance, and that the current literature under-utilises it.

A road less travelled

Exploratory practice-driven research provides an environment for researchers and practitioners to collaborate, with the objective of solving a specific problem in practice *and* developing new theory, thus producing research that is both rigorous and relevant. In contrast to the usual debate around binary choices of rigor/relevance or theory/practice, this approach is simultaneously pursuing good science, which leads to new understanding, and practical solutions to critical problems. This is also known as Pasteur's quadrant (Mason, 2001).

In our view, exploratory practice-driven research is a high-potential approach to developing theory in the IS project management context where:

- Existing theory is inadequate or is of limited applicability;
- Trial and error learning has produced limited performance improvements;
- Identification of alternative theories is problematic;
- The source of the problem is unlikely to be close to its presenting symptoms; and
- Multiple theories are required to explain behaviour.

Practice-led research has an established acceptance and use within the IS discipline and various research designs are available to conduct this style of research, including case study and action research. Techniques to tackle the theory building process are rooted in the classic grounded theory paradigm from Glaser and Strauss (1967) and subsequent developments and debates — see Glaser (1992) and Strauss and Corbin (1997) . A notable application of grounded theory is Eisenhardt (1989), which provides an accessible framework for building theory based on case study research.

However, exploratory practice-driven research has not been extensively utilised in IS project management research. Nor are there clearly articulated steps to follow for theory development to derive theory from gaps in its practice. Instead, IS project management research has generally focused on holes in the existing literature, with researchers exploiting the limited existing theory to develop factor and process models (Markus and Robey, 1988; Robey and Newman, 1996; Sauer, 1999). As contexts appear where these do not hold, researchers introduce contingencies (Shenhar, 1998, 2001) and the various Bodies of Knowledge expand in detail and coverage. For example, as early as 1997, there were over 1,000 methodologies in use by the IS community (Fitzgerald, 1998).

Exploratory research intended to displace the existing dated theory has been limited, with a few notable exceptions such as the application of Adaptive Control Theory (Alleman, 2002) and a growing body of literature on the application, often using simulation techniques, of Complex Systems (Benbya and McKelvey, 2006; Morris, 2002; Williams, 2005). Exploratory practice-led research is all but absent in the IS project management literature.

Research approach

> A model system or controller can only model or control something to the extent that it has sufficient internal variety to represent it. (Law of Requisite Variety or Ashby's Law[1])

> Everything should be made as simple as possible, but not simpler. (Albert Einstein)

In support of the view that exploratory practice-driven research is high potential and under-utilised, this paper reports on a seven-year research program to improve IS project management. The researchers have conducted a series of engagements with practitioners to improve practice through the development of new theory. Each of the research studies draws on a different theoretical framework and generates different insights while building on the earlier engagements to improve project performance. The different frameworks provide the necessary variety, in Ashby's terms, to model and control improvements in project performance.

Examining the IS project management challenge early in the research program, the researchers concluded that there were at least three explanations for the failure to develop effective theories through which to manage large and complex IS project performance:

- Either the research community has failed to identify the right factors or processes, or factor and process models are insufficient by themselves;
- Project performance is subject to high contextual complexity and multiple contingencies; and
- Researchers have looked in the wrong places, wearing the wrong glasses.

---

[1] The larger the variety of actions available to a control system, the larger the variety of perturbations it is able to compensate for. Ashby, R. 1958, 'Requisite variety and its implications for the control of complex systems', Cybernetica, vol.1, no. 2, pp. 1-17.

- All three explanations suggest the challenge needs reframing, reinforcing the search for new theory.

Objective	Step	Description	References
Engagement	Form a multi-disciplinary team	Access to multiple frameworks	Pettigrew (1990)
	Immerse researchers in practice	Role in practice, direct observation, participant observation	
Looking for the gap in practice[a]	Choose the 'gap in practice'	What is the unusual behaviour?	Benbasat and Zmud (1999)
		A prepared mind	
		'The problem of the problem'	
	Articulate the problem	What is done: • What is problematic? • Specific characteristics of that world • Limits of the domain	Klein and Myers (1999)
Finding the theory in that gap	Understand the ontological and epistemological underpinnings	Consider the strengths and limitations of the meta-theoretical assumptions that have either explicitly or implicitly been adopted	Weber (2003)
		What are the strengths and limitations of their implicit assumptions?	
		What embedded assumptions in the world might be relaxed (testing assumptions)?	
	Form the evoked set of theories	Look at data in the gap to signal which things will be useful to point us towards the theories	Whetten (1989)
		Examine perspectives from other fields	
		• Propinquity • Adjacencies • Deep and surface structure	
	Develop a combination and/or permutation of theories	Which theories shed light on the gap or are dispensable?	
		Can multiple theories integrate?	
Account	Develop an account of the phenomena	The explanation of the hypothesised laws: • Constructs • Interactions • States • Lawful transitions	Weber (2003)

Table 3: Theory development approach.

[a] The choice and articulation of the phenomena often occur concurrently rather than as discrete sequenced event. Weber, R. 2003, 'Editor's comments: Theoretically speaking', MIS Quarterly, vol. 27, no. 3, pp. iii-xii.

Table 3 presents the research approach. The approach is iterative within each step and adopts Burrell and Morgan's (1979) *functionalist* paradigm, which views social science as objective and ordered, reflecting the researchers' positivistic orientation.

Engagement

Practice-driven research involves a collaborative effort between a research team and the sponsors of the research effort (Zmud, 1998). This research program consists of a series of engagements with organisations, from both the public and private sectors, undertaking a program of IS-based business change. Engagements extended over a period of three to five years and involved deep immersion of the research team in the organisations followed by periods of reflection and theory development.

Engagements were conducted within various research frameworks, including single-case, multi-case, and longitudinal case studies (Yin, 2003); grounded theory (Eisenhardt, 1989; Strauss and Corbin, 1997) and action research (Baskerville and Pries-Heje, 1999; Susman et and Evered, 1978) .

The engagements provided theory-driven frameworks and recommendations. Researcher participation has ranged from direct observation in executive steering committees to participant observer (Jorgenson, 1989; McCall and Simons, 1969) undertaking project roles as well as being part of the research team. The extent of participant observation provided a unique perspective of operations across the organisations and extensive access to the research subjects. Understanding increases by being there as part of the project control system.

Formal data collection protocols applied to three primary forms of data. First, semi-structured interviews with individual informants were recorded, transcribed and validated. Second, direct observation augmented, compared and corroborated evidence in meetings, reviews and informal gatherings. Third, documents provided information on data gathered from interviews. These documents included strategic plans and business plans, proposals, reviews, policy and procedure manuals, release plans, project plans and specifications, reports, letters, minutes, memoranda and media clippings. Together, these multiple sources of data enabled triangulation of evidence (Carson et al., 2001).

The research background included organisational psychology, philosophy, political science, marketing, systems design and engineering. Some of the researchers have held senior positions in industry. This diverse set of theoretical and practical backgrounds enabled open dialogue and simultaneous engagement in robust debate with senior managers and between the researchers.

Looking for the 'gap in practice'

Weber (2003) describes the *choice* and *articulation* of the phenomena to be explained or predicted via theory as the two most critical tasks undertaken by researchers.

When undertaking exploratory practice-driven research there are two characteristics that help to identify a gap in practice. The first is the absence of practice predicted by current theory. The second is observing practice that is inconsistent with current theory. Together, they strongly suggest that current theory is inappropriate as a basis from which to resolve the problem. Studying such events, which, for some reason, have behaved differently from what established knowledge would prescribe, is consistent with support for in-depth research in a single organisation (Sauer et al., 1997).

The identification of practice-driven research problems requires a prepared mind. Otherwise, the researcher simply treats departures from expectations as errors whereas the research team must be sensitive to such departures and assess them against their different theoretical backgrounds to identify unexpected insights. To do this, problem statements must be clearly articulated. Weick (1989) highlights that:

> ... the problem statements that drive the theorising process are more complex than they appear to be. Not only do they contain an anomaly to be explained, but they also contain a set of assumptions that can be confirmed or disconfirmed.

They require a description of what is problematic, the specific characteristics of and assumptions about the context, and identifications of limits to the domain.

A final challenge in practice-driven research is that the sponsors must also agree on the problem, with the sponsors often subject to stringent time requirements.

Finding the 'theory in the gap'

There is an extensive literature on what constitutes good theory but limited guidance on good theorising or how to develop good theory. Developing new theory to account for practice 'commonly involves borrowing a perspective from other fields, which encourages altering our metaphors and gestalts in ways that challenge the underlying rationales supporting accepted theories' (Whetten, 1989).

A useful place to start is to develop an understanding of the ontological and epistemological underpinnings and look at what researchers have taken for granted. It is then possible to challenge or relax the most accepted propositions in the current theory and to explore alternative explanations of the phenomena. To do the latter (that is, fit an alternative theory to the problem), researchers look for a theory, or theories, that simultaneously define the gap and account for the features in the gap.

Developing an account of the phenomenon

Good guidelines are available for developing a theoretical account of a phenomenon. See, for example, Weber (2003) and Weick (1989). Weber (2003) describes this step as the explanation of the laws that are hypothesised, including their constructs, interactions, states and lawful transitions.

Research progress and discussion

So far, we have argued the case for exploratory practice-driven research and outlined the approach used in a program of research to improve project management. This section provides examples of the theory developed using this approach and discusses three key findings of the research. Specifically:

- the need for multiple theories;
- the value of multidisciplinary thinking; and
- the challenge of sustaining the focus on theory development.

Examples of exploratory practice-driven research

Table 4 describes four engagements, in which an observed gap in practice drove theory development. Two engagements describe situations characterised by an absence of practice predicted by current theory. The other two describe situations where the observed practice was inconsistent with current theory.

Bannerman (2004) provides a capability-based explanation of IS project management performance outcomes, as an alternative to the traditional factor and process view. It presents a theory of performance as the contested outcome of drivers for success (learning) and drivers for failure (liability of newness).

Vlasic and Yetton (2004) provide a time-based explanation of how the variance of tasks on a project generates a cumulative variance in project performance. Drawing on the Total Quality Management literature, they present a theoretical framework to explain poor performance driven by the relationship between task inter-dependence and task variance.

Thorogood and Yetton (2005) provide an explanation of how the currently dominant IT investment model, Net Present Value (NPV), drives the bundling of project delivery. The authors propose an alternative Real Options-based model to unbundle IT investment decisions, with the IT infrastructure investment as the premium paid by an organisation to execute a portfolio of business project options. The business units then assess each optional business project over time, resulting in decisions to execute, delay or discard.

Real Options provides the IT investment decision framework but not 'how' to unbundle projects. Reynolds (2006) addresses IS project complexity and uncertainty, and argues that modularity can unbundle projects to reduce the technical and organisational complexity of IS-based business transformations.

Engagement	NSW Roads and Traffic Authority	South Australian Water	Commonwealth Securities	Commonwealth Bank
Case	Further Down The Open Road	Raise Your Glasses — The Water's Magic!	CommSec: Australia's leading on-line Stockbroker	Building a New Bank: Service Excellence Everyday
Timing	1989 – 2001	2002 – 2003	1994 – 2001	2003 – 2006
Researcher role	Post event description, partial direct observation	Direct observation, participant observation	Post event description, partial direct observation	Direct observation, participant observation, action research
Level of analysis	Project, organisation	Project, department	Project, subsidiary	Project, organisation
Gap in practice Nature Description	Absence of practice predicted by current theory	Absence of practice predicted by current theory	Observed practice inconsistent with current theory	Observed practice inconsistent with current theory
	Observed apparent failure to develop IS-based competencies over time (absence of learning)	Observed large variance at component level of four projects despite the same organisational context	Observed investment in technology platform first and then the development of a portfolio of business applications to respond to market and technology changes	Observed unbundling of a project to reduce technical and organisational interdependencies between project components
Practices current theory would predict	Over time, learning will improve capabilities and the ability to repeat a similar task	The application of a standard methodology in the same context will drive predictable project performance	New application and business processes justify infrastructure changes	Project is optimised for time and cost (as per PERT/ GERT/ GANTT)
The theory in the gap Insight	New technical and organisational conditions reset IS learning and capabilities	Task interdependence and task variance drive project performance	Reframing of projects using real options to unbundle IT infrastructure as the option and a portfolio of business projects	Traditional PM techniques drive technical and organisational inter-dependencies, which increases complexity and reduces project performance
Theoretical base	RBV, Liability of Newness	Total Quality Management	Real Options	Complex Systems
Constructs	Core capabilities	Task inter-dependence Task Variance	Investment models and governance	Uncertainty, Complexity
Account	Bannerman (2004)	Vlasic and Yetton (2004); Thorogood et al. (2004)	Thorogood and Yetton (2004a, 2004b, 2005)	Reynolds et. al. (2005); Reynolds (2006)

Table 4: Application of exploratory practice-driven research.

Multiple theories

Table 4 presents multiple theories, each of which addresses a gap in practice with new theory, drawing from different reference disciplines. This range of theories has been used to provide insight into problems in IS project management performance and to develop new theory that can be applied to make sense of, predict or prescribe practice in IS project management.

If only a single theory were required to fill the IS project management gap, the contention is that it would be easy to develop. Academics and practitioners together would have rapidly applied the theory to solve the identified problem.

Instead, this research shows that the IS field requires multiple theories to support the management of projects, rather than a single theory of project management.

Multi-disciplinary thinking

The ability to draw on multi-disciplinary thinking as described above has three major benefits. First, it enables easy access to alternative theoretical frameworks. Second, it provides access to a wide-range of research methods. Third, it supports deep immersion in the problem, generating strong engagement with practitioners.

The diverse theoretical backgrounds of the researchers supported the search for alternative theoretical frameworks and their initial evaluations. For example, from production engineering, the project critical path was treated as analogous to one run down a production line. The findings from Total Quality Management concerning variance-driven scheduling performance were then evaluated and integrated into the program. Similarly, Real Options Pricing was imported from investment theory to restructure the IS investment decision, with strong implications for both governance and the structure of the project and with both impacting directly on project performance. Looking in different places and through different lenses identified novel and powerful success factors.

A wide range of research methods can be applied. The selection of each is dependent on the research context and has included predominantly qualitative methods such as grounded theory, action research and interpretive case studies. It has also encouraged the research team, in other areas, to draw on quantitative methods such as structural equation modelling to allow simultaneous fitting of the data to the model and of the model to the problem.

Deep immersion in practice, with a multi-disciplinary team, supported a rich dialogue with practitioners. The managers involved in the projects evaluated all insights and this provided an early test against practice. Managers would know whether a proposal had already been tried and failed elsewhere in their industry. It also provided a guard against developing unnecessarily complex explanations, responding to Einstein's call to keep it simple, or as simple as possible. All this illustrates how, within this research approach, there is a natural tension between the need to develop richer theory while, at the same time, maintaining simplicity to explain and guide practice.

Challenges

Following the exploratory practice-driven approach described in this paper requires researchers to address three major challenges:

- avoid early closure;
- extend knowledge in practice; and
- ensure that the application of insights from other fields is used to develop new theory.

The first major challenge requires that researchers remain both problem-focused and theory-focused, even when deeply immersed in practice. Without this discipline, it is easy to become solution-bound. The danger is that the practical problem is solved but the researchers do not generate new theory.

The second major challenge is to improve performance in practice and not just to reflect what is already known. The danger is that the researchers may explain only what is already known in practice. Lee (1999) states that 'with few exceptions, none of much significance, the scientists who turned to [practical needs] for their problems succeeded merely in validating and explaining, not improving, techniques developed earlier and without the aid of science'. This is almost certainly true for mature disciplines and practices. However, in immature areas with poor performance, such as IS project management, this is less of an issue. In addition, the approach of applying multi-disciplinary thinking allows new skills to be applied to practical problems.

The third major challenge is to ensure that the application of insights and models from other fields brings about new theory. To make a theoretical contribution, it is not sufficient to apply a theory from one field to a new context and to show that it works as expected. Whetten (1989) explains that the 'common element in advancing theory development by applying it in new settings is the need for a theoretical feedback loop. Theorists need to learn something about the theory itself as a result of working with it under different conditions. That is, new applications should improve the tool, not merely reaffirm its utility'.

The application of the approach in this paper addresses this by providing deep immersion to evaluate both data and theory. It allows the simultaneous fitting of data to the theory and fitting of the model to the data. In this way, theory is adjusted to reflect the empirical data and, at the same time, it is tested against that data.

Finally, the approach presented above is oriented around the developing of new theory using insights and existing theory from other fields. This, in itself, does not address calls for new theory in the 'core of IS'. Some, including Weber (2003), would argue that the IS discipline relies too much on theories borrowed or adapted from other disciplines. Instead the unique IS theory now becomes the integration of these theories, perhaps to the extent that others will want to borrow it.

Conclusions

Existing theory underpinning IS project management practice is weak, with much of the academic literature focusing on exploitation of the limited existing theory rather than exploration of new theory. In contrast, we argue in this paper that 'exploratory practice-driven research' is a high potential and under-utilised approach to address this challenge, where a multi-disciplinary team of researchers work with practitioners to solve significant problems while developing new theory. An approach is presented that focuses on 'looking for a gap in practice and finding the theory in the gap'. Four examples are presented.

A key finding of this paper is that there are likely to be multiple theories that support the management of IS projects as opposed to a single theory of IS project management. We have not attempted to identify and resolve the different gaps in practice and theory required to fill these gaps. Rather, we have presented a preliminary view based on our background and research program. While many theories can be borrowed from other fields and further developed, the unique challenge for the IS discipline becomes the need to provide an integration of these theories for its own purposes.

Finally, we have provided an approach that may prove fruitful for other areas of IS research where there is both a large and persistent gap in practice, and existing theory is weak and inadequate. In particular, this approach is powerful when there may be multiple problems, multiple theories required, it is not obvious where new theories may come from, and the problems are not close to their presenting symptoms.

Acknowledgements

The authors wish to acknowledge Dr Paul Bannerman, Dr Alan Thorogood, and Dr Anthony Vlasic for their critical role in this research and their feedback and perspectives provided during the development of this paper. In addition, the authors acknowledge the feedback and suggestions made by the two anonymous reviewers.

References

Alleman, G. B. 2002, 'A work in progress: Is there an underlying theory of software project management? (A critique of the transformational and normative views of project management)', Niwot, Colorado, p. 32.

Ambler, S. 1999, 'Comprehensive approach cuts project failures', *Computing Canada*, vol. 25, no. 1, pp. 15-6.

Ashby, R. 1958, 'Requisite variety and its implications for the control of complex systems', *Cybernetica*, vol. 1, no. 2, pp. 1-17.

Bannerman, P. 2004, 'The Liability of newness: Toward a capability-based theory of information systems performance', unpublished PhD thesis, The University of New South Wales, Australian Graduate School Of Management.

Baskerville, R. and Pries-Heje, J. 1999, 'Grounded action research: A method for understanding IT in practice', *Accounting, Management and Information Technologies*, vol. 9, pp. 1-23.

Benbasat, I. and Zmud, R. W. 1999, 'Empirical research in information systems: The practice of relevance', *MIS Quarterly*, vol. 23, no. 1, pp. 3-16.

Benbya, H. and McKelvey, B. 2006, 'Toward a complexity theory of information systems development', *Information Technology & People*, vol. 19, no. 1, pp. 12-35.

Burrell, G. and Morgan, G. 1979, *Sociological Paradigms and Organisational Analysis: Elements of the Sociology of Corporate Life*, Heinemann Educational Books Ltd, London, UK.

Carson, D., Gilmore, A., Perry, C. and Gronhaug, K. 2001, *Qualitative Marketing Research* Sage, London; Thousand Oaks, CA.

Chalmers, A. F. 1999, *What is This Thing Called Science? An Assessment of the Nature and Status of Science and its Methods*, 3rd ed., University of Queensland Press, St Lucia, Qld.

Eisenhardt, K. M. 1989, 'Building theories from case study research', *The Academy of Management Review*, vol. 14, no. 4), pp. 532-50.

Field, T. 1997, 'When bad things happen to good projects', *CIO Magazine*, pp. 55-62.

Fitzgerald, B. 1998, 'An empirical Investigation into the adoption of systems development methodologies', *Information and Management*, vol. 34, no. 6, pp. 317-28.

Glaser, B. and Strauss, A. 1967, *The Discovery of Grounded Theory: Strategies for Qualitative Research*, Aldine Publishing Company, Chicago.

Glaser, B. G. 1992, *Emergence vs. Forcing: Basics of Grounded Theory Analysis*, Sociology Press, Mill Valley, CA.

Hambrick, D. C. 2005, 'Upper echelons theory: Origins, twists and turns, and lessons learned', in Smith, K. G. and Hitt, M. A. (eds), *Great Minds in Management : The Process of Theory Development*, Oxford University Press, New York, pp. 109-27.

Johnson, J., Boucher, K.D., Connors, K. and Robinson, J. 2001, 'Project management: The criteria for success', Software Magazine, vol. 21, no. 1, pp. S3-S11.

Johnson, P. and Duberley, J. 2000, *Understanding Management Research*, Sage, London, UK.

Jorgenson, D. 1989, *Participant observation: A Methodology for Human Studies*, Sage, Newbury Park, CA.

Kahneman, D., Slovic, P. and Tversky, A. 1982, *Judgment Under Uncertainty: Heuristics and Biases*, Cambridge University Press.

Kerzner, H. 1998, *Project Management: A Systems Approach to Planning, Scheduling and Controlling*, 6th ed., Van Nostrand Reinhold, New York.

Kilduff, M. 2006, 'Editor's comments: Publishing theory', The Academy of Management Review, vol. 31, no. 2, pp. 252-55.

Klein, H. K. and Myers, M. D. 1999, 'A Set of principles for conducting and evaluating interpretive field studies in information systems', *MIS Quarterly*, vol. 23, no. 1, pp. 67-93.

Koskela, L. and Howell, G. 2002, 'The underlying theory of project management is obsolete', Proceedings of the Project Management Institute Research Conference, Seattle, WA, pp. 293-301.

Kuhn, T. S. 1996, *The Structure of Scientific Revolutions*, (3rd ed.), University of Chicago Press, Chicago, IL.

Lee, A. S. 1999, 'Rigor and relevance in MIS research: Beyond the approach of positivism alone', *MIS Quarterly*, vol. 23, no. 1, pp. 29-33.

Lewin, K. 1945, 'The research center for group dynamics at Massachusetts Institute of Technology', Sociometry, vol. 8, no. 2), pp. 126-36.

Lundin, R. A. 1995, 'Editorial: Temporary organisations and project management', *Scandinavian Journal of Management*, vol. 11, pp 315—7.

Machiavelli, N. 1513, The Prince, <http://www.sidereus.org/library/the-prince.htm>, Accessed 22 Aug 2007.

March, J. G. 1991, 'Exploration and exploitation in organisational learning', Organisational Science, vol. 2, no. 1, pp. 71-87.

Markus, L. M. and Robey, D. 1988, 'Information technology and organisational change: Causal structure in theory and research', *Management Science*, vol. 34, no. 5, pp. 583-98.

Mason, R. M. 2001, 'Not either/or: Research in Pasteur's quadrant', *Communications of the AIS*, vol. 6, no.16, pp. 1-6.

McCall, G. and Simons, J. 1969, *Issues in Participant Observation*, Addison-Wesley, Reading, MA.

Morris, P. W. G. 2002, 'Science, objective knowledge and the theory of project management', Proceedings of the Institute of Civil Engineering Conference, pp. 82—90.

Packendorff, J. 1996, 'Inquiring into the temporary organisation: New directions for project management research', *Scandinavian Journal of Management*, vol. 11, pp 319—33.

Pettigrew, A. M. 1990, 'Longitudinal field research on change: Theory and practice', *Organisation Science*, vol. 1, no. 3, pp. 267-92.

PMI, 2000, *A Guide to the Project Management Body of Knowledge*, Project Management Institute, Pennsylvania, USA.

Remington, K. and Crawford, L. 2004, 'Illusions of control: Philosophical foundations for project management', in: *Proceedings of IRNOP Conference*, Turku, Finland, pp. 563-77.

Reynolds, P. 2006, 'Managing requirements for a US$1bn IT-based business transformation: New approaches and challenges', *Journal of Systems and Software* (in press).

Reynolds, P., Thorogood, A. F. and Yetton, P. 2005, 'Reframing executive perception: a $1 billion action research IT project', Winter International Symposium on Information and Communications Technology, ACM, Cape Town.

Robey, D. and Newman, M. 1996, 'Sequential patterns in information systems development: An application of a social process model', *ACM Transactions on Information Systems*, vol. 14, no. 1, pp. 30-63.

Sauer, C. 1999, 'Deciding the future for IS failure: Not the choice you might think', in Currie, W. L. and Galliers, R. (eds), *Rethinking Management Information Systems: An Interdisciplinary Perspective*, Oxford University Press, Oxford, UK.

Sauer, C., Yetton, P. W. and Associates 1997, *Steps to the Future: Fresh Thinking on the Management of IT-Based Organisational Transformation*, Jossey-Bass Publishers, San Francisco.

Schwalbe, K. 2002, *Information Technology Project Management*, Thomson Learning, Cambridge, MA.

Shenhar, A. J. 1998, 'From theory to practice: Toward a typology of project-management styles', IEEE Transactions on Engineering Management, vol. 45, no. 1, pp. 33-48.

Shenhar, A. J. 2001, 'Contingency management in temporary, dynamic organisations: The comparative analysis of projects', Journal of High Technology Management Research, vol. 12, no. 2, pp. 239-71.

Soderlund, J. 2001, 'On the development of project management research: Schools of thought and critique', *International Project Management Journal*, vol. 8, pp. 20-31.

Standish Group 2003, 'Latest Standish Group CHAOS Report Shows Project Success Rates have Improved by 50%', p. 1.

Standish Group 2004, 'CHAOS Demographics and Project Resolution', p. 1.

Strauss, A. and Corbin, J. (eds) 1997, *Grounded Theory in Practice*, Sage Publications, London.

Susman, G. I. and Evered, R. D. 1978, 'An assessment of the scientific merits of action research', *Administrative Science Quarterly*, vol. 23, no. 4, pp. 582-603.

Thorogood, A. F. and Yetton, P. 2004a, 'Reducing complexity and market risk in major system upgrades: An extension of Real Options theory to information technology infrastructure', Proceedings of the 8th Pacific Asia Conference on Information Systems, Shanghai, PRC.

Thorogood, A. F. and Yetton, P. 2004b, 'Reducing the technical complexity and business risk of major systems projects', Proceedings of the 37th Hawaii International Conference on System Sciences, IEEE, Big Island, Hawaii.

Thorogood, A. F. and Yetton, P. 2005, 'Transforming the agility of IT infrastructure and projects through Real Options', Proceedings of the 5th European Academy of Management, Munich.

Thorogood, A. F., Yetton, P., Vlasic, A. and Spiller, J. 2004, 'Transforming a public sector utility: IT alignment, governance and outsourcing', *Journal of Information Technology* vol. 19, no. 2, pp. 130-9.

Turner, J. R. 1993, *The Handbook of Project-Based Management*, McGaw-Hill, London, UK.

Van de Ven, A. H. 1989, 'Nothing is quite so practical as a good theory', The Academy of Management Review, vol. 14, no. 4, pp. 486-89.

Vlasic, A. and Yetton, P. 2004, 'Why information systems projects are always late', Proceedings of the 15th Australasian Conference on Information Systems, Hobart, Australia.

Weber, R. 2003, 'Editor's comments: Theoretically Speaking', *MIS Quarterly*, vol. 27, no. 3, pp. iii-xii.

Weick, K. E. 1989, 'Theory construction as disciplined imagination', *The Academy of Management Review*, vol. 14, no. 4, pp. 516-31.

Whetten, D. A. 1989, 'What constitutes a theoretical contribution?', *The Academy of Management Review*, vol. 14, no. 4, pp. 490-95.

Williams, T. 2005, 'Assessing and moving on from the dominant project management discourse in the light of project overruns', IEEE Transactions on Engineering Management, vol. 52, no. 4, pp. 497-508.

Yin, R. K. 2003, *Case Study Research: Design and Methods*, (2nd ed.) Sage, Thousand Oaks, CA.

Zmud, R. W. 1998, 'Conducting and publishing practice-driven research', in Larsen, T.J., Levine, L. and DeGross, J. I. (eds), *Information Systems: Current Issues and Future Changes,* International Federation of Information Processing, pp. 21-33.

A Multi-Paradigm Approach to Grounded Theory

Walter Fernández
School of Accounting and Business Information Systems,
The Australian National University
email: walter.fernandez@anu.edu.au

Michael A. Martin
School of Finance and Applied Statistics,
The Australian National University
email: michael.martin@anu.edu.au

Shirley Gregor
School of Accounting and Business Information Systems,
The Australian National University
email: shirley.gregor@anu.edu.au

Steven E. Stern
School of Finance and Applied Statistics,
The Australian National University
email: steven.stern@anu.edu.au

Michael Vitale
Melbourne Business School, University of Melbourne
email: m.vitale@mbs.edu

Abstract

While grounded theory methodology was intended to be used as a general research method accepting any type of data, most grounded theory studies in the literature refer to research based on qualitative data. This paper aims to address this perceived neglect by describing our experiences and our approach while using grounded theory across qualitative and quantitative research paradigms. The case-based discussion presented in this paper, explains how the combination of these paradigms in exploratory studies can benefit research outcomes. The discussion follows the authors' approach to a competitive research grant opportunity that resulted in a comprehensive study into the use and management of information and communication technology in

Australian organisations. We propose that the use of classic grounded theory as a general research method enables researchers to capitalise on greater opportunities to participate in substantial team-based exploratory research endeavours.

Introduction

When the seminal work of Glaser and Strauss was published in 1967, grounded theory was proposed as a *general method* independent of a particular research paradigm. This early premise rarely, if ever, is mentioned in the current literature and thus many researchers perceive the method as being entirely within the domain of qualitative research, neglecting the fact that one of the cornerstones of the grounded theory method was the quantitative work of Barney Glaser (1964).

Glaser (1964), in an exploratory study of the professional careers of organisational scientists, presented many of the core elements of the grounded theory methodology. His study's goal was 'to explore for and to develop generalised formulations on these careers'. Thus, the research was not about testing preconceived theoretical propositions but rather its purpose was to develop plausible relations between variables that could 'guide sociologists of science — as well as of occupations, professions, and organisations'.

Moreover, Glaser (1964) was able to acknowledge and include two important aspects of studies of sociological processes, namely: that a process exists within multiple contextual conditions and that these contexts are subject to variations as they present several stages or phases. The study described a process in conceptual terms in such a way that variations of context were accounted for in the theoretical formulation emerging from the research. Given this recognition of contextual issues, usually associated with qualitative studies, it may be surprising to some that for his foundational study, Glaser used secondary quantitative data and extant literature as data sources. By using extensive secondary quantitative data to search for patterns and the literature to inform the research, Glaser was able to detect and enrich many emergent concepts.

The exploratory analysis of quantitative data enabled the identification of processes and discovery of properties of these processes. For example, the property of 'integration' in a process of facing career concerns describes the concept of individuals choosing to integrate with peers according to their common circle of concern. By integrating with different members of the circle, the scientists were able to solve their own career concerns and to move forward in their careers. Another example can be found in the process of career advancement, where recognition was a property that resolved scientists' career concerns.

The second book presenting the results of grounded theory research was *Awareness of Dying* (Glaser and Strauss, 1965), which was an exploration of the social process of dying in American hospitals. The overall research approach taken in this study was, in many ways, similar to Glaser (1964) and yet, as Glaser and Strauss conducted intensive fieldwork based on interviews and observations, the data was qualitative in nature. It was this work on dying that consolidated the grounded theory method and gave it its initial recognition.

Glaser and Strauss (1967) clearly state that grounded theory is a general method that accepts both qualitative and quantitative data, and claimed that 'grounded theory is a *general method of comparative analysis*' (emphasis in original). Indeed, Glaser and Strauss (1967) described the 'slices of data' collected for theoretical sampling as varied, providing researchers with limitless options for data gathering including different collection techniques, data types and ways of analysing the data with the objective of generating 'different views or vantage points from which to understand a category and to develop its properties'. In other words, the nature of the data is not important in itself. More significant is the role the data play in providing evidence for useful conceptualisations.

Regardless of early descriptions and evidence, it is difficult to find recent examples of grounded theory studies that have used quantitative data or mixed data approaches. This is clearly the case in information systems (IS) research, a late adopter of the grounded theory method and where, to our knowledge, all published grounded theory studies are of a qualitative nature.

While this situation is neither desirable nor undesirable per se, we suggest that by failing to perceive grounded theory as a general research method, IS grounded theorists could be missing opportunities to participate in important collaborative research endeavours. In IS research it is often necessary to combine qualitative and quantitative research skills to analyse complex socio-technical phenomena and to satisfy the needs of diverse stakeholders. Furthermore, in IS it is important to produce empirical studies that are both academically rigorous and relevant to the information and communication technology (ICT) industry (Benbasat and Zmud, 1999) and grounded theory can contribute to rigorous and relevant research outcomes (Fernández and Lehmann, 2005).

This paper aims to address the apparent neglect of the general nature of the grounded theory method by describing the case of a recent study that used both qualitative and quantitative data. In the study we are about to describe, a team of researchers from different backgrounds decided to adopt key premises from grounded theory methodology for their exploratory investigation; in particular, the detection of patterns and the desire to discover what is going on in a particular substantive field. The ability to use a mixed-data approach was also a differentiation strategy in competing for the research opportunity.

The case of the Australian ICT study

In early 2004, the Australian Government's Department of Communication, Information Technology and the Arts (DCITA) called for a competitive tender to commission a study entitled 'ICT, organisation and management — the strategic management of technology'. DCITA wanted to 'examine the relationship between ICT, organisation and management and the way in which it contributes to productivity, organisational transformation and establishing sustainable competitive advantage'.[1]

To achieve the research objective, DCITA requested that the study:

> [conduct] a comprehensive survey, examining the competitive and business settings under which ICT is implemented by Australian enterprises;

> examine the interaction between ICT and organisational and management strategies and processes such as change management, business process review, strategy alignment, organisational restructuring and competency development;

> contribute to understanding and knowledge of the interdependence between social and economic processes and ICT in enterprises and the factors that influence the adoption of particular management and organisational strategies; and

> report on the outcomes of this research in a form that also provides practical advice to firms, industry and governments on the principles and practices that contribute to successful ICT implementation and management.[2]

DCITA was open to different approaches and, in order to successfully compete, our team needed to produce a convincing conceptual framework and a methodology that could enable the attainment of DCITA's stated research objectives. The research strategy is explained next.

The proposed research framework

Our brief was to examine the circumstances and settings in which ICT is implemented by Australian organisations in a number of industry contexts. In particular, DCITA was interested to explore the relationships between ICT, the environment, the industry, and organisation and management, and the associated contribution of ICT to business value.

As we had only a few months to collect and analyse considerable amounts of data, we needed to use an efficient method. Simultaneously, our methodology

---

[1] DCITA's Tender Brief No. NCON/04/10 p.1
[2] DCITA's Tender Brief No. NCON/04/10 p.2

needed to fulfil DCITA's dual requirements for rigour and relevance and the study had to withstand academic scrutiny as well as provide meaningful lessons and outcomes for the Australian ICT industry.

To compete for the grant, we adopted an integrated multi-paradigm research strategy that involved different types of explorations, building on each other and on previous empirical research. By systematically adding layers of knowledge to our understanding of the problem domain, we could aim to go as far as possible given the time constraints and yet produce rigorous and useful research. To fulfil the requirements of the request for tender, we believed it was critical to follow an efficient theory construction approach in which research actions produced slices of knowledge that can be aggregated and explored in more detail by successive research actions.

Our basic objective was to use statistical methods to discover patterns (also called *data mining*) as well as interviews and focus groups to obtain rich data upon which we could ground our enquiry before the survey and then further develop and explain the patterns emerging from the survey. The design and execution of these activities took advantage of the diverse research skills within the team. We had six people working in the project: three IS experts (one skilled in the use of grounded theory), two statisticians and one project manager/industry consultant.

The study was designed to have three phases, each including data collection and analysis: *Phase One* in which the survey instrument was developed, *Phase Two* in which the survey was conducted and analysed, and *Phase Three*, which involved the conduct and analysis of interviews and the final integration of conceptualisations, as discussed in the following sections.

Phase One: survey instrument development

Critical to our objectives was the development of a survey instrument based on empirical theory from prior research work, and grounded in the current context of the Australian industry. This grounding activity was essential to ensure a sound basis for identification and specification of constructs, rigour in the project methodology and to give legitimacy and credibility to the results. The flow of main tasks and outputs of this phase are represented in Figure 1, which is explained in more detail below.

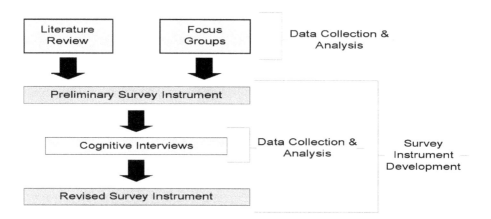

Figure 1: Activities and outcomes — Phase One.

We investigated the literature across empirical studies conducted worldwide. The aim was to find well-tested survey models, although as a starting point only since uncritically relying on those models could ignore peculiarities of the Australian context. In parallel with the literature review, we convened a series of focus groups with business executives and senior ICT managers.

The focus groups were central to the initial development of the survey instrument. A total of 27 organisations took part in four focus groups held in Melbourne, Sydney and Canberra. The results were used to ensure that the survey instrument was grounded in, and relevant to, the current circumstances and settings of Australian organisations across a range of industries, organisation sizes, and geographical locations.

The focus groups used the Nominal Group Technique (Delbecq et al., 1986) to develop and prioritise a list of issues associated with the successful use of ICT. This technique allows the participants to discuss and prioritise their own issues rather than forcing a prioritisation based on extant literature. The experience of the focus group participants regarding the benefits arising from ICT aligned well with previous empirical research that categorised benefits as being strategic, informational and transactional. Factors identified as important to successful ICT use included: strategic planning, education and training, cost, support for ICT, effective client-supplier relationships, business case understanding, and effective management decision making. These key observations from the focus groups were used as inputs to the development of a draft survey instrument.

To help reduce the ambiguity often present in questions, the draft survey instrument was then refined through seven face-to-face cognitive interviews conducted in Sydney and Canberra. Participants were asked to report on how they would arrive at their answer to a particular question rather than on what their answer would be. For example, what meaning did they ascribe to the terms used and what context did they apply when considering their answer.

Based on the results from these interviews, we identified many problems that respondents had in understanding questions, and revised the survey questions accordingly. Finally, the survey instrument was vetted and cleared by the Australian Bureau of Statistics (ABS) Statistical Clearance House, a mandatory step for government-sponsored research in Australia.

Phase Two: conducting and analysing the survey

The aim of Phase Two was to collect and analyse the data, searching for important concepts and their attributes. The flow of main tasks and outputs of this phase are represented in Figure 2, which is explained below.

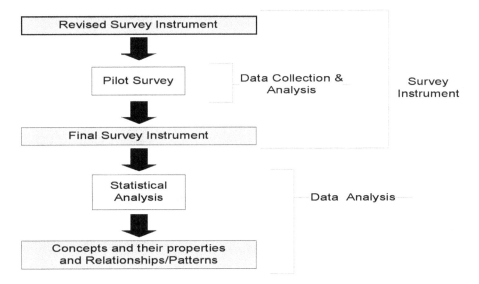

Figure 2: Activities and outcomes — Phase Two.

The data consisted of observations of a number of variables for each of the 1050 organisations surveyed. The sampling frame was drawn from the Dun and Bradstreet database of Australian organisations. The sampling methodology used stratification by business size, so that the final sample included 225 large organisations (100 or more employees), 450 medium organisations (20-99 employees) and 375 small organisations (5-19 employees).

The approach was also intended to cover 15 of the Australian New Zealand Standard Industry Classification (ANZSIC) codes, so initially quotas by industry as well as size were planned. While the allocated sample size was not met for all industries, the number of responses obtained within each of the 15 industries was sufficient for further analysis. The initial sampling frame included 5380 organisations. Advance letters were sent to 2600 of these organisations to increase response rates and 63% of these companies were also contacted by telephone. The response rate was 31%. Details of the actual numbers of responses obtained by industry as well as organisation size are provided in Table 1.

Industry	Number of Responses		
	Small Size	Medium Size	Large Size
Agriculture, Forestry and Fishing	31	37	15
Manufacturing	33	35	17
Electricity, Gas and Water Supply	12	12	18
Construction	27	39	12
Wholesale Trade	37	30	9
Retail Trade	39	32	13
Accomm, Cafes and Restaurants	25	15	8
Transport and Storage	19	29	7
Communication Services	33	35	16
Finance and Insurance	13	31	11
Property and Business Services	42	32	20
Govt Administration and Defence	5	27	22
Education	11	25	22
Health and Community Services	26	36	17
Cultural and Recreational Service	22	35	18
Total	375	450	225

Table 1: Sample sizes.

The survey was telephone-based since this technique enabled survey data from a large number of Australian organisations to be gathered within the required time and cost constraints. Also, to alleviate the problem of the time constraint, we contracted a quality-accredited research organisation, here called Social Research Group (SRG), to collect data for the research team using a computer assisted telephone interviewing (CATI) facility. After the first 20 interviews, which were used as a pilot, all fieldwork was completed in time, between 8 June 2004 and 7 July 2004, and we were ready for the data analysis stage.

The purpose of our data analysis was to *discover patterns* and to detect *significant structure* in the data. Many modern statistical procedures begin with the simple purpose of detecting significant structure in high-dimensional data; that is, where the dimension of the data is in the hundreds of covariates. The term 'significant structure' has many interpretations, the two most useful of which state that a significant structure exists when:

- the data suggest that there is a relationship between a particular variable (variously termed a response or dependent variable) and a subset of the other variables (called predictors or independent variables), and the data suggests the nature of that relationship; and
- the dimension of the covariate space can be reduced by discovering relationships among the predictors. That is, the original high-dimensional

covariate space has a meaningful lower-dimensional subspace that possesses most of the important properties of the original space.

These interpretations reflect the broad principle of parsimony. That is, they attempt to answer the question 'can the information carried in a high-dimensional data set be adequately understood in a low-dimensional analogue?' and, further, to explore and interpret relevant relationships within the resultant low-dimensional space.

Structure of the first kind has classically been captured by parametric regression models, which seek to represent the structure in terms of straightforward linear models relating response and covariates. The strength of such models is that they are very compact, low-dimensional representations of the data, but their main drawback is that in cases where the underlying structure is not simple or linear they can fundamentally fail to capture what is really going on in the data. A broad overview of statistical modelling techniques for discovering structure in data of the type we describe in this paper is given in an excellent monograph entitled *The Elements of Statistical Learning* (Hastie et al, 2001). This book describes basic parametric techniques and discusses in detail the strengths and weaknesses of the classical parametric approach to model fitting.

More modern, non-parametric techniques relax classical linearity and distributional assumptions, thereby allowing more flexible and realistic models, which are inherently data-based. Examples of such methods include:

- generalised linear models (Nelder and Wedderburn, 1972; McCullagh and Nelder, 1989) that allow for non-normal error assumptions and certain types of non-linear relationships;
- generalised additive models (Hastie and Tibshirani, 1986) that seek to find the best fitting additive relationship between transformed versions of the response and covariates; and
- regression trees (Breiman et al., 1983) that recursively partition the high dimensional space into homogeneous subspaces using simple binary decision rules at each step.

The key advantage of these techniques is their flexibility — they essentially trade off extremely compact descriptions of the response surface (such as simple lines or planes) against better fitting but more complex models.

In our analysis, the response variable — that is, the construct we wished to model in terms of other properties of the businesses involved — was not initially precisely defined as the outcome to a single survey question but was rather summarised in survey responses to 22 interview questions. In other words, the response space was initially a 22-dimensional space, and the first goal of the analysis was to isolate a smaller space spanned by interpretable variables that could be used as response variables in our model, and which adequately captured the important properties of the original 22-dimensional response space.

We employed a classical multivariate technique, factor analysis, to discover meaningful structure amongst covariates, and to provide low-dimensional analogues to high-dimensional covariate spaces.

Factor analysis seeks to account for variability in the original high-dimensional space by identifying relatively few common, underlying factors (linear combinations of the original covariates) that explain similar variability to that possessed by the original high-dimensional space. Further, factor analysis attempts to assign simple meanings to the resultant factors based on the characteristics of their constituent variables. Factor analysis specifically posits the existence of a small number of common factors that account for a reasonable proportion of the variability in the higher-dimensional space up to a set of 'unique' elements that cannot be accounted for by the small set of common factors. Factor analysis is described in detail in many texts on multivariate statistical methods — see, for example, Lattin et al. (2003).

We carried out a factor analysis in an attempt to reduce the complex 22-question response into a form that was both lower-dimensional and easily interpretable in terms of constructs isolated in the foregoing qualitative analysis. A four-factor solution isolated four broad types of value arising from the use of ICT: *informational* (i.e. increasing the quality, quantity and availability of valuable information), *strategic* (i.e. creating a competitive advantage), *transactional* (i.e. leading to efficiencies) and *transformational* (i.e. enabling organisational change).

The four-factor solution allows a compact representation of the complex response space in terms of easily interpreted factors, the features of which arose from the earlier, qualitative phase of our investigation. These four factors together explained over 60% of the variation present in the original 22-dimensional response space, and so this solution allowed for both significant dimension reduction as well as a confirmation of existing notions of what sorts of benefits might arise from ICT implementation.

Phase Three: interviews and reporting

The third and final phase of the project was designed to expand and explain concepts emerging from the previous phases and to integrate these concepts into a report. To achieve this aim, we used both quantitative and qualitative techniques. Figure 3 represents the activities of this phase, which are explained in more detail below.

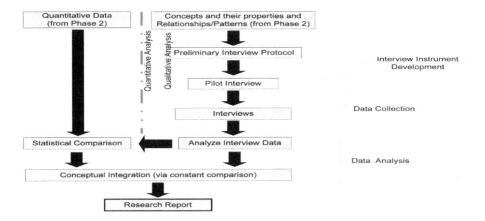

Figure 3: Activities and outcomes — Phase Three.

As described above, Phase One was mainly qualitative and Phase Two was mainly quantitative. In Phase Three, however, this distinction becomes to a certain extent meaningless. Once the analysis of our interview data started to result in concept emergence, we were engaged in an almost simultaneous process of comparing ideas and concepts emerging from the interviews with the quantitative data from the survey. Through the constant comparison of these concepts against the raw data collected in Phase Two, we were able to test the conceptual validity of what we considered important. Nevertheless, to explain how we conducted our work, the next two subsections describe the qualitative and quantitative components separately.

Qualitative component

Fifty structured interviews were conducted between the 2nd and 23rd July 2004. Participants were recruited by SRG by contacting those who indicated during the large-scale survey stage that they would be willing to participate in further research for this project. The conduct of the interviews was also outsourced to SRG. The majority of these interviews were performed face-to-face, others by telephone. The purpose of the interviews was to collect data regarding specific contextual and managerial aspects related to ICT use and implementations considered as significant by the survey participants. The interviews were designed to collect descriptions of:

- How the use and implementation of ICT impacted the organisation;
- How the organisation managed these uses and implementations;
- Results achieved from using and implementing ICT;
- Contribution of ICT to overall organisational change; and
- Current organisational challenges and the role of ICT in facing these challenges.

An interview protocol was developed to ensure a consistent approach was taken to the interviews. We conducted four pilot interviews to fine-tune the questions before conducting the remaining 46 interviews. The final protocol allowed different interviewers to conduct the interviews in different Australian states, in similar fashion and using the same questions. Yet the questions were *open*, allowing the participants to tell their own stories and thus enabling us to collect rich information. The interviewers took comprehensive notes, which were manually coded using *ATLAS.ti*, a software tool for text analysis. The analysis of interview notes resulted in 301 pages of quotations.

The initial aim of the analysis was to produce a set of quotations that could be used to illustrate the findings from the extensive survey previously conducted. However, the interviews were extremely valuable as they revealed interesting examples supporting the findings of the telephone based survey and they also showed core patterns interrelating human and organisational behaviour with benefit realisation, in particular as follows:

- *Being ICT aware.* Awareness of ICT capabilities influenced the style of management adopted and also increased the likelihood of achieving benefits from organisational learning and organisational transformation.
- *Being open to organisational transformation.* Organisations that achieved the most significant benefits from ICT were able to exploit their new ICT capabilities to transform their business processes and to create new opportunities.
- *Being persistent in benefit realisation.* The process of benefit realisation is governed by time. This is so because successful use of ICT demands a continuous effort to learn and to change, causing a lag between implementing ICT and realising the full benefits of that implementation.

Our research indicated that ICT benefit realisation is mainly influenced by managerial choices and behaviours. We found a widespread realisation of value from ICT in which organisations with clear and strategic reasons for ICT investment (internal ICT impetus), good practice in ICT management and openness to organisational transformation and change were associated with the achievement of significant benefits. Contrary to expectations, we also found that size of firm, size of ICT investment, ICT applications adopted, ICT support type, size of in-house ICT team, ICT decision maker type and perceived inhibitors were not so important.

The analysis of the notes indicated a pattern in which being ICT savvy was perceived as a major factor in benefiting from ICT implementations. This pattern was interesting because it was not related to the size of the companies; rather, it appeared across our sample of organisations. Furthermore, the pattern took the shape of self-fulfilling prophecies or virtuous/vicious circles as used by Weick (1979) to explain the effect of multiple causal loops on the fate of the system. Contrary to other studies, our data was showing that one of the most important factors influencing benefit realisation from ICT in Australia was related to human will and attitudes towards technology. To further explore this pattern, we used a number of statistical techniques to search for significant relationships relating business value to other business features.

Quantitative component

Having isolated a low-dimensional response, the next step in the analysis was to relate those responses to the other business features through an explicit modelling step designed to isolate which business features were most associated with high business value being achieved. Simple linear regression, though compact and easy to understand, was not a reasonable approach in this case because of the lack of a clear linear relationship between response and covariates. Rather, a non-parametric method, regression tree modelling, was used to find significant relationships between the response(s) and the predictors.

Tree methods use an approach called recursive partitioning to model the high-dimensional relationship in terms of local features of the data. The basic premise of regression tree modelling is to seek binary splits in the data that yield large differences in the response, and then to recursively split on subsequent variables to find finer structure. A reasonable analogy that may be helpful in visualising tree modelling is that of representing a smooth surface using building blocks; locally, the blocks are flat, but if different-sized blocks are used and sufficiently many blocks employed, a smooth surface can be approximated reasonably well. Such techniques are most effective when simple linear models fail to adequately capture the relationships in the data. These techniques are also very flexible since they can adapt to 'shapes' in the relationship by splitting repeatedly on a small set of variables, revealing complex interactive effects that simple linear models can fail to capture. Classification and regression trees (CART) were developed by Breiman et al (1983) as a non-parametric alternative to traditional parametric classification and regression procedures. In the current context, regression, rather than classification, trees were used in our analysis. The use and broad features of regression tree models are discussed in detail by Hastie et al (2001).

The results of our analyses revealed that the covariates that most reliably predicted high business value arising from ICT implementation were related to ICT awareness in businesses along with the persistence with which businesses pursued their ICT strategies. The results of our tree models repeatedly showed that these variables were those on which the tree preferred to split, with other 'demographic' variables such as business size and so on only appearing fairly low in the tree structure. This statistical procedure was conducted to discover how business benefits were achieved, and was carried out in parallel with the qualitative activities described above.

Critically, the results of our quantitative analysis independently affirmed our main qualitative findings while also helping to refine our understanding of how concepts such as 'ICT awareness' might be measured. Further, the constant comparison between incidents and the further grounding of emerging concepts in quantitative data was a powerful feature of our research approach.

Conclusion

We have described a research case and the main actions taken to fulfil the research objectives and, to conclude, we present some thoughts regarding what we did and the lessons we learned.

The interviews were extremely valuable in allowing us to detect patterns and move beyond the limited goal of simple description. That is, while the data gathered from the interviews provided some interesting examples to support the findings of the telephone based survey, it also showed core patterns relating human and organisational behaviour with benefit realisation. These patterns were important because they allowed us to engage in further exploration of the quantitative data through the use of sophisticated data mining statistical techniques.

Going beyond description is one of the most important and powerful aspects of grounded theory. We feel that while more could have been achieved in this regard, we were able to detect important concepts and their interrelationships in such a way that it was possible to present a theory. For example, the comparison of concepts across qualitative and quantitative data resulted in the identification of three core concepts that we used to explain the relationship between ICT, organisation and management and the way in which it contributes to productivity, organisational transformation and establishing sustainable competitive advantage (Gregor et al., 2005).

The study had a number of limitations. Non-response bias may have influenced the results. However, we have no direct evidence of non-response bias and the use of industry best practice standards by SRG in conducting the survey assisted in reducing the non-response bias to the minimum possible in such circumstances. Yet, the patterns observed 'worked' in the studied substantive field, and concerns regarding non-response bias are arguable from the classic grounded theory perspective since the unexpressed concerns of indifferent or unsuccessful managers would only add another dimension to the study rather than negate the validity of the findings in the studied substantive field.

Another issue with this study relates to its depth. This was accepted as a limitation of scope and time imposed by the organisation that commissioned the study. However, by adopting a grounded theory approach we were able to produce meaningful results in a short period of time and also to provide the foundations for a second study to extend the theory.

Before the study, the team thought that a diverse research team could work together cohesively by following a grounded theory approach. However, it was through our research actions that we found answers to questions such as:

- Is it possible for grounded theory techniques and principles to contribute to other approaches?
- Are these principles and techniques flexible enough?
- Is this approach efficient enough to meet the deadline?
- Is the approach effective enough to meet expectations of relevance?

We now believe that the answer to these questions is *yes*. In *doing* the research we gained understanding of our team strengths and complementary skills, discovered key synergies between our qualitative and quantitative team components, and developed further research capabilities. This approach can work successfully for us; it enhances our team's capabilities to both gain access to grants and to produce research that is rigorous and relevant to our target community.

References

Benbasat, I. and Zmud, R. W. 1999, MIS Quarterly, vol. 23, pp. 3-16.

Breiman, L., Friedman, J. H., Olshen, R. A., and Stone, C. J. 1983, *CART: Classification and Regression Trees*. Wadsworth: Belmont, CA.

Delbecq, A., Van de Ven, A. H. and Gustafson, D. 1986, *Group Techniques for Program Planning: A Guide to Nominal Group and Delphi Processes.*, Green Briar Press, Middleton, Wisconsin, USA.

Fernández, W. D. and Lehmann, H. P. 2005, The grounded theory review: An international journal, vol. 5, pp. 79-107.

Glaser, B. G. 1964, *Organisational Scientists: Their Professional Careers,* The Bobbs-Merrill Company, Inc., Indianapolis.

Glaser, B. G. and Strauss, A. L. 1965, *Awareness of Dying,* Aldine Publishing Company, New York.

Glaser, B. G. and Strauss, A. L. 1967, *The Discovery of Grounded Theory: Strategies for Qualitative Research,* Aldine Publishing Company, New York.

Gregor, S. D., Fernández, W. D., Holtham, D., Martin, M. A., Stern, S. E. and Vitale, M. R. 2005, *Achieving Value from ICT: Key Management Strategies,* Department of Communications, Information Technology and the Arts, Canberra.

Hastie, T. and Tibshirani, R. 1986, 'Generalised additive models', Statistical Science, vol. 1, pp. 297-318.

Hastie, T., Tibshirani, R. and Friedman, J. 2001, *The Elements of Statistical Learning*, Springer-Verlag, New York.

Lattin, J., Carroll, D. and Green, P. E. 2003, *Analysing Multivariate Data*, Duxbury Press, Belmont, CA.

McCullagh, P. and Nelder, J. 1989, *Generalised Linear Models*, Chapman and Hall, London.

Nelder, J. A. and Wedderburn, R. W. M. 1972, 'Generalised linear models', Journal of the Royal Statistical Society, Series A (General), vol. 135, no. 3, pp. 370-84.

Weick, K. E. 1979, *The Social Psychology of Organising*, Addison-Wesley, Reading, Mass.

The Methodological and Theoretical Foundations of Decision Support Systems Research

David Arnott
Faculty of Information Technology, Monash University
email: david.arnott@infotech.monash.edu.au

Graham Pervan
School of Information Systems, Curtin University of Technology
email: graham.pervan@cbs.curtin.edu.au

Abstract

Decision support systems (DSS) is the part of the information systems (IS) discipline that is focused on supporting and improving managerial decision making. The field covers personal DSS, group support systems, negotiation support systems, intelligent DSS, knowledge management-based DSS, executive information systems/business intelligence, and data warehousing. Our long-term project on the intellectual foundations of DSS research has revealed a conservative field that needs to re-orient its research agendas to achieve greater quality and impact. This paper furthers this project and explores what we feel may be at the core of the field's problems — its methodological and theoretical foundations. A number of recommendations for improving the quality and relevance of DSS research are made. As DSS is a significant proportion of IS research, the lessons and recommendations from this study may be of use to all IS researchers.

Introduction

Decision support systems (DSS) is the part of the information systems (IS) discipline that is focused on supporting and improving managerial decision making. Essentially, DSS is about developing and deploying IT-based systems to support decision processes. It is perhaps the most buoyant area of contemporary IS practice (Graham, 2005) and the decisions made using these systems can fundamentally change the nature of an organisation. To help define the field, Arnott and Pervan (2005) presented a history of DSS that focused on the evolution of a number of sub-groupings of research and practice. These DSS types are:

- *Personal DSS*: usually small-scale systems that are normally developed for one manager, or a small number of independent managers, for one decision task;
- *Group Support Systems*: the use of a combination of communication and DSS technologies to facilitate the effective working of groups;
- *Negotiation support systems*: DSS where the primary focus of the group work is negotiation between opposing parties;
- *Intelligent DSS*: the application of artificial intelligence techniques to DSS;
- *Knowledge Management-based DSS*: systems that support decision making by aiding knowledge storage, retrieval, transfer and application by supporting individual and organisational memory and inter-group knowledge access;
- *Executive Information Systems/Business Intelligence*: data-oriented and model-oriented DSS that provide reporting about the nature of an organisation to management; and
- *Data Warehousing*: systems that provide the large-scale data infrastructure for decision support.

This paper arises from a long-term project investigating the intellectual foundations of the DSS field. The foundation of the project is the content analysis of 1,093 DSS articles published in 14 major journals from 1990 to 2004. The first, descriptive, results were presented in Arnott et al (2005b). Pervan et al (2005) presented a critical analysis of group support research from 1990 to 2003; Arnott et al (2005a) analysed the funding of all types of DSS research; Arnott and Pervan (2005) analysed published DSS research using a number of dimensions including journal publishing patterns, research paradigms and methods, decision support focuses, and professional relevance; Pervan and Arnott (2006) analysed data warehousing and business intelligence research; and Dodson et al (2006) investigated the role of the client and user in DSS research.

Our analysis of DSS research has revealed a conservative field that needs to re-orient its research agendas to achieve greater quality and impact. The practical relevance of DSS research is declining and it is underrepresented in 'A' journals (Arnott and Pervan, 2006). This means that it faces problems with both its key constituencies of industry and academe. Our paper addresses what we feel may be a major cause of these problems — the theoretical and methodological foundations of the field.

The paper is structured as follows: first, the project's research method and design is outlined. This is followed by an analysis of the article sample and discussion in terms of research paradigms, research design and methods, judgement and decision-making foundations, and discipline coherence. As DSS is a significant proportion of IS research, the lessons and recommendations from this study may be of use to all IS researchers.

Research method

The overall project aims to understand the nature of the DSS discipline using literature analysis. There have been a number of other critical reviews of DSS publications. Sean Eom's series of analyses have used bibliometric approaches, including co-citation analysis, to analyse the intellectual structure of the field (Eom, 1995, 1996, 1999; Eom and Lee, 1990, 1993). Other reviews have examined the content of articles but have usually concentrated on only one aspect of the field. For example, Benbasat and Nault (1990) examined empirical research while Pervan (1998) analysed group support systems. The literature analysis at the heart of this project included all DSS types. It involved the protocol-based content analysis of each paper in the sample. This form of data capture has the disadvantage that it is a very labour intensive process but, importantly, it has the advantage that it can illuminate the deep structure of the field in a way that is difficult with citation studies.

The time period of published research chosen for analysis in this project is 1990 to 2004 (although some of the earlier papers that reported on parts of the project ended their analysis in 2002 or 2003). The start of this analysis period is marked by two much-cited reviews: Eom and Lee (1990) and Benbasat and Nault (1990). Both of these reviews covered the DSS field from its inception to the late 1980's. A third review paper focusing on DSS implementation (Alavi and Joachimsthaler, 1992) provides a further anchor for the starting date of our analysis, as does the TIMS/ORSA and National Science Foundation sponsored discipline assessment (Stohr and Konsynski, 1992). The period 1990 to 2004 also marks an interesting period in the development of the information systems discipline because it witnessed a significant growth in the use of non-positivist research methods. Also, in industry, the analysis period saw the deployment of several new generations of DSS, especially the large-scale approaches of executive information systems (EIS), data warehousing (DW), and business intelligence (BI). To help identify trends in DSS research, the sample was divided into three five-year eras: 1990-1994, 1995-1999, and 2000-2004.

The sample of articles used in the project is shown in Table 1. We adopted a large set of quality journals as a basis of the sample because we believe that this best represents the invisible college of DSS research. Previous analyses of information systems research have used a similar sampling approach (Benbasat and Nault, 1990; Alavi and Carlson, 1992; Pervan, 1998). Alavi and Carlson (1992) used eight North American journals for their sample. However, Webster and Watson (2002) have criticised the over emphasis on North American journals in review papers. In response to this criticism, we included four European information systems journals (*ISJ, EJIS, JIT,* and *JSIS*) in our sample. The quality of journals was classified as 'A' level or 'Other'. This classification was based on a number of publications that address journal ranking (Gillenson and Stutz,

1991; Hardgrave and Walstrom, 1997; Holsapple et al., 1994; Mylonopoulos and Theoharakis, 2001; Walstrom et al., 1995; Whitman et al., 1999) and on discussions with a number of journal editors. The articles were selected electronically by examining key words and titles. A manual check was performed of the table of contents of each issue of each journal. In addition, the text of each potential article for analysis was examined to verify its decision support content.

Journal	Journal Area and Ranking	Journal Orientation	No. of DSS Articles Published	Total No. of Articles Published	DSS Articles as a Percentage of Published Articles
Decision Sciences (DS)	US 'A'	MS/OR	64	665	9.6
Decision Support Systems (DSS)	US 'Other'	Specialist DSS	466	857	54.4
European Journal of Information Systems (EJIS)	Europe 'A'	General IS	24	348	6.9
Group Decision and Negotiation (GD&N)	US 'Other'	Specialist DSS	122	321	38.0
Information and Management (I&M)	US 'Other'	General IS	98	818	12.0
Information and Organization (I&O)	US 'Other'	General IS	16	169	9.4
Information Systems Journal (ISJ)	Europe 'A'	General IS	15	183	8.2
Information Systems Research (ISR)	US 'A'	General IS	34	303	11.2
Journal of Information Technology (JIT)	Europe 'Other'	General IS	22	378	5.8
Journal of Management Information Systems (JMIS)	US 'Other'	General IS	80	523	15.3
Journal of Organizational Computing and Electronic Commerce (JOC&EC)	US 'Other'	General IS	71	225	31.5
Journal of Strategic Information Systems (JSIS)	Europe 'Other'	General IS	8	240	3.3
Management Science (MS)	US 'A'	MS/OR	39	1,807	2.1
MIS Quarterly (MISQ)	US 'A'	General IS	34	347	9.8
Total			1,093	7,184	15.2

Table 1: Article sample by journal.

The sample comprised 1,093 papers that concern the development and use of IT-based systems that support management decision-making. Table 1 shows the distribution of these papers by journal as well as identifying the percentage of papers in each journal that were classified as DSS. Overall, 15.2% of published papers between 1990 and 2004 were in the DSS field. When only the general IS journals are examined, the proportion of DSS articles is still a healthy 11.4%. Each of these measures indicate that DSS is an important part of the IS discipline.

The protocol used to code each paper appears in Arnott and Pervan (2005). Some papers, termed 'example articles', were selected as being representative of the various article types. To calibrate the coding process, the example articles were coded independently and compared. A small number of changes to the initial assessments were made. The remaining articles were then coded by the two authors and a research assistant working independently. The time taken to code each article varied considerably, ranging from over an hour for large, complex papers, to ten minutes for the straightforward coding of a known paper. In coding each paper the emphasis was on the dominant attribute of each factor for each paper. For consistency, the coding of articles by the research assistant was reviewed by the first author. The coded protocols were entered into an SPSS database for analysis by the second author, who also performed statistical consistency checks on the coding.

Research methods and paradigms

Table 2 shows the empirical papers in the sample coded for research paradigm. The papers were coded as positivist, interpretivist, critical, or mixed. We followed the approach of Chen and Hirschheim (2004) and only coded empirical papers for paradigm. Only one paper, in Personal DSS, was coded as mixed. Surprisingly, no DSS paper in the sample adopted a critical paradigm. The analysis period saw a significant increase in non-positivist research in IS with an increasing presence of interpretivist case studies in the highest quality journals. Table 2 shows that DSS research is overwhelmingly dominated by the positivist paradigm with 92.3% of empirical studies following that approach. Chen and Hirschheim's (2004) study of general IS research from 1991 to 2001 reported that 81% of papers had a positivist orientation with 19% using an interpretivist approach. Thus, DSS research is more dominated by positivism than general IS research and DSS researchers have been more conservative than their general IS colleagues in embracing philosophical diversity.

	Positivist		Interpretivist		Total
	No of Articles	% of Type	No of Articles	% of Type	No of Articles
Personal DSS	250	96.5	8	3.1	259
Group Support Systems	202	87.4	29	12.6	231
EIS/BI	50	83.3	10	16.7	60
Data Warehouse	11	78.6	3	27.4	14
Intelligent DSS	86	98.0	1	1.1	87
Knowledge Mgt-based DSS	14	87.5	2	12.5	16
Negotiation Support Systems	17	94.4	1	5.6	18
Many	31	96.9	1	3.1	32
Total	662	92.3	54	7.5	717

Table 2: DSS types by research paradigm.

Arnott and Pervan (2005) found that only 9.6% of DSS papers were of high or very high professional relevance. One strategy for improving the relevance of DSS research is to increase the number of case studies, especially interpretive case studies. Put simply, a field that is so removed from practice needs case study work to ensure that the questions it is addressing are both relevant and important. Interpretive case studies can illuminate areas of contemporary practice in ways that natural science-like studies such as laboratory experiments and surveys cannot (Cavaye, 1996; Eisenhart, 1989). Importantly, they can inspire researchers to focus on issues of current importance and build lasting links between academics and senior professionals, a process that will assist with grant funding as well. Table 2 shows that data warehousing and EIS/BI have the highest proportion of interpretivist studies (although the number of DW papers is probably too small to make firm conclusions), while intelligent DSS and personal DSS have almost ignored non-positivist paradigms. It is interesting that the more modern types of DSS are being researched with a more contemporary mix of paradigms than older types of DSS. Further analysis of the interpretivist studies reveals that almost all are focused on the theory development stage of research, thus confirming their importance in developing new theory in DSS.

Table 2 also shows the dominance of the oldest types of DSS in the agendas of researchers. While DW and EIS/BI have been mainstream in practice since the mid 1990s they only account for 9% of empirical papers (8.4% of all papers). Arnott and Pervan (2006) confirmed this dominance of the oldest aspects of the field.

	Article Type	Number	%
Non-Empirical			
Conceptual	DSS Frameworks	51	4.7
	Conceptual Models	28	2.6
	Conceptual Overview	48	4.4
	Theory	22	2.0
Illustrative	Opinion and Example	22	2.0
	Opinion and Personal Experience	5	0.5
	Tools, Techniques, Methods, Model Applications	126	11.5
Applied Concepts	Conceptual Frameworks and Their Application	65	5.9
Empirical			
Objects	Description of Type or Class of Product, Technology, Systems etc.	36	3.3
	Description of Specific Application, System etc.	194	17.7
Events/Processes	Lab Experiment	204	18.7
	Field Experiment	19	1.7
	Field Study	36	3.3
	Positivist Case Study	58	5.3
	Interpretivist Case Study	39	3.6
	Action Research	4	0.4
	Survey	73	6.7
	Development of DSS Instrument	4	0.4
	Secondary Data	26	2.4
	Simulation	33	3.0

Table 3: Sample by article type.

Table 3 shows an analysis of the sample using the IS research classification developed by Alavi and Carlson (1992) and revised by Pervan (1998). The highest level of the classification divides papers into empirical and non-empirical categories. The lowest level addresses research designs and methods. Table 3 shows that around one-third (33.6%) of DSS research is non-empirical, with the remaining two-thirds (66.4%) being empirical. Chen and Hirschheim's (2004) analysis of overall IS research reported a different split between non-empirical (40%) and empirical (60%) research, showing that DSS research has significantly more empirical research than general IS. The most popular single research method since 1990, using the Alavi and Carlson (1992) taxonomy, has been the laboratory experiment. This, in part, reflects the methodological focus of North American business schools.

What is noteworthy in Table 3 is the 21% of papers in the empirical-objects categories. DSS was founded on the development of experimental systems for managers and has a long history of publication of descriptions of DSS applications that are novel or important. This is part of what is now called design science (Hevner et al., 2004). There could also be a significant amount of design-science research in the 'Tools, Techniques, Methods, Model Applications' and 'Conceptual Frameworks and Their Application' article types. As a result, design science could be the largest major category of DSS research. DSS researchers have much to offer the current debate on IS design science methodologies; it may even be the most significant contribution that DSS can make to its parent discipline.

Judgement and decision making foundations

It is axiomatic that research in DSS should be grounded in quality judgement and decision-making (JDM) research since it is focused on supporting and improving management decision making. In coding and analysing this JDM grounding, special care was taken to distinguish between merely citing reference theory in introductory or focussing discussion and using reference theory in the design of the research and interpretation of results. Only the second, integral, use of reference theory was coded in this project. Surprisingly, the result was that 47.8% of papers did not use any reference research in judgement and decision-making. Further, the percentage of papers that explicitly use JDM reference research is falling slightly over time. Table 4 shows the mean number of citations to JDM reference research per paper for each type of DSS. Group and Negotiation Support, and Personal DSS have the most reference citations, with the current professional mainstream of data warehousing having the poorest grounding.

	No of Articles	Mean	Standard Deviation	Median
Personal DSS	389	2.15	3.72	0.00
Group Support Systems	319	2.62	3.15	2.00
EIS	76	1.55	2.84	0.00
Data Warehouse	16	0.00	0.00	0.00
Intelligent DSS	160	0.73	1.61	0.00
Knowledge Management Based DSS	22	1.82	3.11	0.00
Negotiation Support Systems	43	2.33	2.61	1.00
Many	68	2.71	4.68	1.00
Total	1,093	2.04	3.31	1.00

Table 4: Cited judgement and decision making references by DSS type.

Another aspect of the intellectual structure of a field is the degree of coherence between different sub-fields. Arnott and Pervan (2005), using an historical analysis, characterised DSS as a set of partially connected sub-fields. The 'partially connected' descriptor hints at a field that may not be as coherent as may be imagined. Table 5 shows the top five judgement and decision-making reference articles for each DSS type. The total number of references per type is shown in the left column and the right column shows the reference ranking and reference frequency for each type. The 'many' classification in KM-based DSS and NSS indicates a large number of reference articles with one or two citations in the sample. These 'many' articles are different to those cited elsewhere in the table. This analysis of the JDM foundation citations can provide an indication of the coherence of the field. If the key references across different DSS types are similar then the discipline has a high level of coherence.

What immediately stands out in the table is the major disconnect between the grouping of GSS and Negotiation Support Systems, and the other DSS types; there are no common key references between these two groupings. This suggests that they may even be considered as separate academic fields, a notion that is supported by the conduct of separate specialist conferences and the publishing of separate specialist journals. The lack of any JDM references in data warehousing research indicates that it could also be regarded as a separate academic field. Data structures, data quality, and information delivery seems to be this DSS type's core concerns. Another interesting observation is the integrating nature of Simon's behavioural theory of decision making across Personal DSS, EIS/BI, Intelligent DSS, and KM-based DSS. The strength of this referencing does indicate intellectual coherence among these DSS types.

DSS Type	Key Reference Articles — Frequency
Personal DSS	1. Simon (1960) — 30
(389 papers, 828 references)	2. Newell & Simon (1972) — 22
	3. Keeney & Raiffa (1976) - 17
	4. Tversky & Kahneman (1974), Mintzberg et al. (1976) — 15
Group Support Systems	1. DeSanctis & Gallupe (1987) — 82
(319 papers, 834 references)	2. McGrath (1984) — 35
	3. Daft & Lengel (1986) — 19
	4. Nunamaker et al. (1991) — 16
	5. Steiner (1972) — 15
EIS/BI	1. Mintzberg (1973), Isenberg (1984) — 5
(76 papers, 117 references)	2. Newell & Simon (1972), Simon (1957), Mintzberg et al. (1976), Cyert & March (1963)
Data Warehouse	No key references
(16 papers, 0 references)	
Intelligent DSS	1. Newell & Simon (1972), Saaty (1980) — 5
(160 papers, 115 references)	2. Keeney & Raiffa (1976) — 4
	3. Simon (1960), Simon (1977) — 3
KM-based DSS	1. Newell & Simon (1972) — 3
(22 papers, 40 references)	2. Many — 1
Negotiation Support Systems	1. Raiffa (1982) — 5
(43 papers, 101 references)	2. Shakun (1988), Mumpower (1991) — 4
	3. DeSanctis & Gallupe (1987) — 3
	4. Many — 2

Table 5: Key reference articles per DSS type.

This analysis of Table 5 indicates that the DSS field is fragmented with marked disconnects between important sub-fields. In terms of judgement and decision-making reference theory, there appears to be three disjoint groups of DSS research:

- GSS and Negotiation Support Systems;
- Personal DSS, EIS/BI, Intelligent DSS, and KM-based DSS;
- Data Warehousing.

A further aspect of Table 5 is the relative age and scope of the reference research. Although the article sample spans 1990 to 2004, the major references are quite old and many are from the 1970s; only two frequently cited references are from the 1990s. This is another aspect of discipline conservatism. In particular, the early behavioural decision theory associated with Herbert Simon is dominant. This could be a negative consequence of Simon's Nobel Prize and it could be that the academic standing of Nobel Prize winning theory has prevented or discouraged the search for other reference theory. An author is unlikely to be criticised for basing their research on Nobel Prize winning theory. More contemporary theory is often the subject of vigorous debate and can be a riskier prospect with journal editors and reviewers. Daniel Kahneman won a Nobel Prize in 2002 for his behavioural decision theory based on heuristics and biases and the effect of this more recent prize may be to counteract the evident Simon-based conservatism of DSS research.

Conclusions

DSS has a long history of success in scholarship and practice. BI and Personal DSS systems are now an integral part of most managers' work and DSS scholars have contributed significantly to IS theory in areas such as evolutionary systems development, multi-dimensional data structures, critical success factors, group processes, and managerial information behaviours. Despite this history of achievement, the discipline is at an important turning point. It is increasingly removed from practice, is relatively unsuccessful in major competitive grant funding, and does not have the presence in 'A' journals that it should. The analysis of the methodological and theoretical foundations of DSS provided in this paper gives important insight into the field's underperformance.

A major theme of our analysis is the conservatism of the field. The evidence for this lies with:

- The small proportion of non-positivist research;
- The relatively low proportion of non-empirical research;
- The continuing dominance of Personal DSS and Group SS in research agendas; and
- The reliance on an aging and narrow reference foundation in judgement and decision making.

This evidence provides the foundations for our major recommendations. First, DSS must embrace more contemporary reference theory in judgement and decision making. This applies to research on all types of DSS. DSS researchers should look for this reference research not only in psychology, but in business and other social science fields as well. Second, researchers should shift their objects of study toward data warehousing and EIS/BI. In effect, such a shift would move researchers from a well accepted, well established comfort zone to the messy reality of current practice. The fundamental research questions of DSS that relate to how to support managers in important decision tasks would need little change. Third, DSS researchers need to embrace more diversity in epistemology and methodology. In an applied field struggling for professional relevance, a significant amount of theorising and exploratory research needs to be undertaken. This research should be focused on concepts and theory that will lead to the reshaping of the ideas and methods of influential professionals (Lyytinen, 1999). This attention to research with fundamental and long lasting effect on practice is much more important than orienting projects towards the short term concerns of CIOs.

The design science heritage of DSS is very important for IS as a whole since the parent discipline shares DSS's problem of declining professional relevance, albeit to a lesser extent (Benbasat and Zmud, 1999; Argarwal and Lucas, 2005). One aspect of the relevance decline has been the pursuit of research rigor; another has been a decline in the number of quality studies that address systems development. A number of influential IS researchers have called for greater attention on the IT artifact in research designs and the greater use of quality design-science designs (Orlikowski and Iacono, 2001; Markus et al., 2002). DSS's long experience with design science can inform its increasing application in general IS. For example, in the landmark *MIS Quarterly* paper on the conduct of design science research in IS (Hevner et al., 2004) two of the three exemplar studies analysed were from DSS. Importantly, design-science research can link researchers to practitioners in creative and influential ways.

Related to the analysis in this paper, two further investigations of the intellectual foundations of DSS are under way. The first is a critical review of DSS design-science research using the guidelines developed by Hevner et al. (2004). The aim of this analysis is to provide prescriptions for improving the rigor and relevance of DSS design science research. The second project is a more detailed analysis of the judgement and decision-making foundations of DSS research with a special emphasis on the role Simon's theory of behavioural decision-making has played in shaping the field.

We finish this paper with a call-to-arms to other IS researchers. The IS discipline faces a critical period in its development. There has been a significant downturn in IS-related IT activities and spending in OECD countries. There are also serious questions over the direction and relevance of IS research (Benbasat and Zmud, 2003). An important aspect of understanding our current situation and developing research agendas for the future is the rigorous analysis of high-quality published research. The literature analysis project described in this paper can support DSS disciplinary development. Other branches of IS scholarship need to follow this lead.

Acknowledgements

We thank Gemma Dodson for her research assistance on the project especially in sourcing the papers and her contribution to the article coding.

References

Alavi, M. and Carlson, P. 1992, 'A review of MIS research and disciplinary development', Journal of Management Information Systems, vol. 8, no. 4, pp. 45-62.

Alavi, M. and Joachimsthaler, E. A. 1992, 'Revisiting DSS implementation research: A meta-analysis of the literature and suggestions for researchers', MIS Quarterly, vol. 16, no. 1, pp. 95-116.

Argarwal, R. and Lucas, H. C., Jr. 2005, 'The information systems identity crisis: Focusing on high-visibility and high-impact research', MIS Quarterly, vol. 29, no. 3, pp. 381-98.

Arnott, D. and Pervan, G. 2005, 'A critical analysis of Decision Support Systems research', Journal of Information Technology, vol. 20, no. 2, pp. 67-87.

Arnott, D. and Pervan, G. 2006, 'Eight key issues in Decision Support Systems research', in Adam, F., Brezillon, P., Carlsson, S. and Humphreys, P. (eds) Creativity and Innovation in Decision Making and Decision Support, Ludic Publishing, pp. 946-68.

Arnott, D., Pervan, G. and Dodson, G. 2005a, 'Who pays for Decision Support Systems research? Review, directions and issues', Communications of the Association for Information Systems, vol. 16, pp. 356-80.

Arnott, D., Pervan, G. and Dodson, G. 2005b, 'A descriptive analysis of Decision Support Systems research from 1990 to 2003', Australian Journal of Information Systems, vol. 12, no. 2, pp. 178-91.

Benbasat, I. and Nault, B. 1990, 'An evaluation of empirical research in managerial support systems', Decision Support Systems, vol. 6, pp. 203-26.

Benbasat, I. and Zmud, R. W. 1999, 'Empirical research in information systems: The practice of relevance', MIS Quarterly, vol. 23, no. 1, pp. 3-16.

Benbasat, I. and Zmud, R. W. 2003, 'The identity crisis within the IS discipline: Defining and communicating the discipline's core properties', MIS Quarterly, vol. 27, no. 2, pp. 183-94.

Cavaye, A. L. M. 1996, 'Case study research: A multi-faceted research approach for IS', Information Systems Journal, vol. 6, pp. 227-42.

Chen, W. S. and Hirschheim, R. 2004, 'A paradigmatic and methodological examination of information systems research from 1991 to 2001', Information Systems Journal, vol. 14, pp. 197-235.

Cyert, R. M. and March, J. G. 1963, A Behavioral Theory of the Firm, Prentice-Hall, New York

Daft, R. L. and Lengel, R. H. 1986, 'Organisational information requirements, media richness and structural design', Management Science, vol. 32, no. 5, pp. 554-71.

DeSanctis, G. and Gallupe, R. B. 1987, 'A foundation for the study of Group Decision Support Systems', Management Science, vol. 33, no. 5, pp. 589-609.

Dodson, G., Arnott, D. and Pervan, G. 2006, 'The client and user in Decision Support Systems: Review and research agenda', in Adam, F., Brezillon, P., Carlsson, S. and Humphreys, P. (eds) Creativity and Innovation in Decision Making and Decision Support, Ludic Publishing, pp. 466-487.

Eisenhart. K. M. 1989, 'Building theories from case study research', Academy of Management Review, vol. 14, pp. 532-50.

Eom, S. B. 1995, 'Decision Support Systems research: Reference disciplines and a cumulative tradition', Omega: The International Journal of Management Science, vol. 23, no. 5, pp. 511-23.

Eom, S. B. 1996, 'Mapping the intellectual structure of research in Decision Support Systems through author cocitation analysis (1971-1993)', Decision Support Systems, vol. 16, no. 4, pp. 315-38.

Eom, S. B. 1999, 'Decision Support Systems research: Current state and trends', Industrial Management and Data Systems, vol. 99, no. 5, pp. 213-20.

Eom, S. B. and Lee, S. M. 1990, 'A survey of Decision Support System applications (1971-1988)', Interfaces, vol. 20, pp. 65-79.

Eom, S. B. and Lee, S. M. 1993, 'Leading universities and most influential contributors in DSS research: A citation analysis', Decision Support Systems, vol. 9, no. 3, pp. 237-44.

Gillenson, M. L. and Stutz, J. D. 1991, 'Academic issues in MIS: Journals and books', MIS Quarterly, vol. 15, no. 4, pp. 447-52.

Graham, C. 2005, Business Intelligence Software Market Grows by 12% (Gartner Research Report ID. G00130216), Gartner Inc, Stamford, CT.

Hardgrave, B. C. and Walstrom, K. A. 1997, 'Forums for MIS scholars', Communications of the ACM, vol. 40, no.11, pp. 119-24.

Hevner, A. R., March, S. T., Park, J. and Ram, S. 2004, 'Design Science in information systems research', MIS Quarterly, vol. 28, no. 1, pp. 75-106.

Holsapple, C., Johnson, L., Manakyan, H. and Tanner, J. 1994, 'Business computing research journals: A normalised citation analysis', Journal of Management Information Systems, vol. 11, no. 1, pp. 131-40.

Isenberg, D. J. 1984, 'How senior managers think', Harvard Business Review, vol. 84, no. 6, pp. 81-90.

Keeney, R. L. and Raiffa, H. 1976, Decision with Multiple Objectives, John Wiley , New York.

Lyytinen, K. 1999, 'Empirical research in information systems: On the relevance of practice in thinking of IS research', MIS Quarterly, vol. 23, no. 1, pp. 25-8.

Markus, M. L., Majchrzak, A. and Gasser, L. 2002, 'A design theory for systems that support emergent knowledge processes'. MIS Quarterly, vol. 26, no.3, pp. 179-212.

McGrath, J. E. 1984, Groups: Interaction and Performance, Prentice-Hall, New Jersey.

Mintzberg, H. 1973, *The Nature of Managerial Work*, Prentice-Hall, Englewood Cliffs, NJ.

Mintzberg, H., Raisinghani, D. and Theoret, A. 1976, 'The structure of "unstructured" decision processes', Administrative Science Quarterly, vol. 21, no. 6, pp. 246-75.

Mumpower, J. 1991, 'The judgement policies of negotiators and the structure of negotiation problems', Management Science, vol. 37, pp. 1304-24.

Mylonopoulos, N. A. and Theoharakis V. 2001, 'Global perceptions of IS journals: Where is the best IS research published?', Communications of the ACM, vol. 44, no. 9, pp. 29-33.

Newell, A. and Simon, H. A. 1972, *Human Problem Solving*, Prentice Hall, Englewood Cliffs, NJ.

Nunamaker, J. F., Jr., Dennis, A. R., Valacich, J. S., Vogel, D. R. and George, J. F. 1991, 'Electronic meeting systems to support group work', Communications of the ACM, vol. 34, no. 7, pp. 40-61.

Orlikowski, W. J. and Iacono, C. S. 2001, 'Desperately seeking the "IT" in IT Research — A call to theorising the IT artifact', Information Systems Research, vol. 12, pp. 121-34.

Pervan, G. 1998, 'A review of research in Group Support Systems: Leaders, approaches and directions', Decision Support Systems, vol. 23, no. 2, pp. 149-59.

Pervan, G. and Arnott, D. 2006, 'Research in Data Warehousing and Business Intelligence: 1990-2004', in Adam, F., Brezillon, P., Carlsson, S. and Humphreys, P. (eds) *Creativity and Innovation in Decision Making and Decision Support*, Ludic Publishing, pp. 985-1003.

Pervan, G., Arnott, D. and Dodson, G. 2005, 'Trends in the study of Group Support Systems', in Kersten, G. E., Shakun, M. F. and Vetschera, R. (eds), *Group Decision and Negotiation 2005*, University of Vienna.

Raiffa, H. 1982, *The Art and Science of Negotiation*, Harvard University Press, Cambridge, MA.

Saaty, T. L. 1980, *The Analytic Hierarchy Process*, McGraw-Hill, New York.

Shakun, M. F. 1988, *Evolutionary Systems Design: Policy Making under Complexity and Group Decision Support Systems*, Holden-Day, Oakland, CA.

Simon, H. A. 1957, *Models of Man*, Wiley, New York.

Simon, H. A. 1977, *The New Science of Management Decision* (revised ed.), Prentice-Hall, Englewood Cliffs, NJ, (Original work published 1960).

Steiner, I. D. 1972, *Group Process and Productivity*, Academic Press, New York.

Stohr, E. A. and Konsynski, B. R. (eds) 1992, *Information Systems and Decision Processes*, IEEE Computer Society Press, Los Alamitos, CA.

Tversky, A. and Kahneman, D. 1974, 'Judgment under uncertainty: Heuristics and biases', Science, vol. 185, pp. 1124-31.

Walstrom, K. A., Hardgrave, B. C. and Wilson, R. L. 1995, 'Forums for management information systems scholars', Communications of the ACM, vol. 38, no. 3, pp. 93-107.

Webster, J. and Watson, R. T. 2002, 'Analysing the past to prepare for the future: Writing a literature review', MIS Quarterly, vol. 26, no. 2, pp. xiii-xxiii.

Whitman, M. E., Hendrickson, A. R. and Townsend, A. M. 1999, 'Academic rewards for teaching, research and service: Data and discourse', Information Systems Research, vol. 10, no. 2, pp. 99-109.

www.ingramcontent.com/pod-product-compliance
Lightning Source LLC
LaVergne TN
LVHW071357070326
832902LV00028B/4632